By

Rev. Luis A. Betances

T0365037

WHAT WE SHOULD

KNOW ABOUT

DEMONS

LIBERATION MANUAL

Copyright © 2012 Rev. Luis A. Betances

All rights reserved. No part of this book may be used or reproduced by any means, graphic, electronic, or mechanical, including photocopying, recording, taping or by any information storage retrieval system without the written permission of the publisher except in the case of brief quotations embodied in critical articles and reviews.

WestBow textbooks can be ordered in bookstores or by directly contacting WestBow Press Division of Thomas Nelson at the following addresses or phone numbers:

WestBow Press
A Division of Thomas Nelson
1663 Liberty Drive
Bloomington, IN 47403
www.westbowpress.com
1-(866) 928-1240

Because of the dynamic nature of the Internet, any web addresses or links contained in this book may have changed since publication and may no longer be valid. The views expressed in this work are solely those of the author and do not necessarily reflect the views of the publisher, and the publisher hereby disclaims any responsibility for them.

ISBN: 978-1-4497-6406-7 (sc)

Library of Congress Control Number: 2012915177

Printed in the United States of America

WestBow Press rev. date: 8/27/2012

INDEX

Index... 3

Dedication.. 6

Prologue.. 7

Introduction....................................... 12

PART I   14

Do you believe in the Devil?..................... 15

Do you believe in Jesus and His Power?........ 38

The Power of Jesus................................ 49

What does Jesus want with us?.................. 55

PART II   60

Spirit, Soul and Body............................ 60

In The Gap.. 81

Battle in the Spirit World...................... 88

PART III

THEME 1
Attitude and Perspective For
The Liberation.................................... 98

THEME 2
Preparation for Release.......................... 109

THEME 3
 Disease of the spirit........................... 118

THEME 4
How the Demons can enter in
people, entry door................................   133

THEME 5
Steps in the Liberation..............................   171

The Form..   173
Questionnaire.......................................   176
Legal Statement.....................................   178
Questionnaire Part I...............................   182
                Part II.............................   196
                Part III............................   211
                Part IV.............................   219
Questionnaire Suggestions Part I..................   223
                            Part II................   235
                            Part III...............   251
                            Part IV................   264

STEP 1
Place, Minister the Release Team...................   268

STEP 2
The Fight against the Demons.......................   273

STEP 3
Tie, Tie and Tie...................................   289

STEP 4
Legal Right (Name of the Spirit   299

STEP 5
Inner Healing......................................   317

STEP 6
Untie, Untie and Untie   319

STEP 7
Test if the Spirit Left ……......................   336

STEP 8
Baptism in the Holy Spirit ….................   338

STEP 9
The Block.......................................   342

STEP 10
Recommendation and Monitoring.............   350

Home Release   351
Bibliography.......................................   371

DEDICATION

I dedicate this book to all my brothers and sisters in Christ Jesus, who have the call of our Lord Jesus Christ, hoping in God and His Holy Spirit to leave them with an understanding of how to read this book and to allow them to discern and put it in practice.

A special dedication to my dear wife Dinorah Betances, for all the support she has always given me and the time she has sacrificed in the making of this book.

Also I dedicate this book to my children: Marta Patricia, Luis Miguel, Edward, Alice, Luis Alfredo, Luis Armando and Paola Altagracia.

May God make a special call to them to recognize Jesus as their Savior and Lord and work in his vineyard and bear fruit to hundredfold.

God bless you all.

Rev. Luis A. Betances

PROLOGUE

Over 20 years ago a book came into my hands from Monsignor Luis Gomez with the title "He Came to Set the Captives Free" by Dr. Rebecca Brown.

After reading it I got so interested in it that I asked my friend Rosalie who was traveling to Miami to do me the favor of buying a copy.

I still have that book, which is highlighted for the most parts, when I finished reading it for the second time I realized I had highlighted the most important points.

One of the questions that are in the book translated into Spanish on page 173called my attention and came to be the beginning of something that bothered me long after I had received the Baptism in the Holy Spirit or New Outpouring of the Holy Spirit or whatever you want to call it.

The question is this:
Are you willing to get in the gap for someone else?

This question is based on the following Biblical quotation:

EZEKIEL 22, 30 – 31
30
I LOOKED FOR A MAN AMONG THEM WHO WOULD BUILD UP THE WALL AND STAND BEFORE ME IN THE GAP ON BEHALF OF THE LAND SO I WOULD NOT HAVE TO DES- TROY IT, BUT I FOUND NONE.

31
SO I WILL POUR OUT MY WRATH ON THEM AND CONSUME THEM WITH MY FIERY ANGER, BRINGING DOWN ON THEIR OWN HEADS ALL THEY HAVE DONE, DECLARES THE SOVEREIGN LORD.

Today I'm thinking and I wonder. Where is the army of Christians to be put in the gap before Him?

We're not exactly in the same situation, today we see churches of all nominations in each corner, each day the temples are larger, more beautiful and comfortable.

But are the churches fulfilling two of the most important commandments that Jesus told us?

JOHN 13, 34
A NEW COMMAND I GIVE YOU: LOVE ONE ANOTHER. AS I HAVE LOVED YOU, SO YOU MUST LOVE ONE OTHER.

MARK 16, 15 – 18
15
HE SAID TO THEM, GO INTO ALL THE WORLD AND PREACH THE GOOD NEWS TO ALL CREATION,

16
WHOEVER BELIEVES AND IS BAPTIZED WILL BE SAVED, BUT WHOEVER DOES NOT BELIEVE WILL BE CONDEMNED.

17
AND THESE SIGNS WILL ACCOMPANY THOSE WHO BELIEVE: IN MY NAME THEY WILL DRIVE OUT DEMONS; THEY WILL SPEAK IN NEW TONGUES;

18
THEY WILL PICK UP SNAKES WITH THEIR HANDS; AND WHEN THEY DRINK DEADLY POISON, IT WILL NOT HURT THEM AT ALL; THEY WILL PLACE THEIR HANDS ON SICK PEOPLE, AND THEY WILL GET WELL.

I've had conversations with many pastors, ministers and priests, also with many Christians of different nominations related to this.

All are taught in God's Word (the Bible), Religion or go to Sunday Mass and other Services, we could say that they are experts, theologians, especially to the point of view of the interpretation they give to the word of God, many others do works of charity to the poor and visit the sick and people who are incarcerated.

Many visit the homes of family to preach God's Word according to the interpretation and that of the Church they belong to.

But I wonder why they don't comply with the mandate of Jesus?

I'm not who, nor is my intention to judge anyone, but several reasons come to mind

> **LACK OF FAITH.**
> **NO TRUST IN THE WORD OF JESUS.**
> **LACK OF THE HOLY SPIRIT PRESENCE AND CHA-RISMS.**
> **DO NOT RECEIVE INSTRUCTIONS OR PRACTICES.**
> **BELIEVE THAT BY PREACHING THE WORD ALL IS SATISFIED.**

Let me tell you something that is very clear in God's Word (the Bible):

1 CORINTHIANS 4, 20
FOR THE KINGDOM OF GOD IS NOT A MATTER OF TALK BUT OF POWER.

If you are not fulfilling Jesus' command to preach the word of God **With Power**, with all due respect, all they are making is the work of a parrot, repeat, repeat and repeat. In Acts, when Peter became filled with the Holy Spirit he converted 3000 people with a single speech, the biblical quotation ends like this:

ACTS 2, 43
EVERYONE WAS FILLED WITH AWE, AND MANY WONDERS AND MIRACULOUS SIGNS WERE DONE BY THE APOSTLES.

It is clear that after the preaching of the Word came the other party that Jesus commands us, healings, deliverances, etc.

No one is expert in the field, only God, Jesus and the Holy Spirit have the answer to everything.

This book is based on some information from various books and personal experiences that we hope can help you, teach you and guide you in giving you a very clear light in how to fulfill these commandments of our beloved Jesus.

I only ask God to allow these lines to awaken many people that are asleep and may they be prepared to go along with Jesus in the gap and make a defense wall (fenced) so that our brothers can be healed, liberated and achieve salvation of their soul.

I recognize that there are many who are fulfilling Jesus' commands and that their books are inspiring and full of accomplishment and let very clear that they are in the fight in the army of Jesus Christ Our King.

As one expression "I tip my hat" before Carlos Annacondia who wrote the book with the title " Listen to Me Satan!, When this book came to my hands and I started to read it and as he turned the pages, saying to myself **"This man knows what this is all about",** I mean that I am 100% agreeing with his way of preaching, by which I pray that there will be millions of Carlos Annacondia with simplicity and modesty in saving thousands of people to Jesus Christ.

I humbly recommend this book to all Christians, all those who lead churches to see that you do not need a huge temple, full of gardens and air conditioning.

What is needed is trust in the Word of Jesus and to preach the Word with power from the Holy Spirit with signs and wonders, healings, physical healings and inner healings, etc.

Carlos Annacondia used tents and moved them to all parts of his country Argentina preaching the Word of God with power and driving out demons in Jesus' name, I hope that we can all follow his example, God bless him and his family and allow me to someday meet him personally and to shake his hands.

INTRODUCTION

One day I made the decision to seek within the Church which I belonged to (Catholic Church), where I could serve the Lord, I searched, searched and searched and when I was tired of searching I was introduced to a priest, José Maldonado who we affectionately called Father Pepito.

When I was introduced to him I got down on my knees and said: "Please, do not disappoint me too", because I had visited many priests but none was in the charismatic wave, I started to work with him and once a month in the Church San Pio X in the Dominican Republic in which he was the parish priest, we had a mass of healing to pray for the sick.

During the mass, he asked me to help him pray for all the faithful present, the Church was completely filled and at the center there were two rows, one to the priest and another to me, curiously, the row of the father was filled with hundreds of people and in my row were about 8 or 10 people.

Some people are always incredulous and think that the priest or Pastor or Minister, is who will heal, they take their eyes off from Jesus who is the healer, and put their faith in a human being.

I remember on one occasion a group of us went to a family home to pray for a child who was sick since birth, the mother greeted us asking "When is Father Emiliano Tardif coming to pray for my child"?, I am a little bit rebellious and my answer was "We are here with one further greater than Father Emiliano, His name is Jesus, I always remember that Father Emiliano always said he was the donkey of Jesus, meaning that Jesus is the Lord who heals.

Returning to the above as our Lord Jesus knows it all and uses all His children to open their hearts to serve Him, that day Jesus healed people, mainly on the side that I was.

When the healing prayer had finished, Father Pepito in front of the altar asked me if I wanted him to pray for me, I quickly said "Yes" I got down on my knees to receive the laying of his hands and hear the beautiful prayer and the request he made to God for me, when I got up I asked him if he wanted me to pray for him, immediately he said Yes, which took me for surprise, as honestly, not too many priests liked to be prayed for by a common man like me.

I am 6 feet tall, about 72 inches and Father Pepito is a person of short stature, at the time of praying for him, when I had just lifted my hand to him, he fell to the floor in front of all the faithful, for a period of about 8 to 12 minutes he stayed on the floor, in all honesty at that time I did not know what was happening and didn't know what to do so I got closer to his face and whispered in his ear: " Father wake up, wake up"!, I did not know what to do! He finally stood up and finished the mass.

Back then little was known or talked about the "rest or ecstasy in the spirit" as we know it today; like servants, the Holy Spirit come through us and the people who receive the Holy Spirit cannot resist the Great Power of God pouring His blessings into our hearts: what the Lord is doing then, only He knows, many times He heals physically or internally, often evil spirits can manifest and these people are released from them and others receive the merciful love of God in a beautiful resting in the spirit or small ecstasy.

When Father Pepito moved from Dominican Republic to Puerto Rico, I was an orphan again searching and searching where to serve God.

I was introduced to Monsignor Luis Gómez and I started working with him, his main Ministry was to pray for the people in the field of Liberation and Exorcism.

PART I

THE HELL UP
IN THE SOUP

EZEKIEL 3, 18

**WHEN I SAY TO A WICKED MAN,
YOU WILL SURELY DIE, AND YOU
DO NOT WARN HIM OR SPEAK
OUT TO DISSUADE HIM FROM HIS EVIL
WAYS IN ORDER TO SAVE HIS LIFE,
THAT WICKED MAN WILL DIE FOR HIS SIN,
AND I WILL HOLD YOU
ACCOUNTABLE FOR HIS BLOOD.**

DO YOU BELIEVE IN THE DEVIL?

Many people do not believe in devils' existence, but the word of God (the Bible) says just the opposite.

From Genesis to Revelation the Bible tell us about this character referring to Satan, Demon, Devil, Azazel, Beelzebú and Belial.

In Isaiah and Ezekiel an account of who this character is, is found:

EZEKIEL 28, 13 – 19
13
YOU WERE IN EDEN, THE GARDEN OF GOD; EVERY PRE-CIOUS STONE ADORNED YOU: RUBY, TOPAZ, AND EMERALD, CHRYSOLITE, ONYX AND JASPER, SAPPHIRE, TURQUOISE AND BERYL. YOUR SETTINGS AND MOUNTINGS WERE MADE OF GOLD; ON THE DAY YOU WERE CREATED THEY WERE PREPARED.

14
YOU WERE ANOINTED AS A GUARDIAN CHERUB, FOR SO I ORDAINED YOU. YOU WERE ON THE HOLY MOUNT OF GOD; YOU WALKED AMONG THE FIERY STONES.

15

YOU WERE BLAMELESS IN YOUR WAYS FROM THE DAY YOU WERE CREATED TILL WICKEDNESS WAS FOUND IN YOU.

16

THROUGH YOUR WIDESPREAD TRADE YOU WERE FILLED WITH VIOLENCE, AND YOU SINNED. SO I DROVE YOU IN DISGRACE FROM THE MOUNT OF GOD, AND I EXPELLED YOU, O GUARDIAN CHERUB, FROM AMONG THE FIERY STONES.

17

YOUR HEART BECAME PROUD ON ACCOUNT OF YOUR BEAUTY, AND YOU CORRUPTED YOUR WISDOM BECAUSE OF YOUR SPLENDOR. SO I THREW YOU TO THE EARTH; I MADE A SPECTACLE OF YOU BEFORE KINGS.

18

BY YOUR MANY SINS AND DISHONEST TRADE YOU HAVE DESECRATED YOUR SANCTUARIES. SO I MADE A FIRE COME OUT FROM YOU, AND IT CONSUMED YOU, AND I REDUCED YOU TO ASHES ON THE GROUND IN THE SIGHT OF ALL WHO WERE WATCHING.

19

ALL THE NATIONS WHO KNEW YOU ARE APPALLED AT YOU; YOU HAVE COME TO A HORRIBLE END AND WILL BE NO MORE.

ISAIAH 14, 12 – 16
12

HOW YOU HAVE FALLEN FROM HEAVEN, O MORNING STAR, SON OF THE DAWN! YOU HAVE BEEN CAST DOWN TO THE EARTH, YOU WHO ONCE LAID LOW THE NATIONS!

13

YOU SAID IN YOUR HEART, I WILL ASCEND TO HEAVEN; I WILL RAISE MY THRONE ABOVE THE STARS OF GOD; I WILL SIT ENTHRONED ON THE MOUNT OF ASSEMBLY ON THE UTMOST HEIGHTS OF THE SACRED MOUNTAIN.

14

I WILL ASCEND ABOVE THE TOPS OF THE CLOUDS; I WILL MAKE MYSELF LIKE THE MOST HIGH.

15

BUT YOU ARE BROUGHT DOWN TO THE GRAVE, TO THE DEPTHS OF THE PIT.

16

THOSE WHO SEE YOU STARE AT YOU, THEY PONDER YOUR FATE: IS THIS THE MAN WHO SHOOK THE EARTH AND MADE KINGDOMS TREMBLE,

God created the angels, among them was one adorned with many attributes, including having a great brightness and extraordinary beauty, named **Lucifer** which means full of light or light bearer, in Ezekiel is determined as a Great Cherub and protector.

Lucifer defied the will of God together with a third of the angels, there arose a great spiritual battle between these angels and the angels faithful to God were guided by the Archangel Michael.

Lucifer was cast from heaven like lightning.

Another name given to this angel is Satan meaning obstacle in Greek known as Apolión, meaning Hebrew for destructive Abaddon.

Other names that occur:

- ➤ **PRINCE DES TÉNEBRES.**
- ➤ **ADVERSAIRE.**
- ➤ **ACCUSANT.**
- ➤ **DECEIVER.**
- ➤ **DRAGON.**
- ➤ **MENTEUR.**
- ➤ **LEVIATHAN.**
- ➤ **KILLER.**
- ➤ **SNAKE.**
- ➤ **GOD OF THIS WORLD.**
- ➤ **PRINCE OF THIS WORLD.**
- ➤ **SEDUCER IN THE WORLD.**

We do not intend to tire you out with innumerable Bible citations in relation to the existence of demons. Each one of these events has a lesson that will give us the necessary knowledge to understand and learn the teachings and experiences of this book.

We also want you to take conscience of a reality that our fight is not with the flesh but with the spirits of evil.

EPHESIANS 6, 12
FOR OUR STRUGGLE IS NOT AGAINST FLESH AND BLOOD, BUT AGAINST THE RULERS, AGAINST THE AUTHORITIES, AGAINST THE POWERS OF THIS DARK WORLD AND AGAINST THE SPIRITUAL FORCES OF EVIL IN THE HEAVENLY RALMS.

When we pray, we see that some people heal physically, we are amazed by this, and thank God, we tell all the people with whom we speak and we gather by the thousands to see lay brothers, pastors, Ministers and priests that Jesus has given the gift of healing and the Holy Spirit.

We are going after them to be healed by Jesus; However when there is a spiritual healing (Liberation), we want to hide this healing from other people, we don't want to tell people about it and nevertheless, seek those whom Jesus chose to do these healings as if it was not the same Jesus the one who does the healing, breaks the captivity and saves this soul.

In the Biblical stories in the New Testament we find as many releases as physical healings done by Jesus, and in any case was made in private, but on the contrary in the midst of thousands of people to serve as a testimony to the great mercy of Him and His Father.

Why do we want to hide these healings?

Of course the devil plays an important role because he does not want us to see that he is defeated and that thru Jesus, God has given the power to defeat all powers.

MATTHEW 28, 18
THEN JESUS CAME TO THEM AND SAID, ALL AUTHORITY IN HEAVEN AND ON EARTH HAS BEEN GIVEN TO ME.

When a person is physically healed, everyone comes out to tell about that healing, even the same person that was healed starts to give testimony in the groups and in the Church.

But when there is a healing thru liberation, everybody keeps quiet, the world remains silent, and nobody says anything and even the healed and freed person don't say a word, because it feels ashamed or embarrassed, to say what God in His great mercy had done for him. Many are in favor of doing the liberation in private out of respect for the person who is being released of evil spirits.

Jesus in the Gospels never made a release in private, quite the contrary he even commanded the demon possessed man to go back to his village and to give testimony of what God had done for him.

Many times we hear or see healings done by witches, shamans, healers that heal and operate thru entities or spirits, which reminds me of when we take a pill that is coated so that our palate not savor the substance that typically are bitter and unpleasant, likewise these entities and spirits are wrapped demons that act out thru these people or mediums, etc.

There is nothing hidden that will not revealed in the light, and Jesus and his disciples made these releases in front of the village to build their faith.

Jesus himself tells us that if by one finger he can expel the demons is that the Kingdom of heaven has come.

I guarantee you brothers that it is not the same that the Kingdom of heaven comes to you, bringing salvation, love, peace, mercy, understanding, etc. On the other hand, the Kingdom of Satan and his demons bring condemnation, heartbreak, anxiety, pressure, evil, envy, disunity and death, etc.

MATTHEW 12, 28
BUT IF I DRIVE OUT DEMONS BY THE SPIRIT OF GOD, THEN THE KINGDOM OF GOD HAS COME UPON YOU.

I know that healing is very nice and we are happy to see how Jesus continues to act today and forever, and that is nothing pleasant to see a release, with a person shouting, wallow on the ground and throwing out foam from the mouth, but I can give testimony that the love and mercy that is felt when Jesus liberates a brother and rescues him from the bonds of Satan you can't express in words, we must feel it firsthand and in the heart.

LUKE 13, 16 – 17

16

THEN SHOULD NOT THIS WOMAN, A DAUGHTER OF ABRAHAM, WHOM SATAN HAS KEPT BOUND FOR EIGHTEEN LONG YEARS, BE SET FREE ON THE SABBATH DAY FROM WHAT BOUND HER?

17

WHEN HE SAID THIS, ALL HIS OPPONENTS WERE HUMILIATED, BUT THE PEOPLE WERE DELIGHTED WITH ALL THE WONDERFUL THINGS HE WAS DOING.

I hope that these biblical quotations give us a conviction that the Kingdom of Satan and his demons are real and the importance of fighting against them. Don't want to ignore that there are human spirits that act and are a bad or as worse than the demons.

We must do what Jesus has entrusted to us and let's be prepared for the battle, because our enemies are thrown here on Earth.

REVELATION 12, 12

THEREFORE REJOICE, YOU HEAVENS AND YOU WHO DWELL IN THEM! BUT WOE TO THE EARTH AND THE SEA, BECAUSE THE DEVIL HAS GONE DOWN TO YOU!

In the book of Revelation we can read about a great final battle between these angels, in which Saint Michael Archangel will defeat Satan forever, and will be thrown into the Lake of eternal fire with all his angels and his followers.

REVELATION 12, 7 – 9

7

AND THERE WAS WAR IN HEAVEN. MICHAEL AND HIS ANGELS FOUGHT AGAINST THE DRAGON, AND THE DRAGON AND HIS ANGELS FOUGHT BACK.

8

BUT HE WAS NOT STRONG ENOUGH, AND THEY LOST THEIR PALACE IN HEAVEN.

9

THE GREAT DRAGON WAS HURLED DOWN THAT ANCIENT SERPENT CALLED THE DEVIL, OR SATAN, WHO LEADS THE WHOLE WORLD ASTRAY. HE WAS HURLED TO THE EARTH, AND HIS ANGELS WITH HIM.

JOHN 12, 31
NOW IS THE TIME FOR JUDGMENT ON THIS WORLD; NOW THE PRINCE OF THIS WORLD WILL BE DRIVEN OUT.

JUDE 1, 6
AND THE ANGELS WHO DID NOT KEEP THEIR POSITIONS OF AUTHORITY BUT ABANDONED THEIR OWN HOME THESE HE HAS KEPT IN DARKNESS, BOUND WITH EVERLASTING CHAINS FOR JUDGMENT ON THE GREAT DAY.

OTHER BIBLE VERSICLES:

GENESIS 3, 1
DANIEL 10, 13
MATTHEW 12, 24
MATTHEW 12, 25
MATTHEW 23, 33

These biblical citations clearly shows us the reality of the existence of demons; Satan is approximately named 50 times in the Bible, the word demon roughly about 70 times and devil about 40 times

SATAN - SATAN

JOB 1, 6 – 9

6

ONE DAY THE ANGELS CAME TO PRESENT THEMSELVES BEFORE THE LORD AND SATAN ALSO CAME WITH THEM.

7

THE LORD SAID TO SATAN, WHERE HAVE YOU COME FROM? SATAN ANSWERED THE LORD, FROM ROAMING THROUGH THE EARTH AND GOING BACK AND FORTH IN IT,

8

THEN THE LORD SAID TO SATAN, HAVE YOU CONSIDERED MY SERVANT JOB? THERE IS NO ONE ON EARTH LIKE HIM; HE IS BLAMELESS AND UPRIGHT, A MAN WHO FEARS GOD AND SHUNS EVIL.

9

DOES JOB FEAR GOD FOR NOTHING? SATAN REPLIED.

ZACHARIAH 3, 1

THEN HE SHOWED ME JOSHUA THE HIGH PRIEST STANDING BEFORE THE ANGEL OF THE LORD, AND SATAN.

REVELATION 12, 10

THEN I HEARD A LOUD VOICE IN HEAVEN SAY:
NOW HAVE COME THE SALVATION AND THE POWER AND THE KINGDOM OF OUR GOD, AND THE AUTHORITY OF HIS CHRIST. FOR THE ACCUSER OF OUR BROTHERS, WHO ACCUSES THEM BEFORE OUR GOD DAY AND NIGHT, HAS BEEN HURLED DOWN.

ZACHARIAH 3, 2
THE LORD SAID TO SATAN, "THE LORD REBUKE YOU, SATAN! THE LORD, WHO HAS CHOSEN JERUSALEM, REBUKE YOU! IS NOT THIS MAN A BURNING STICK SNATCHED FROM THE FIRE?"

ECCLESIASTICUS / SIRACH 21, 27
WHEN THE IMPIOUS CURSES TO SATAN, HIMSELF TO BE CURSES

MATTHEW 4, 10
JESUS SAID TO HIM, AWAY FROM ME, SATAN! FOR IT IS WRITTEN: WORSHIP THE LORD YOUR GOD, AND SERVE HIM ONLY.

MARK 1, 13
AND HE WAS IN THE DESERT FORTY DAYS, BEING TEMPTED BY SATAN. HE WAS WITH THE WILD ANIMALS, AND ANGELS ATTENDED HIM.

MARK 4, 15
SOME PEOPLE ARE LIKE SEED ALONG THE PATH, WHERE THE WORD IS SOWN. AS SOON AS THEY HEAR IT, SATAN COMES AND TAKES AWAY THE WORD THAT WAS SOWN IN THEM.

LUKE 10, 18
HE REPLIED, I SAW SATAN FALL LIKE LIGHTNING FROM HEAVEN.

LUKE 22, 3
THEN SATAN ENTERED JUDAS, CALLED ISCARIOT, ONE OF THE TWELVE.

LUKE 22, 31
SIMON, SIMON, SATAN HAS ASKED TO SIFT YOU AS WHEAT.

JOHN 13, 27
AS SOON AS JUDAS TOOK THE BREAD, SATAN ENTERED INTO HIM.

ACTS 5, 3
THEN PETER SAID, ANANIAS HOW IS IT THAT SATAN HAS SO FILLED YOUR HEART THAT YOU HAVE LIED TO THE HOLY SPIRIT AND HAVE KEPT FOR YOURSELF SOME OF THE MONEY YOU RECEIVED FOR THE LAND?

ACTS 26, 18
TO OPEN THEIR EYES AND TURN THEM FROM DARKNESS TO LIGHT, AND FROM THE POWER OF SATAN TO GOD, SO THAT THEY MAY RECEIVE FORGIVENESS OF SINS AND A PLACE AMONG THOSE WHO ARE SANCTIFIED BY FAITH IN ME.

ROMANS 16, 20
THE GOD OF PEACE WILL SOON CRUSH SATAN UNDER YOUR FEET. THE GRACE OF OUR LORD JESUS BE WITH YOU.

1 CORINTHIANS 5, 5
HAND THIS MAN OVER TO SATAN, SO THAT THE SINFUL NATURE MAY BE DESTROYED AND HIS SPIRIT SAVED ON THE DAY OF THE LORD.

1 CORINTHIANS 7, 5
DO NOT DEPRIVE EACH OTHER EXCEPT BY MUTUAL CONSENT AND FOR A TIME, SO THAT YOU MAY DEVOTE YOURSELVES TO PRAYER. THEN COME TOGETHER AGAIN SO THAT SATAN WILL NOT TEMPT YOU BECAUSE OF YOUR LACK OF SELFCONTROL.

2 CORINTHIANS 11, 14
AND NO WONDER, FOR SATAN HIMSELF MASQUERADES AS AN ANGEL OF LIGHT.

1 THESSALONIANS 2, 18
FOR WE WANTED TO COME TO YOU CERTAINLY I, PAUL, DID, AGAIN AND AGAIN BUT SATAN STOPPED US.

2 THESSALONIANS 2, 9
THE COMING OF THE LAWLESS ONE WILL BE IN ACCORDANCE WITH THE WORK OF SATAN DISPLAYED IN ALL KINDS OF COUNTERFEIT MIRACLES, SIGNS AND WONDERS,

1 TIMOTHY 1, 20
AMONG THEM ARE HYMENAEUS AND ALEXANDER, WHOM I HAVE HANDED OVER TO SATAN TO BE TAUGHT NOT TO BLASPHEME.

1 TIMOTHY 5, 15
SOME HAVE IN FACT ALREADY TURNED AWAY TO FOLLOW SATAN.

REVELATION 2, 9
I KNOW YOUR AFFLICTIONS AND YOUR POVERTY YET YOU ARE RICH! I KNOW THE SLANDER OF THOSE WHO SAY THEY ARE JEWS AND ARE NOT, BUT ARE A SYNAGOGUE OF SATAN.

REVELATION 2, 24
NOW I SAY TO THE REST OF YOU IN THYATIRA, TO YOU WHO DO NOT HOLD TO HER TEACHING AND HAVE NOT LEARNED SATAN'S SOCALLED DEEP SECRETS (I WILL NOT IMPOSE ANY OTHER BURDEN ON YOU):

REVELATION 12, 9
THE GREAT DRAGON WAS HURLED DOWN THAT ANCIENT SERPENT CALLED THE DEVIL, OR SATAN, WHO LEADS THE WHOLE WORLD ASTRAY. HE WAS HURLED TO THE EARTH, AND HIS ANGELS WITH HIM.

REVELATION 20, 2
HE SEIZED THE DRAGON, THAT ANCIENT SERPENT, WHO IS THE DEVIL, OR SATAN, AND BOUND HIM FOR A THOUSAND YEARS.

REVELATION 20, 7
WHEM THE THOUSAND YEARS ARE OVER, SATAN WILL BE RELEASED FROM HIS PRISON

DEMON – DEMONS

TOBIT 3, 8 (It is one of the Deuterocanonical books)
FOR SHE HAD BEEN GIVEN IN MARRIAGE SEVEN TIMES, AND ASMODEUS, THE WORST OF DEMONS, HAD KILLED HER BRIDEGROOMS ONE AFTER ANOTHER BEFORE EVER THEY HAD SLEPT HER AS MAN WITH WIFE. THE SERVANT-GIRL SAID, YES, YOU KILL YOUR BRIDEGROOMS YOURSELF. THAT MAKES SEVEN ALREADY TO WHOM YOU HAVE BEEN GIVEN, AND YOU HAVE NOT ONCE BEEN IN LUCK YET.

MATTHEW 9, 33
AND WHEN THE DEMON WAS DRIVEN OUT, THE MAN WHO HAD BEEM MUTE SPOKE. THE CROWD WAS AMAZED AND SAID, "NOTHING LIKE THIS HAS EVER BEEN SEEN IN ISRAEL".

MATTHEW 11, 18
FOR JOHN CAME NEITHER EATING NOR DRIN-KING, AND THEY SAY, HE HAS A DEMON.

MATTHEW 17, 18
JESUS REBUKED THE DEMON, AND IT CAME OUT OF THE BOY, AND HE WAS HEALED FROM THAT MOMENT.

MARK 7, 26
THE WOMAN WAS A GREEK, BORN IN SYRIAN PHOENICIA. SHE BEGGED JESUS TO DRIVE THE DEMON OUT OF HER DAUGHTER.

MARK 7, 29 - 30

29

THEN HE TOLD HER, "FOR SUCH A REPLY, YOU MAY GO; THE DEMON HAS LEFT YOUR DAUGHTER

30

SHE WENT HOME AND FOUND HER CHILD LYING ON THE BED, AND THE DEMON GONE.

LUKE 4, 33

IN THE SYNAGOGUE THERE WAS A MAN POSSESSED BY A DEMON, AN EVIL SPIRIT. HE CRIED OUT AT THE TOP OF HIS VOICE.

LUKE 4, 35

"BE QUIET!" JESUS SAID STERNLY. "COME OUT OF HIM!" THEN THE DEMON THREW THE MAN DOWN BEFORE THEM ALL AND CAME OUT WITHOUT INJURING HIM.

LUKE 9, 42

EVEN WHILE THE BOY WAS COMING, THE DEMON THREW HIM TO THE GROUND IN A CONVULSION. BUT JESUS REBUKED THE EVIL SPIRIT, HEALED THE BOY AND GAVE HIM BACK TO HIS FATHER.

LUKE 11, 14

JESUS WAS DRIVING OUT A DEMON THAT WAS MUTE. WHEN THE DEMON LEFT, THE MAN WHO HAD BEEN MUTE SPOKE, AND THE CROWD WAS MAZED.

JOHN 7, 20

YOU ARE DEMON POSSESSED, THE CROWD ANSWERED. "WHO IS TRYING TO KILL YOU?"

MARK 16, 9

WHEN JESUS ROSE EARLY ON THE FIRST DAY OF THE WEEK, HE APPEARED FIRST TO MARY MAGDALENE, OUT OF

WHOM HE HAD DRIVEN SEVEN DEMONS.

MARK 16, 17
AND THESE SIGNS WILL ACCOMPANY THOSE WHO BELIEVE: IN MY NAME THEY WILL DRIVE OUT DEMONS; THEY WILL SPEAK IN NEW TONGUES;

LUKE 8, 27
WHEN JESUS STEPPED ASHORE, HE WAS MET BY A DEMON-POSSESSED MAN FROM THE TOWN. FOR A LONG TIME THIS MAN HAD NOT WORN CLOTHES OR LIVED IN A HOUSE, BUT HAD LIVED IN THE TOMBS.

LUKE 8, 30
JESUS ASKED HIM, "WHAT IS YOUR NAME?" "LEGION," HE REPLIED, BECAUSE MANY DEMONS HAD GONE INTO HIM.

LUKE 8, 33
WHEN THE DEMONS CAME OUT OF THE MAN, THEY WENT INTO THE PIGS, AND THE HERD RUSHED DOWN THE STEEP BANK INTO THE LAKE AND WAS DROWNED.

LUKE 9, 1
WHEN JESUS HAD CALLED THE TWELVE TOGETHER, HE GAVE THEM POWER AND AUTHORITY TO DRIVE OUT ALL DEMONS AND TO CURE DISEADES,

LUKE 10, 17
THE SEVENTY RETURNED WITH JOY AND SAID, "LORD, EVEN THE DEMONS SUBMIT TO US IN YOUR NAME.

LUKE 11, 15
BUT SOME OF THEM SAID, "BY BEELZEBUB, THE PRINCE OF DEMONS HE IS DRIVING OUT OF DEMONS."

LUKE 11, 19 – 20
19
NOW IF DRIVE OUT DEMONS BY BEELZEBUB, BY WHOM DO YOUR FOLLOWERS DRIVE THEM OUT? SO THEN, THEY WILL BE YOUR JUDGES.

20
BUT IF I DRIVE OUT DEMONS BY THE FINGER OF GOD, THEN THE KINGDOM OF GOD HAS COME TO YOU

LUKE 13, 32
HE REPLIED, "GO TELL THAT FOX, I WILL DRIVE OUT DEMONS AND HEAL PEOPLE TODAY AND TOMORROW, AND ON THE THIRD DAY I WILL REACH MY GOAL.

1 CORINTIOS 10, 20 - 21
20
NO, BUT THE SACRIFICES OF PAGANS ARE OFFERED TO DEMONS, NOT TO GOD, AND I DO NOT WANT YOU TO BE PARTICIPANTS WITH DEMONS.

21
YOU CAN NOT DRINK THE CUP OF THE LORD AND THE CUP OF DEMONS TOO; YOU CAN NOT HAVE A PART IN BOTH THE LORD'S TABLE AND THE TABLE OF DEMONS.

JAMES 2, 19
YOU BELIEVE THAT THERE IS ONE GOD. GOOD!
EVEN THE DEMONS BELIEVE THAT AND SHUDDER.

REVELATION 9, 20
THE REST OF MANKIND THAT WHERE NOT KILLED BY THESE PLAGUES STILL DID NOT REPENT OF THE WORK OF THEIR HANDS; THEY DID NOT STOP WORSHIPING DEMONS, AND IDOLS OF GOLD, SILVER, BRONZE, STONE AND WOOD IDOLS THAT CANNOT SEE OR HEAR OR WALK.

REVELATION 16, 14
THEY ARE SPIRITS OF DEMONS PERFORMING MIRACULOUS SIGNS, AND THEY GO OUT TO THE KINGS OF THE WHOLE WORLD, TO GATHER THEM FOR THE BATLE ON THE GREAT DAY OF GOD ALMIGHTY.

REVELATION 18, 2
WITH A MIGHTY VOICE HE SHOUTED:
FALLEN! FALLEN IS BABYLON THE GREAT!
SHE HAS BECOME A HOME FOR DEMONS AND A HAUNT FOR EVERY EVIL SPIRIT A HAUNT FOR EVERY UNCLEAN AND DETESTABLE BIRD.

DEVIL

WISDOM 2, 24
DEATH CAME INTO THE WORLD ONLY THROUGH THE DEVIL'S ENVY, AS THOSE WHO BELONG TO HIM FIND TO THEIR COST.

MATTHEW 4, 1
THEN JESUS WAS LED BY THE SPIRIT INTO THE DESERT TO BE TEMPTED BY THE DEVIL.

MATTHEW 4, 5
THEN THE DEVIL TOOK HIM TO THE HOLY CITY AND HAD HIM STAND ON THE HIGHEST POINT OF THE TEMPLE.

MATTHEW 4, 8
AGAIN, THE DEVIL TOOK HIM TO A VERY HIGH MOUNTAIN AND SHOWED HIM ALL THE KINGDOMS OF THE WORLD AND THEIR SPLENDOR.

MATTHEW 4, 11
THEN THE DEVIL LEFT HIM, AND ANGELS CAME AND ATTENDED HIM.

MATTHEW 25, 41
THEN HE WILL SAY TO THOSE ON HIS LEFT, DEPART FROM ME, YOU WHO ARE CURSED, INTO THE ETERNAL FIRE PREPARED FOR THE DEVIL AND HIS ANGELS.

LUKE 4, 6
AND HE SAID TO HIM, "I WILL GIVE YOU ALL THEIR AUTHORITY AND SPLENDOR, FOR IT HAS BEEN GIVEN TO ME, AND I CAN GIVE IT TO ANYONE I WANT TO.

LUKE 4, 13
WHEN THE DEVIL HAD FINISHED ALL THIS TEMPTING, HE LEFT HIM UNTIL AN OPPORTUNE TIME.

JOHN 8, 44
YOU BELONG TO YOUR FATHER, THE DEVIL, AND YOU WANT TO CARRY OUT YOUR FATHER'S DESIRE. HE WAS A MURDERER FROM THE BEGINNING NOT HOLDING TO THE TRUTH, FOR THERE IS NO TRUTH IN HIM. WHEN HE LIES, HE SPEAKS HIS NATIVE LANGUAGE, FOR HE IS A LIAR AND THE FATHER OF LIES.

JOHN 13, 2
THE EVENING MEAL WAS BEING SERVED, AND THE DEVIL HAD ALREADY PROMPTED JUDAS ISCARIOT, SON OF SIMON, TO BETRAY JESUS.

ACTS 10, 38
HOW GOD ANOINTED JESUS OF NAZARETH WITH THE HOLY SPIRIT AND POWER, AND NOW HE WENT AROUND DOING GOOD AND HEALING ALL WHO WERE UNDER THE POWER OF THE DEVIL, BECAUSE GOD WAS WITH HIM.

ACTS 13, 10
YOU ARE A CHILD OF THE DEVIL AND AN ENEMY OF EVERYTHING THAT IS RIGHT! YOU ARE FULL OF ALL KINDS OF DECEIT AND TRICKERY. WILL YOU NEVER STOP PERVERTING THE RIGHT WAYS OF THE LORD?

EPHESIANS 4, 27
AND DO NOT GIVE THE DEVIL A FOOTHOLD.

EPHESIANS 6, 11
PUT ON THE FULL ARMOR OF GOD SO THAT CAN TAKE YOUR STAND AGAINST THE DEVIL'S SCHEMES.

1 TIMOTHY 3, 6 - 7
6
HE MUST NOT BE A RECENT CONVERT, OR HE MAY BECOME CONCEITED AND FALL UNDER THE SAME JUDGMENT AS THE DEVIL.

7
THEY MUST ALSO HAVE A GOOD REPUTATION WITH OUTSIDERS, SO THAT HE WILL NOT FALL INTO DISGRACE AND INTO THE DEVIL'S TRAP.

JAMES 3, 15
SUCH "WISDOM" DOES NOT COME DOWN FROM HEAVEN BUT IS EARTHLY, UNSPIRITUAL, OF THE DEVIL.

1 TIMOTHY 4, 1
THE SPIRIT CLEARLY SAYS THAT IN LATER TIMES SOME WILL ABANDON THE FAITH AND FOLLOW DECEIVING SPIRITS AND THINGS TAUGHT BY DEMONS.

2 TIMOTHY 2, 26
AND THAT THEY WILL COME TO THEIR SENSES AND ESCAPE FROM THE TRAP OF THE DEVIL, WHO HAS TAKEN THEM CAPTIVE TO DO HIS WILL.

HEBREWS 2, 14
SINCE THE CHILDREN HAVE FLESH AND BLOOD, HE TOO SHARED IN THEIR HUMANITY SO THAT BY HIS DEATH HE MIGHT DESTROY HIM WHO HOLDS THE POWER OF DEATH THAT IS, THE DEVIL.

JAMES 4, 7
SUBMIT YOURSELVES, THEN, TO GOD. RESIST THE DEVIL, AND HE WILL FLEE FROM YOU.

1 PETER 5, 8
BE SELF-CONTROLLED AND ALERT. YOUR ENEMY THE DEVIL PROWLS AROUND LIKE A ROARING LION LOOKING FOR SOMEONE TO DEVOUR.

1 JOHN 3, 8
HE WHO DOES WHAT IS SINFUL IS OF THE DEVIL, BECAUSE THE DEVIL HAS BEEN SINNING FROM THE BEGINNING. THE REASON THE SON OF GOD APPEARED WAS TO DESTROY THE DEVIL'S WORK.

1 JOHN 3, 10
THIS IS HOW WE KNOW WHO THE CHILDREN OF GOD ARE AND WHO THE CHILDREN OF THE DEVIL ARE: ANYONE WHO DOES NOT DO WHAT IS RIGHT IS NOT A CHILD OF GOD; NOR IS ANYONE WHO DOES NOT LOVE HIS BROTHER.

JUDE 1, 9
BUT EVEN THE ARCHANGEL MICHAEL, WHEN HE WAS DISPUTING WITH THE DEVIL ABOUT THE BODY OF MOSES, DID NOT DARE TO BRING A SLANDEROUS ACCUSATION AGAINST HIM, BUT SAID, "THE LORD REBUKE YOU!"

OTHER REFERENCES

GENESIS 3, 1

TOBIT 3, 17
TOBIT 6, 8
TOBIT 6, 14
TOBIT 6, 16 -17
TOBIT 8, 3

DANIEL 10, 13

1 CHRONICLES 21, 1

JOB 1, 12
JOB 2, 1 – 7

DEUTERONOMY 6, 13
DEUTERONOMY 32, 17

LEVITICUS 16, 8   AZAZEL
LEVITICUS 16, 10   AZAZEL
LEVITICUS 16, 26   AZAZEL

NAHUM 1,11
NAHUM 2, 1

BARUCH 4, 7
BARUCH 4, 35

PSALMS 18, 5
PSALMS 106, 37

2 SAMUEL 22, 5   BELIAL

MATTHEW 7, 22
MATTHEW 8, 31
MATTHEW 9, 34
MATTHEW 10, 8
MATTHEW 10, 25
MATTHEW 12, 24 – 25
MATTHEW 12, 26
MATTHEW 12, 27 – 28
MATTHEW 13, 39
MATTHEW 16, 23
MATTHEW 23, 33

MARK 1, 34
MARK 1, 39
MARK 3, 15
MARK 3, 22
MARK 3, 23
MARK 3, 26
MARK 6, 13
MARK 8, 33
MARK 9, 38

LUKE 4, 2 – 3
LUKE 4, 33
LUKE 4, 41
LUKE 7, 33
LUKE 8, 2
LUKE 8, 12
LUKE 8, 29
LUKE 8, 35
LUKE 8, 38
LUKE 9, 49
LUKE 11, 15
LUKE 11, 18 - 19
LUKE 10, 20 – 21

JOHN 6, 70
JOHN 8, 48 – 49
JOHN 8, 52

1 CORINTHIANS 4,

2 CORINTHIANS 2, 11
2 CORINTHIANS 6, 15
2 CORINTHIANS 12, 7

1 JOHN 3, 10

REVELATION 2, 10
REVELATION 2, 13
REVELATION 3, 9
REVELATION 9, 11 ABADDON
REVELATION 20, 2
REVELATION 20, 10

DO YOU BELIEVE IN JESUS AND HIS POWER?

Many people in our world by ignorance do not believe in Jesus, others believe, but do not trust Him and His salvific work, if we still have not read the Bible, which is the word of God, then is logical not to believe in Jesus and His power. But there is a statement given by God's damnation to one who does not believe and trust in Jesus.

JOHN 3, 18
WHOEVER BELIEVES IN HIM IS NOT CONDEMNED, BUT WHOEVER DOES NOT BELIEVE STANDS CONDEMNED ALREADY BECAUSE HE HAS NOT BELIEVED IN THE NAME OF GOD'S ONE AND ONLY SON.

If we Christians regardless of the nomination to which you belong do not teach and talk about who Jesus is, if we are not fulfilling their mandates, the stones would then speak.

LUKE 19, 40
"I TELL YOU" HE REPLIED, "IF THEY KEEP QUIET, THE STONES WILL CRY OUT."

Talk about the Kingdom of God, Jesus and the Holy Spirit and salvation plan is a mandate and a duty of all Christians; we must preach the word of God **(With Power)** and give live testimony of what God has done in each of us.

Recently a book was released that later became a film titled "The Da Vinci Code", I don't want to comment concerning the book nor the film, but my comment is about the number of people who believe in a written book of science fiction that are pure lies.

But few people we speak the word of God to (the Bible) and do not believe certain acts, however they believe in what they hear in newscasts and newspapers, especially any information of horoscopes, a divination, etc. Believe in the power of the devil and his demons in his healings and their divinations. But do not believe in the prophecies, releases, or healings done by Jesus, these must be in studies and trials scientists, especially if it's a miracle.

Let's use our imagination for a moment:
We pretend that we are recording a baseball game between the Boston Red Sox and the New York Yankees, after finishing the recording of the game Boston Red Sox won 7 to 3.

The following day we play back the recording to watch the game, and I say to you, I bet $1,000.00 that the Red Sox are the winners and I doubled up that bet saying that the Red Sox scored 7 runs. **Would you bet?** I am sure that you would say "Of course not, I am not a fool."

So if Jesus defeated the world, defeated Satan and was given all power in heaven and on earth and every knee must double up in the heavens and on the earth in front of Him, how it is possible to go after the idols, deities, soothsayers that only are disguised demons?; We know that they lost, but bet and we submit to them as fools.

Many times we hear criticism about the Jehovah's witnesses and the Mormons, but if we ask ourselves this question in our heart:

Are they doing what God has commanded them? Comfortable are we sometimes and our churches that we don't understand the mandate of Jesus; we, who we called ourselves Christians.

MARK 16, 15 – 18
15
HE SAID TO THEM, "GO INTO ALL THE WORLD AND PREACH THE GOOD NEWS TO ALL CREATION."

16
WHOEVER BELIEVES AND IS BAPTIZED WILL BE SAVED, BUT WHOEVER DOES NOT BELIEVE WILL BE CONDEMNED.

17
AND THESE SIGNS WILL ACCOMPANY THOSE WHO BELIEVE: IN MY NAME THEY WILL DRIVE OUT DEMONS; THEY WILL SPEAK IN NEW TONGUES;

18
THEY WILL PICK UP SNAKES WITH THEIR HANDS; AND WHEN THEY DRINK DEADLY POISON, IT WILL NOT HURT THEM AT ALL; THEY WILL PLACE THEIR HANDS ON SICK PEOPLE, AND THEY WILL GET WELL.

Believe me brothers, that I am not writing this as criticism of anyone, but to wake up from the slumber and do what Jesus has commanded us, I do not know why we believe that only the priests, religious, nuns, ministers are trained for it. We are in a complete mistake; this mandate is for everyone who believes.

All Christians have received baptism, but to receive it is not everything, must activate it and confirm it in our hearts so that the Holy Spirit is the guide of our lives.

Without this confirmation which we call activation in the Holy Spirit we can't speak of our salvation, or Jesus, or of the Kingdom of God, much less understand the word of God (the Bible).

We are going to make a comparison, imagine that they give us a new Digital HD TV and we installed it in our favorite site, we sit down to watch it….. but if we don't turn it on, we will never see our favorite show, although we have the latest model digital TV in our house; the same goes with The Holy Spirit, we have the holy spirit that dwells in us in a passive way, but if we never activate it we won't be guided by Him, fulfilling his commandments, not can we have the gifts and fruits of the spirit, nor understand the word of God (the Bible) we cannot know who is Jesus and will not have communion with Him.

ROMANS 8, 9
YOU, HOWEVER, ARE CONTROLLED NOT BY THE SINFUL NATURE BUT BY THE SPIRIT, IF THE SPIRIT OF GOD LIVES IN YOU. AND IF ANYONE DOES NOT HAVE THE SPIRIT OF CHRIST, HE DOES NOT BELONG TO CHRIST.

Brothers ask Jesus to send us His Spirit; He awarded it to anyone who requests it with a clean and pure heart. Jesus Himself tells us:

LUKE 11, 13
IF YOU THEN, THOUGH YOU ARE EVIL, KNOW HOW TO GIVE GOOD GIFTS TO YOUR CHILDREN, HOW MUCH MORE WILL YOUR FATHER IN HEAVEN GIVE THE HOLY SPIRIT TO THOSE WHO ASK HIM!

When the apostles were sad for the departure of Jesus to the heavens; He told them of the convenience of His departure to the Father, so our Heavenly Father can send us His Holy Spirit.

JOHN 16, 7

BUT I TELL YOU THE TRUTH: IT IS FOR YOUR GOOD THAT I AM GOING AWAY UNLESS I GO AWAY, THE COUNSELOR WILL NOT COME TO YOU; BUT IF I GO, I WILL SEND HIM TO YOU.

JOHN 7, 38

WHOEVER BELIEVES IN ME, AS THE SCRIPTURE HAS SAID, STREAMS OF LIVING WATER WILL FLOW FROM WITHIN HIM.

The Holy Spirit is the key communication and understanding with God and His beloved Son Jesus Christ; Jesus Himself makes his works by the power of the Holy Spirit.

MATTHEW 3, 16

AS SOON AS JESUS WAS BAPTIZED, HE WENT UP OUT OF THE WATER. AT THAT MOMENT HEAVEN WAS OPENED, AND HE SAW THE SPIRIT OF GOD DESCENDING LIKE A DOVE AND LIGHTING ON HIM.

MATTHEW 12, 28

BUT IF I DRIVE OUT DEMONS BY THE SPIRIT OF GOD, THEN THE KINGDOM OF GOD HAS COME UPON YOU.

In one way or another we **believe in Jesus** but **trust in Jesus** and his words is a different thing. We know by the word of God that even the demons believe and know who Jesus is.

MARK 5, 7

HE SHOUTED AT THE TOP OF HIS VOICE, "WHAT DO YOU WANT WITH ME, JESUS, SON OF THE MOST HIGH GOD? SWEAR TO GOD THAT YOU WON'T TORTURE ME!"

Mark tells us as one of the miracles of Jesus shows us how to work the Holy Spirit through Jesus.

MARK 5, 28, 30, 33 – 34
28
BECAUSE SHE THOUGHT, "IF I JUST TOUCH HIS CLOTHES, I WILL BE HEALED."

30
AT ONCE JESUS REALIZED THAT POWER HAD GONE OUT FROM HIM. HE TURNED AROUND IN THE CROWD AND ASKED, "WHO TOUCHED MY CLOTHES?"

33
THEN THE WOMAN, KNOWING WHAT HAD HAPPENED TO HER, CAME AND FELL AT HIS FEET AND, TREMBLING WITH FEAR, TOLD HIM THE WHOLE TRUTH.

34
HE SAID TO HER, "DAUGHTER, YOUR FAITH HAS HEALED YOU. GO IN PEACE AND BE FREED FROM YOUR SUFFERING.

Faith and the self-confidence of this woman in Jesus made it possible for her to receive healing and be saved, the fear of this woman was that she was in an unclean condition and it was forbidden at that time to approach a person while having a blood flow, they should purify themselves before entering the city, and much less could touch a Rabbi or anyone until it was clean.

Isaiah confirms to us that we must have full confidence in God and in Jesus:

ISAIAH 26, 3 – 4
3
YOU WILL KEEP IN PERFECT PEACE HIM WHOSE MIND IS STEADFAST, BECAUSE HE TRUSTS IN YOU.

4
TRUST IN THE LORD FOREVER, FOR THE LORD, IS THE ROCK ETERNAL.

JOHN 16, 33
I HAVE TOLD YOU THESE THINGS, SO THAT IN ME YOU MAY HAVE PEACE. IN THIS WORLD YOU WILL HAVE TROUBLE. BUT TAKE HEART! I HAVE OVERCOME THE WORLD.

In verse 5, 30 in the Gospel of St. Mark talk about how power left Jesus, and Jesus Himself told His disciples to stay in the city until they were vested with the power of the Holy Spirit.

LUKE 24, 49
I AM GOING TO SEND YOU WHAT MY FATHER HAS PROMISED; BUT STAY IN THE CITY UNTIL YOU HAVE BEEN VESTED WITH POWER FROM ON HIGH.

The same St. Paul tells the Corinthians of the importance of this power that we all must have who we are in Christ:

1 CORINTHIANS 2, 4 - 5
4
MY MESSAGE AND MY PREACHING WERE NOT WITH WISE AND PERSUASIVE WORDS, BUT WITH A DEMONSTRATION OF THE SPIRIT'S POWER,

5
SO THAT YOUR FAITH MIGHT NOT REST ON MEN'S WISDOM, BUT ON GOD'S POWER.

1 CORINTHIANS 4, 20
FOR THE KINGDOM OF GOD IS NOT A MATTER OF TALK BUT OF POWER.

Let's say a well-known Spanish saying, **"Clearer does not sing a rooster"**, St. Paul tells us that neither by eloquent speakers, nor by wonderful preaching, nor by human wisdom theology courses, retreats, etc.: but with demonstration of power through us, for which we will obtain faith and that this faith it will not be grounded in wisdom of men but in the power of God given by God through the gifts of the Holy

Spirit so that it pleases all those who **believe** and **trust** in the word of Jesus, so with this power we can fulfill their mandates.

With this I do not mean that we must not read, take courses, retreats, search the word of God (the Bible); now, what the Gospel teaches us is that the preaching of the word of God, must be accompanied by signs and wonders, healings and freeing the captives by demons.

MARK 16, 15 – 18
15
HE SAID TO THEM, "GO INTO ALL THE WORLD AND PREACH THE GOOD NEWS TO ALL CREATION."

16
WHOEVER BELIEVES AND IS BAPTIZED WILL BE SAVED, BUT WHOEVER DOES NOT BELIEVE WILL BE CONDEMNED.

17
AND THESE SIGNS WILL ACCOMPANY THOSE WHO BELIEVE: IN MY NAME THEY WILL DRIVE OUT DEMONS; THEY WILL SPEAK IN NEW TONGUES;

18
THEY WILL PICK UP SNAKES WITH THEIR HANDS; AND WHEN THEY DRINK DEADLY POISON, IT WILL NOT HURT THEM AT ALL; THEY WILL PLACE THEIR HANDS ON SICK PEOPLE, AND THEY WILL GET WELL.

The promise of God and his beloved son Jesus is the Holy Spirit in each of us, He is the guide of our lives and He is who gives us authority and power through the gifts of the Holy Spirit to serve Him, this promise was recounted in several passages of the word of God (the Bible),

Life in the Holy Spirit gives us and fills us with power and activities; thru these activities we know the life He gives us and how to serve Him.

LEVITICUS 26, 12
WILL WALK AMONG YOU AND BE YOUR GOD, AND YOU WILL BE MY PEOPLE.

EZEKIEL 37, 27
MY DWELLING PLACE WILL BE WITH THEM; I WILL BE THEIR GOD, AND THEY WILL BE MY PEOPLE.

REVELATION 21, 3
AND I HEARD A LOUD VOICE FROM THE THRONE SAYING, "NOW THE DWELLING OF GOD IS WITH MEN, AND HE WILL LIVE WITH THEM. THEY WILL BE HIS PEOPLE, AND GOD HIMSELF WILL BE WITH THEM AND BE THEIR GOD."

1 CORINTHIANS 3, 16
DON'T YOU KNOW THAT YOU YOURSELVES ARE GOD'S TEMPLE AND THAT GOD'S SPIRIT LIVES IN YOU?

1 CORINTHIANS 6, 19
DO YOU NOT KNOW THAT YOUR BODY IS A TEMPLE OF THE HOLY SPIRIT, WHO IS IN YOU, WHOM YOU HAVE RECEIVED FROM GOD? YOU ARE NOT YOUR OWN;

2 CORINTHIANS 6, 16
WHAT AGREEMENT IS THERE BETWEEN THE TEMPLE OF GOD AND IDOLS? FOR WE ARE THE TEMPLE OF THE LIVING GOD AS GOD HAS SAID: "I WILL LIVE WITH THEM AND WALK AMONG THEM, AND I WILL BE THEIR GOD, AND THEY WILL BE MY PEOPLE".

Beautiful would be that everyone can say as Saint Paul:

GALATIANS 2, 20
*I HAVE BEEN CRUCIFIED WITH CHRIST AND I NO LONGER
LIVE, BUT CHRIST LIVES IN ME. THE LIFE I LIVE IN THE
BODY, I LIVE BY FAITH IN THE SON OF GOD, WHO LOVED
ME AND GAVE HIMSELF FOR ME.*

In Romans 7, 6; St. Paul tells us that we should serve under the new
spirit system and not under the old regime of the letter.

We are not trying to judge anyone, but how many brothers, pastors,
Ministers and priests, etc., still today in the regime of the letters and not
the new regime of the spirit; do not realize that their churches and
temples are dying and are full of rebukes and calls for money to make
buildings that only are vanities for the human growth and not of saved
souls.

We must ask ourselves brothers in Christ, in how many of our church or
temple, does the Holy Spirit dwells, and have the authority and the
power of the spirit?

God will not ask us if we know the Bible from heart or if we built a
large and beautiful church, I do not think that this is the fruit that we
must give. The question would be **how many have we brought to
Christ in spirit and truth?**

Look at our churches and temples, how many of those are living the life
of the spirit and how many are benchwarmers who only go to church on
Sunday and spend years doing studies.

Jesus looked for simple people to carry the Gospel to the ends of the
Earth, today we are looking for theologians, doctors, ministers, pastors
or priests, or what is worse, people with a good bank account to give a
good tithing; Perhaps everyone has the best of intentions, but they lack
the basics, a living Holy Spirit, that inject their church to a living Jesus,
full of charismas to cast out demons and heal the sick and all of it's

47

parishioners work for the Lord and not a tiny group of arrogant leaders because they have a position or appointment.

How beautiful is it when we go to a temple or church and there is praising to the Lord of Heaven and He in His infinite goodness heals, performs miracles, releases, inner healings to our brothers and sisters who full of faith, mercy and the Holy Spirit give us the infinite love that God provides us.

THE POWER OF JESUS

Many Bible quotes tell us that from the body of Jesus power went off when he was performing healings. Where does this power come from?

MATTHEW 22, 29
JESUS REPLIED, "YOU ARE IN ERROR BECAUSE YOU DO NOT KNOW THE SCRIPTURES" OR THE POWER OF GOD.

The power of Jesus is the Holy Spirit; Jesus received the Holy Spirit with the baptism of John in the Jordan.

Jesus gave them power to his disciples to expel demons and heal the sick:

LUKE 9, 1
WHEN JESUS HAD CALLED THE TWELVE TOGETHER, HE GAVE THEM POWER AND AUTHORITY TO DRIVE OUT ALL DEMONS AND TO CURE DISEASES.

Not only gave them power to the 12 disciples but that gave them power to 70 other versions say 72.

LUKE 10, 17
THE SEVENTY RETURNED WITH JOY AND SAID, "LORD, EVEN THE DEMONS SUBMIT TO US IN YOUR NAME.

LUKE 10, 19
HAVE GIVEN YOU AUTHORITY TO TRAMPLE ON SNAKES AND SCORPIONS AND TO OVERCOME ALL THE POWER OF THE ENEMY; NOTHING WILL HARM YOU.

Jesus promises to send the promise of His Father and be vested with power:

LUKE 24, 49
I AM GOING TO SEND YOU WHAT MY FATHER HAS PROMISED; BUT STAY IN THE CITY UNTIL YOU HAVE BEEN VESTED WITH POWER FROM ON HIGH.

ACTS 1, 8
BUT YOU WILL RECEIVE POWER WHEN THE HOLY SPIRIT COMES ON YOU; AND YOU WILL BE MY WITNESSES IN JERUSALEM, AND IN ALL JUDEA AND SAMARIA, AND TO THE ENDS OF THE EARTH.

Not only pray for the disciples, but for all of us:

JOHN 17, 20
MY PRAYER IS NOT FOR THEM ALONE. I PRAY ALSO FOR THOSE WHO WILL BELIEVE IN ME THROUGH THEIR MESSAGE,

It gives us the same promise He gave to the Apostles to believe and trust in Jesus.

MARK 16, 16
WHOEVER BELIEVES AND IS BAPTIZED WILL BE SAVED, BUT WHOEVER DOES NOT BELIEVE WILL BE CONDEMNED.

When we believe in Jesus, we receive the Holy Spirit and receive the power from on high to serve Him as his disciples.

MARK 16, 17
AND THESE SIGNS WILL ACCOMPANY THOSE WHO BELIEVE:
IN MY NAME THEY WILL DRIVE OUT DEMONS; THEY WILL
SPEAK IN NEW TONGUES;

Now the next question is why the majority of Christians today, do not have these signals and this power?

There is no easy answer, but I think that we must ask ourselves the following questions:

1.- Do we believe in Jesus?
2.- Do we trust in Him?
3.- How do we activate the Holy Spirit?
4.- Have we forgiven those who offended us?
5.- Are we regretful and are we converted?
6.- Have we given ourselves unconditionally to serve Him?
7.- Have we received the Holy Spirit through the imposition of the hands?
8.- Have we have received gifts of the Holy Spirit or have we rejected them?
9.- Have we turned off the Holy Spirit and His gifts?
10.- Are we ready to give up our lives for our brothers and sisters?
11.- Do we obey men rather than obey the mandate of God?

I can only tell you that God's promise is fulfilled, God can not lie in His Word, we just have to believe and trust Him fully and give us up to unconditionally serve Him, this promise is for everyone.

Having faith is a gift of God, this wonderful gift we ask that He gives us and that increases it every day; Jesus himself often admonished His disciples and followers for having such little faith.

MATTHEW 8, 26
HE REPLIED, "YOU OF LITLE FAITH, WHY ARE YOU SO AFRAID?" THEN HE GOT UP AND REBUKED THE WINDS AND THE WAVES, AND IT WAS COMPLETELY CALM.

MATTHEW 17, 20
BECAUSE YOU HAVE SO LITTLE FAITH; I TELL YOU THE TRUTH, IF YOU HAVE FAITH AS SMALL AS A MUSTARD SEED, YOU CAN SAY TO THIS MOUNTAIN, MOVE FROM HERE TO THERE AND IT WILL MOVE. NOTHING WILL BE IMPOSSIBLE FOR YOU.

But the beautiful thing is that it happen just the opposite when we have faith:

MATTHEW 8, 13
THEN JESUS SAID TO THE CENTURION, "GO! IT WILL BE DONE JUST AS YOU BELIEVE IT WOULD."

MATTHEW 9, 22
JESUS TURNED AND SAW HER. "TAKE HEART, DAUGHTER," HE SAID, "YOUR FAITH HAS HEALED YOU." AND THE WOMAN WAS HEALED FROM THAT MOMENT.

MATTHEW 15, 28
THEN JESUS ANSWERED, "WOMAN, YOU HAVE GREAT FAITH! YOUR REQUEST IS GRANTED." AND HER DAUGHTER HEALED FROM THAT VERY HOUR.

HISTORY OF TIGHTROPE:

A tightrope walker in New York City placed a cable from one building to another which crossed the street with the intention of crossing it using a pole.

Many people crowded the streets below to watch it.

The tightrope walker asked the crowd of people as follows:

Do you have faith in me that I can cross to the other side by the cable?

Everyone told him, "Yes, yes, you can, you can cross it, you can".

The tightrope walker crossed from one of the buildings to the other succeeding.

The audience began to applaud and yell: Bravo, Bravo!

Despite the fact that it was very windy, the tightrope walker again addressed the crowd telling them:

I will cross again but this time I will be without the pole, only with my hands.

Do you believe in me that I can achieve this?

This time only a few of the crowd told him:

Yes, yes we believe that you can do it, you will.
The tightrope walker started again to cross only with his arms out stretched and he did it! He crossed over to the other building.

The audience applauded loudly and congratulated him on his success.

The tightrope walker again addressed the crowd who was amazed and announced:

I will now cross pushing a wheelbarrow.

And asked the public **below: "Do you trust that I will once again cross?**

The public stayed completely in silence, the man asked them again and there was only silence from below, all of the sudden only one looked up and say:

Yes, yes I trust that you will do it! "You are going to cross again!.

The tightrope walker asked the man:

"If you really trust me then get up here and get in the wheel-barrow."

To have faith in Jesus is a gift from God which awakens the belief in Him, but to trust Him is an act of our will and our spiritual maturity. Ask God that His Holy Spirit would give you that trust in Jesus and that you will begin to experience what God will act in you in the name of Jesus.

"BROTHERS IN CHRIST, GET ON THE WHEELBARROW"

WHAT DOES JESUS WANT IN US?

In the book of Daniel there is a very important story that reveals a spiritual fight:

DANIEL 10, 13
BUT THE PRINCE OF THE PERSIAN KINGDOM RESISTED ME FOR TWENTYONE DAYS. THEN MICHAEL, ONE OF THE CHIEF PRINCES, CAME TO HELP ME, BECAUSE I WAS DETAINED THERE WITH THE KING OF PERSIA.

In this story note that the spiritual fight is continuous, when one prince ends the other comes in to aid in the fight. But it is interesting to see in the next verse that nobody appears to help in this fight except Michael.

DANIEL 10, 21
BUT FIRST I WILL TELL YOU WHAT IS WRITTEN IN THE BOOK OF TRUTH. (NO ONE SUPPORTS ME AGAINST THEM EXCEPT MICHAEL, YOUR PRINCE.)

It is very clear that in the spiritual struggle against the demons, no body helps except Michael the Archangel. Jesus himself asks the disciples to ask the Father to send laborers to the harvest and sends them to fight against the demons with authority and cast them out.

MATTHEW 9, 37 - 38

37

THEN HE SAID TO HIS DISCIPLES, "THE HARVEST IS PLENTIFUL BUT THE WORKERS ARE FEW.

38

ASK THE LORD OF THE HARVEST, THEREFORE, TO SEND OUT WORKERS INTO HIS HARVEST FIELD."

All of us when we follow Jesus become His disciples, and we must obey and do the will of our Heavenly Father.

Those who belong to Jesus live spiritually and crucify the flesh; the same St. Paul tells us in Ephesians that our fight is not with flesh or with people but with the evil spirits, with heavenly hosts of evil, in other words with evil spirits, against demons.

EPHESIANS 6, 12

FOR OUR STRUGGLE IS NOT AGAINST FLESH AND BLOOD, BUT AGAINST THE RULERS, AGAINST THE AUTHORITIES, AGAINST THE POWER OF THIS DARK WORLD AND AGAINST THE SPIRITUAL FORCES OF EVIL IN THE HEAVENLY REALMS.

In one of His mandates, Jesus tells us to preach the Gospel to the ends of the Earth with the power of the Holy Spirit, and with this same power that He gives us through the Holy Spirit tells us that we release our brothers of the ties of the demons, to cast them out and to heal the sick.

He warns us that we open the eyes of the people so that they turn from darkness to light and that they receive the forgiveness of sins through faith in Jesus Christ.

The "god" of this century has blinded the understanding of unbelievers, so they won't see the light of the Gospel.

ACTS 26, 18
TO OPEN THEIR EYES AND TURN THEM FROM DARKNESS TO LIGHT, AND FROM THE POWER OF SATAN TO GOD, SO THAT THEY MAY RECEIVE FORGIVENESS OF SINS AND A PLACE AMONG THOSE WHO ARE SANCTIFIED BY FAITH IN ME.

2 CORINTHIANS 4, 4
THE god OF THIS AGE HAS BLINDED THE MINDS OF UNBELIEVERS, SO THAT THEY CANNOT SEE THE LIGHT OF THE GOSPEL OT THE GLORY OF CHRIST, WHO IS THE IMAGE OF GOD.

In the history of the Bible, God was choosing people to fulfill different missions, including Abraham, Moses, Isaac, Jacob, the prophets, David, and all the characters of the Bible.

God chooses Mary for the mission to have His beloved son, also choose John Baptist to be the precursor of the mission entrusted to His beloved Son, Jesus.

Jesus chooses his disciples to fulfill the Mission of bringing the Gospel to the ends of the world.

MATTHEW 4, 18 - 19
18
AS JESUS WAS WALKING BESIDE THE SEA OF GALILEE, HE SAW TWO BROTHERS, SIMON CALLED PETER AND HIS BROTHER ANDREW. THEY WERE CASTING A NET INTO THE LAKE, FOR THEY WERE FISHERMEN.

19
COME, FOLLOW ME, JESUS SAID, "AND I WILL MAKE YOU FISHERS OF MEN.

Jesus also gives us this mission to all of us.

MATTHEW 28, 19
*THEREFORE GO AND MAKE DISCIPLES OF ALL NATIONS.
BAPTIZING THEM IN THE NAME OF THE FATHER AND OF
THE SON AND OF THE HOLY SPIRIT,*

God Himself calls us that we may be in accordance with the image of
His son Jesus:

ROMANS 8, 28 - 29
28
*AND WE KNOW THAT IN ALL THINGS GOD WORKS FOR THE
GOOD OF THOSE WHO LOVE HIM, WHO HAVE BEEN CALLED
ACCORDING TO HIS PURPOSE,*

29
*FOR THOSE GOD FORENEW HE ALSO PREDESTINED TO BE
CONFORMED TO THE LIKENESS OF HIS SON, THAT HE
MIGHT BE THE FIRSTBORN AMONG MANY BROTHERS.*

God wants us, in modern terms, to be a perfect photocopy of His son
Jesus.

Jesus tells us to go in pursuit of Him, if we are with Him we will give
fruits in abundance and that we can do nothing without him.

LUKE 14, 27
*AND ANYONE WHO DOES NOT CARRY HIS CROSS AND
FOLLOW ME CANNOT BE MY DISCIPLE.*

MATTHEW 12, 30
*HE WHO IS NOT WITH ME IS AGAINST ME, AND HE WHO
DOES NOT GATHER WITH ME SCATTERS.*

The great Commission that Jesus delegated into us is to save our
brothers and sisters and to make disciples to carry His word to the ends
of the Earth.

MATTHEW 10, 7 - 8

7

AS YOU GO, PREACH THIS MESSAGE: THE KINGDOM OF HEAVEN IS NEAR.

8

HEAL THE SICK, RAISE THE DEAD, CLEANSE THOSE WHO HAVE LEPROSY, DRIVE OUT DEMONS. FREELY YOU HAVE RECEIVED, FREELY GIVE.

1 CORINTHIANS 15, 58

THEREFORE, MY DEAR BROTHERS, STAND FIRM LET NO-THING MOVE YOU. ALWAYS GIVE YOURSELVES FULLY TO THE WORK OF THE LORD, BECAUSE YOU KNOW THAT YOUR LABOR IN THE LORD IS NOT IN VAIN.

It very clear what Jesus wants from us to do, He Himself tells us that it is our duty and we are only useless servants fulfilling what we have been ordered to do.

LUKE 17, 10

SO YOU ALSO, WHEN YOU HAVE DONE EVERYTHING YOU WERE TOLD TO DO, SHOULD SAY, WE ARE UNWORTHY SERVANTS; WE HAVE ONLY DONE OUR DUTY.

But the love of Jesus is so great that before ascending to the heavens He told his disciples that they will no longer be called servants but **Friends.**

JOHN 15, 15

I NO LONGER CALL YOU SERVANTS, BECAUSE A SERVANT DOES NOT KNOW HIS MASTER'S BUSINESS. INSTEAD, I HAVE CALLED YOU FRIENDS, FOR EVERYTHING THAT I LEARNED FROM MY FATHER I HAVE MADE KNOWN TO YOU.

PART II

SPIRIT, SOUL AND BODY

The body, soul and human spirit is very important, we have an obligation to understand. Let's see the following biblical passages:

1 THESSALONIANS 5, 23
MAY GOD HIMSELF, THE GOD OF PEACE, SANCTIFY YOU THROUGH AND THROUGH. MAY YOUR WHOLE SPIRIT, SOUL AND BODY BE KEPT BLAMELESS AT THE COMING OF OUR LORD JESUS CHRIST.

Paul teaches us in this event, we are tripartite beings. That is, we have three parts:

> ➢ **BODY.**

> ➢ **SOUL (THAT IS OUR INTELLECT, WILL AND CONS-CIOUS EMOTIONS).**

> ➢ **AND SPIRIT.**

He clearly states that the three parts should be cleaned and given to Christ, and Christ Himself must enable us to maintain the three **"without rebuke"** until his return.

GENESIS 2, 7

THE LORD GOD FORMED THE MAN FROM THE DUST OF THE GROUND AND BREATHED INTO HIS NOSTRILS THE BREATH OF LIFE AND THE MAN BECAME A LIVING BEING

In other words, Adam gained life and self-awareness. In essence our SELF is our soul manifested in:

> ➢ **OUR MIND.**

> ➢ **OUR WILL.**

> ➢ **OUR EMOTIONS.**

1 CORINTHIANS 15, 44b
IF THERE IS A NATURAL BODY, THERE IS ALSO A SPIRITUAL BODY.

This is a verse that we neglect very much. Our spirit has shape and figure, body which corresponds to our physical body.

The Satanists, and those involved in things such as the astral projection knows very well, but very few realize this.

FIGURE 1

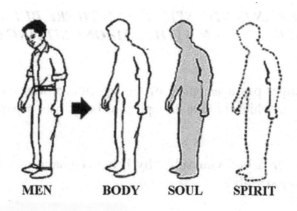

MEN   BODY   SOUL   SPIRIT

2 CORINTHIANS 12, 2 – 4

2

I KNOW A MAN IN CHRIST WHO FOURTEEN YEARS AGO WAS CAUGHT UP TO THE THIRD HEAVEN. WHETHER IT WAS IN THE BODY OR OUT OF THE BODY I DO NOT KNOW GOD KNOWS.

3

AND I KNOW THAT THIS MAN WHETHER IN THE BODY OR APART FROM THE BODY I DO NOT KNOW, BUT GOD KNOWS.

4

WAS CAUGHT UP TO PARADISE, HE HEARD INEXPRESSIBLE THINGS, THINGS THAT MAN IS NOT PERMITTED TO TELL.

REVELATIONS 4, 1 – 2

1

AFTER THIS I LOOKED, AND THERE BEFORE ME WAS A DOOR STANDING OPEN IN HEAVEN. AND THE VOICE I HAD FIRST HEARD SPEAKING TO ME LIKE A TRUMPET SAID, "COME UP HERE, AND I WILL SHOW YOU WHAT MUST TAKE PLACE AFTER THIS."

2

AT ONCE I WAS IN THE SPIRIT, AND THERE BEFORE ME WAS A THRONE IN HEAVEN WITH SOMEONE SITTING ON IT.

These and other passages speak of an experience perceived in the spirit of the person, which is that the spiritual body was separated from the physical body.

Have you ever asked yourself why it is necessary to talk about soul and spirit separately?

According to the mentioned verses the soul and the spirit can be separated.

The first Adam before the fall; could relate to the spiritual world and see it as it was with the physical world.

How? Making use of his spiritual body, this is demonstrated by the ease with which could walk and talk with God in the Garden of Eden.

He was aware of his spiritual body in the same way that it had of their physical body,

His **soul** (intellect and conscious will) controlled his spiritual body and its physical body.

But with the fall occurred spiritual death: Adam and his descendants ceased to be aware of their spiritual body, and could not have with God the same communion he had before.

FIGURE 2

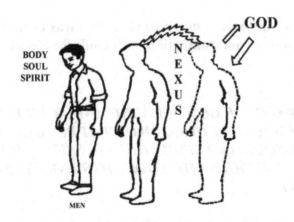

**Before the fall, Adam was the only man made
image of God. Adam could communicate with God**

FIGURE 3

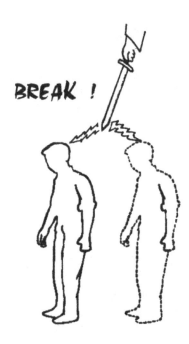

The fall was a disaster. The mysterious link was broken. This put an end to free communication with God, see Hebrews 4, 12

HEBREWS 4, 12
FOR THE WORD OF GOD IS LIVING AND ACTIVE. SHARPER THAN ANY DOUBLE EDGED SWORD, IT PENETRATES EVEN TO DIVIDE SOUL AND SPIRIT (HUMAN SPIRIT), JOINTS AND MARROW; IT JUDGES THE THOUGHTS AND ATTITUDES OF THE HEART.

When the Holy Spirit comes and we accept Jesus as our Lord and Savior, our spiritual body is reborn or is rejuvenated so that we may have communion with the Lord and worship him as Adam did before the fall.

The fact that it is through our human spirit that we find God (with the help of the Holy Spirit) is demonstrated in the following words of Jesus:

JOHN 4, 23 – 24
23
YET A TIME IS COMING AND HAS NOW COME WHEN THE TRUE WORSHIPERS WILL WORSHIP THE FATHER IN SPIRIT (HUMAN SPIRIT) AND TRUTH, FOR THEY ARE THE KIND OF WORSHIPERS THE FATHER SEEKS.

24
GOD IS SPIRIT, AND HIS WORSHIPERS MUST WORSHIP IN SPIRIT (HUMAN SPIRIT) AND IN TRUTH.

Note that in these two verses when it says that God is "Spirit" the word is written in capital letters. (See the Bible). However to refer to the human spirit differs by being clearly written in (see the Bible).

Therefore, only a spirit can communicate with the spiritual world. Only a spirit can worship God the Father, who is spirit (see Figure 4.)

In the Bible it is also clear that the angels are spiritual beings:

PSALM 104, 4 (103)
HE MAKES WINDS HIS MESSENGERS (REFERRED TO GODS) FLAMES OF FIRE HIS SERVANTS.

FIGURE 4

GOD

HOLY
SPIRIT

THE TRUE CHRISTIAN

This nexus activates only at
God's will and it makes you:

- To understand the bible.
- To make us aware of his
  presence.
- To give us understanding
  of the spirit, etc.

Soul and Body   Spirit

Paul quotes the passage from Psalm 104, 4 in Hebrews 1, 7 and
Hebrews 1, 13-14

13
TO WHICH OF THE ANGELS DID GOD EVER SAY, "SIT AT MY RIGHT HAND UNTIL I MAKE YOUR ENEMIES A FOOTSTOOL FOR YOUR FEET"

14
ARE NOT ALL ANGELS MINISTERING SPIRITS SENT TO SERVE THOSE WHO WILL INHERIT SALVATION?

Satan and the demons are spirits. Before they were angels in the service of God but they revolted. Jesus Himself defines these creatures such as angels and therefore spirits. A verse in this regard is:

MATTHEW 25, 41
THEN HE WILL SAY TO THOSE ON HIS LEFT, DEPART FROM ME, YOU WHO ARE CURSED, INTO THE ENTERNAL FIRE PREPARED FOR THE DEVIL AND HIS ANGELS.

Through the Holy Spirit, our spirit can communicate with God and worship him, but Hebrews 4.12 shows that it is not God's will that we gain control of our body spiritual while we are on the earth in our sinful condition.

That is why the sword of the spirit breaks up the soul and spirit. Once this break has been done, the soul (mind, intellect, will) can't still control the spiritual body.

It is also for this reason that the Lord so insists on:

1 THESSALONIANS 5, 23
MAY GOD HIMSELF, THE GOD OF PEACE, SANCTIFY YOU THROUGH AND THROUGH. MAY YOUR WHOLE SPIRIT, SOUL AND BODY BE KEPT BLAMELESS AT THE COMING OF OUR LORD JESUS CHRIST.

The Lord wants that our spirit is under the lordship of Christ, as well as our physical body and our soul.

Revelation 18, 11-13 is a very interesting passage. Referring to the fall of Babylon says:

REVELATION 18, 11, 13
11
THE MERCHANTS OF THE EARTH WILL WEEP AND MOURN OVER HER BECAUSE NO ONE BUYS THEIR CARGOES ANY MORE

13
CARGOES OF CINNAMON AND SPICE, OF INCENSE, MYRRH AND FRANKINCENSE, OF WINE AND OLIVE OIL, OF FINE FLOUR AND WHEAT; CATTLE AND SHEEP; HORSES AND CARRIAGES; AND BODIES ANS SOULS OF MEN;

Why the difference between (slaves or serfs) bodies and souls of men?

Because there is a phenomenal amount of power and intelligence in spiritual human bodies especially when these spiritual bodies are under control of the soul;

Satan has been working since Adam until now to use the spiritual bodies for their evil plans.

The physical body is weak and very unhelpful for Satan; but the spiritual body under the conscious control of the soul is very different.

The goal of Satan is to teach humans to regain the conscious control of their spiritual bodies. Many do.

Once that is achieved, the person can perceive the spiritual world as easily as the physical world. You can talk to demons, leaving the physical body with the spiritual body, and in full conscience go to different places and do things that for the average man is a power supernatural.

God does not want His people to control their spiritual bodies this way. If we did, we would not only be exposed to terrible temptations, but would not have to depend on Him alone and would be constantly aware and exposed to Satan and his kingdom.

There is types of demon which usually call **"power Devil"** which apparently provides **"the glue"** that establish the link between the soul and the spiritual body and the person can take conscious control of his spiritual body.

The imagination is a basic bridge to develop the link between the soul and the spirit. That is why it is so important we take captive every thought to the obedience to Christ.

2 CORINTHIANS 10, 3 – 5
3
FOR THOUGH WE LIVE IN THE WORLD, WE DO NOT WAGE WAR AS THE WORLD DOES.

4
THE WEAPONS WE FIGHT WITH ARE NOT THE WEAPONS OF THE WORLD. ON THE CONTRARY, THEY HAVE DIVINE POWER TO DEMOLISH STRONGHOLDS.

5
WE DEMOLISH ARGUMENTS AND EVERY PRETENSION THAT SETS ITSELF UP AGAINST THE KNOWLEDGE OF GOD, AND WE TAKE CAPTIVE EVERY THOUGHT TO MAKE IT OBEDIENT TO CHRIST.

A good example of the imagination as a link with the spiritual world we find in occult fantasy games. (See figures 5, 6, 7 and 8.)

We have found that we can save lots of time and effort with regard to releases if we clarify to people that request to be released (and it has gone in the occult)to ask the Lord to cast out first, the demon of power.

FIGURE 5

AFTER THE FALL

PICTURE A

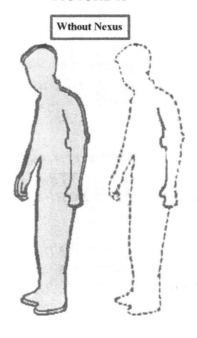

Wthout Nexus

**Adam begat a son in the image and
Likeness of Adam…. Not God**

FIGURE 5

Satan a demonic force to spend a corrupt nexus in the fallen man.

FIGURE B

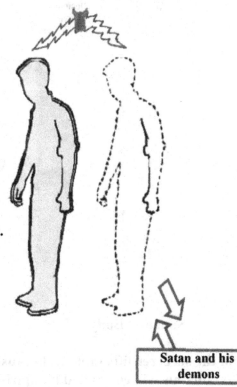

This gives man consciousness about his spiritual body.

This link allows him to communicate with world thru his own spirit.

Satan and his demons

FIGURE 6

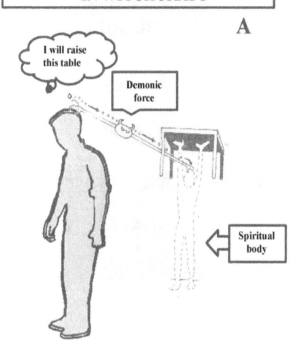

Soul and Body

The will of the sorcerer lifts table.... because through the Satanic link his will controlled his spiritual body.

B

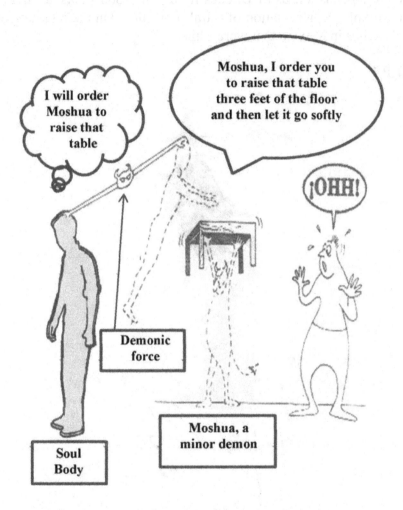

The witch uses his spirit to submit and order the demon that he lift the table. The observer does not know of this communication …….. remember that the physical body may not see or hear what happens in the spiritual world.

FIGURE 7

Ancient legends tell us of witches flying on broomsticks at night. This is a symbolic representation of astral projection. On the internet you can see Witches in Mexico that were filmed.

STEP 1

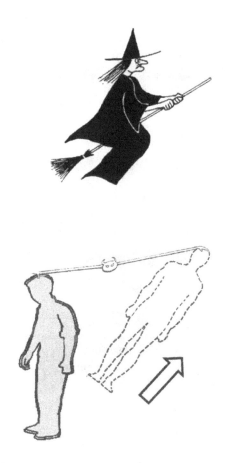

True astral projection; the soul consciously controls the spiritual body.

FIGURE 8

STEP 2

The spirit is sent to hear the conversation

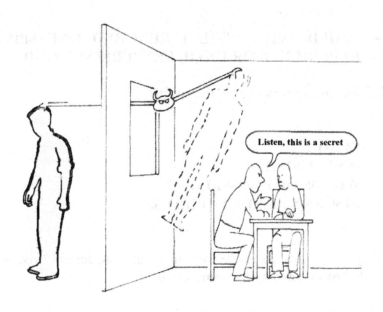

Miles away

This is the projection astral...... the spirit hears the conversation.

If someone is not well determined to achieve liberation, or if is trying to deceive us, it immediately will retract when it finds out that once the demon is cast out from him, will instantly lose the ability to use his/her spiritual body.

A person after being freed may perceive the spiritual world **only** when the Lord wants to give such perception. His spirit will be from that time on, totally under the lordship of Jesus Christ.

Christians should not learn to control their spirit. I have heard many say:

> ➢ **I MEDITATE UNTIL I REACHED ONE SPIRITUAL EXPERIENCE OR UNTIL I EXPERIENCE GOD.**

Christians have experiences in the spirit:

> ➢ **VISIONS.**
> ➢ **DISCLOSURES.**
> ➢ **WORDS OF KNOWLEDGE.**
> ➢ **DISCERNMENT OF SPIRITS.**

But they are always under the control of our Lord Jesus Christ and never controlled or initiated by the same person.

If a Christian wants to determine when to have spiritual experiences, I have to say that I doubt very much that such experiences come from God. It is likely that they come from Satan.

Too many Christians think that they must leave the mind blank so that the Holy Spirit can speak through them or "control". The Bible clearly says that we must **actively** cooperate with the Holy Spirit.

Every time we leave the mind blank, chances are that the spirit who speaks through us is not the Holy Spirit.

Many prophecies of people that leave the mind blank thinking that they are being controlled by the Holy Spirit are demonic prophecies.

They forget that Satan knows every detail of our lives. The only things he don't know are our thoughts and intentions of our heart.

These biblical quotations teach us where should be our thoughts:

2 CORINTHIANS 10, 5b
AND WE TAKE CAPTIVE EVERY THOUGHT TO MAKE IT OBEDIENT TO CHRIST.

ISAIAH 26, 3
YOU WILL KEEP IN PERFECT PEACE HIM WHOSE MIND IS STEADFAST, BECAUSE HE TRUSTS IN YOU.

PHILIPPIANS 4, 7
AND THE PEACE OF GOD, WHICH TRANSCENDS ALL UNDERSTANDING, WILL GUARD YOUR HEARTS AND YOUR MINDS IN CHRIST JESUS.

There is this teaching currently in the United States:
The lesson is that our psychic man must be subjected to our spiritual man because once the Holy Spirit dwells in us, our spirit is without sin.

There are two errors in this teaching:

First:
The only way to put the soul under the authority of the spirit is to establish conscious contact between the soul and spirit. **That is pure witchcraft**.

In 1 Peter 1, 22 say:

1 PETER 1, 22
NOW THAT YOU HAVE PURIFIED YOURSELVES BY OBEYING THE TRUTH SO THAT YOU HAVE SINCERE LOVE FOR YOUR BROTHERS, LOVE ONE ANOTHER DEEPLY, FROM THE HEART.

Note that here "Spirit" is written with capital letter, because it is referring to the Holy Spirit, **not** to our human spirit.

Second:
In 1 Thessalonians 5, 23 clearly say that our spirit is prone to falling into sin, so Jesus Christ has to save us blameless until his coming.

The task of save it is continuous. Let's look at the verse again:

1 THESSALONIANS 5, 23
MAY GOD HIMSELF, THE GOD OF PEACE, SANCTIFY YOU THROUGH AND THROUGH. MAY YOUR WHOLE SPIRIT, SOUL AND BODY BE KEPT BLAMELESS AT THE COMING OF OUR LORD JESUS CHRIST.

Certainly 1 John 1, 8-9 does not agree with that teaching

1 JOHN 1, 8 – 9
8
IF WE CLAIM TO BE WITHOUT SIN, WE DECEIVE OUR-SELVES AND THE TRUTH IS NOT IN US.

9
IF WE CONFESS OUR SINS, HE IS FAITHFULL AND JUST AND WILL FORGIVE US OUR SINS AND PURIFY US FRON ALL UNRIGHTEOUSNESS.

God does not relieve our spirits of the vulnerability of falling into sin.

The purpose of the break between the soul and spirit is ridding the spirit of the influence of natural desires that we have in the soul.

If a Christian walks in submission to God, will originate anything;   It we will rather wait listen quietly to the voice of the Holy Spirit in its spirit and then will act in accordance with the guidance of the Holy Spirit.

A Christian who is in conscious contact with his own spirit will not wait in submission to the Holy Spirit to speak. It will take the initiative, and it is likely that the voice he is listening to **is not** the voice of the Holy Spirit.

Satan will use the spiritual body of that person if given the opportunity without the person realizing it.

1 JOHN 3, 15 (a) dice:
ANYONE WHO HATES HIS BROTHER IS A MURDERER .....

How can one be a murderer by an emotion, such as hatred, if it hasn't done anything physically to cause death to the hated person?

This verse I was intrigued by until I understood the concept of the spiritual body.

Hatred is a conscious sin. As such, it gives Satan a legal basis in our lives if we allow him to stay in our hearts.

If one hates someone, Satan can intervene and avail of our spiritual body to attack the hated person.

Such an attack can cause all kinds of illness, accident, emotional problem and even physical death.

The person who hates not often realizes that Satan is using his spiritual body. The hated person usually not realizes the true origin of their grief.

That is why we have to be careful to ask Jesus Christ that He clean us and keep us pure in our three parts:

> **BODY.**
> **SOUL.**
> **SPIRIT** (HUMAN).

That's why Jesus Christ left us so many commandments as to forgive others. Forgiveness puts a stop to hatred.

Christians must ask the Lord regularly to cleanse us of any sin.

PSALM 51, 10
CREATE IN ME A PURE HEART O GOD, AND RENEW A STEADFAST SPIRIT (REFERRING TO THE HUMAN SPIRIT) WITHIN ME,

Again, note the initial lower case (see the Bible) of the word spirit. It is clear that the sin of the heart of David had also affected the spirit.

Note:
Some notes and figures were taken from the book "He Came to Set the Captives Free" by Dr. Rebecca Brown, as of the utmost importance

IN THE GAP

EZEKIEL 22, 30 – 31

30

I LOOKED FOR A MAN AMONG THEM WHO WOULD BUILD UP THE WALL AND STAND BEFORE ME IN THE GAP ON BEHALF OF THE LAND SO I WOULD NOT HAVE TO DESTROY IT, BUT I FOUND NONE.

31

SO I WILL POUR OUT MY WRATH ON THEM AND CONSUME THEM WITH MY FIERY ANGER, BRINGING DOWN ON THEIR OWN HEADS ALL THEY HAVE DONE, DECLARES THE SOVEREIGN LORD.

When I read the book "He Came to Set the Captives Free" written by Rebecca Brown, MD, it was a great teaching for me and I think that every true Christian must be willing to be put in the gap as command us Jesus Himself.

Wake up you who sleep and form the Christian army to fight the enemy and defend our brothers.

The question that all have to ask ourselves is this:

> ➢ **ARE WE WILLING TO GET IN THE GAP FOR SO-MEONE ELSE?**

One can be put in the gap in different ways.

We must ask the Lord that will allow us to be in the gap in favor of a person so it can have the opportunity to hear the Gospel without demonic interference.

2 CORINTHIANS 4, 3 - 4
3
AND EVEN IF OUR GOSPEL IS VEILED, IT IS VEILED TO THOSE WHO ARE PERISHING.

4
THE god OF THIS AGE HAS BLINDED THE MINDS OF UNBELIEVERS, SO THAT THEY CANNOT SEE THE LIGHT OF THE GOSPEL OF THE GLORY OF CHRIST, WHO IS THE IMA-GE OF GOD.

In Ezekiel God is looking for someone that is willing to stand and fight against Satan and the demons so that they stop blinding people and they could see the need of a Savior.

Why could not God find such a person? He said that it would have to shed his wrath and punish His people for their sins

As Christians soldiers we must be prepared to get in the gap and fight **in the spiritual field** to break the demonic forces that keep people blind.

Paul is very clear when he said to the Ephesians:

EPHESIANS 6, 12
FOR OUR STRUGGLE IS NOT AGAINST FLESH AND BLOOD, BUT AGAINST THE RULERS, AGAINST THE AUTHORITIES, AGAINST THE POWERS OF THIS DARK WORLD AND AGAINST THE SPIRITUAL FORCES OF EVIL IN THE HEAVENLY REALMS.

We often can pray this way:

> ➤ **"LORD, LET ME GET IN THE GAP FOR (NAME OF PERSON) AND FIGHT FOR HIM SO THAT HIS EYES ARE OPEN AND BE FREE FROM THE BONDAGE OF DEMONIC TIES SO HE OR SHE CAN SEE THE NEED IT HAS OF JESUS".**

The Lord has shown us another way to get into the gap.

Consider the following passages:

ISAIAH 58, 6
IS NOT THIS THE KIND OF FASTING I HAVE CHOSEN: TO LOOSE THE CHAINS OF INJUSTICE AND UNTIE THE CORDS OF THE YOKE, TO SET THE OPPRESSED FREE AND BREAK EVERY YOKE?

GALATIANS 6, 2
CARRY EACH OTHER'S BURDENS, AND IN THIS WAY YOU WILL FULFILL THE LAW OF CHRIST.

JOHN 15, 13
GREATER LOVE HAS NO ONE THAN THIS THAT HE LAY DOWN HIS LIFE FOR HIS FRIENDS.

These passages tell us clearly that the Lord expects that we help carry burdens and pains of our brothers and sisters in Christ as well as fight when necessary for freedom of demonic oppression.

Get in the gap is a way of doing this.

Every day we see more and more incredible scandals, pastors, Ministers and priests; but what can we do for them?

Are we willing to be put in the gap for our Pastor, Minister or priests and ask the Lord to allow us to fight for them?

In other words, any demonic power that is launched against our Pastor, Minister or priests, must first go through us.
This implies:

- ➤ **PHYSICAL SUFFERING.**
- ➤ **EMOTIONAL SUFFERING.**
- ➤ **MAY NOT BE GOING TO CHURCH BECAUSE IS TOO SICK.**
- ➤ **MAYBE THE MEMBERS OF THE CHURCH ARE LAUNCHING FALSE ACCUSATIONS.**

Are we prepared to support this type of accusations and remain silent as to the real reason why can't attend church?

Put one in the gap for the other is a way of putting up your life for a friend.

One can't be put in the gap by oneself. Only the Lord can do so because only the Lord controls your spiritual body.

What he has to do is ask the Father that he puts them there and if it is His will as well.

One has to be willing to have the Lord work in you in any way He wants, for the benefit of another person. One can't decide what form has to be used.

Let me clarify something. Rarely will you be aware that you are **"in the gap"**. This is because the Lord has complete control of our spiritual body.

We do not always see the spiritual world as it is the case with the physical world. Only on special occasions the Lord enables us to see the world spiritual and usually brief glances.

One knows that he is or has been in the gap only when the Lord tells us, or by problems arising in our physical body, what the Lord will confirm to us if it is the result of having the spiritual body in the gap.

Have you experienced once that after a period of intercessory prayer you have felt totally exhausted?

It is because while you prayed with the physical body and the mind, God took you spiritual body and put it in battle with the demonic forces against which has been praying on the battlefield of the spiritual world.

The fatigue you feel is due to the tension that the spiritual body experiences. The wounds received in the spiritual body at times also manifest with symptoms in the physical body.

Sorcerers and witches aged at an accelerated pace. They pay a high price in their physical body by relating to the spiritual world with the frequency with which do.

There are several interesting references in the Bible that confirm this. Some are in the book of Daniel 8.

Daniel begins by saying that he had had a vision where he saw the spiritual world and spoke with the Angel Gabriel.

At the end of the experience with the spiritual world says:

DANIEL 10, 7 – 18

7

DANIEL, WAS THE ONLY ONE WHO SAW THE VISION; THE MEN WITH ME DID NOT SEE IT, BUT SUCH TERROR OVERWHELMED THEM THAT THEY FLED AND HID THEM-SELVES.

8

SO I WAS LEFT ALONE, GAZING AT THIS GREAT VISION; I HAVE NO STRENGTH LEFT, MY FACE TURNED DEATHLY PALE AND I WAS HELPLESS.

9

THEN I HEARD HIM SPEAKING, AND AS I LISTENED TO HIM, I FELL INTO A DEEP SLEEP, MY FACE TO THE GROUND.

10

A HAND TOUCHED ME AND SET ME TREMBLING ON MY HANDS AND KNEES,

11

HE SAID, DANIEL, YOU WHO ARE HIGHLY ESTEEMED, CONSIDER CAREFULLY THE WORDS I AM ABOUT TO SPEAK TO YOU, AND STAND UP, FOR I HAVE NOW BEEN SENT TO YOU. AND WHEN HE SAID THIS TO ME, I STOOD UP TREMBLING.

12

THEN HE CONTINUED, DO NOT BE AFRAID, DANIEL. SINCE THE FIRST DAY THAT YOU SET YOUR MIND TO GAIN UNDERSTANDING AND TO HUMBLE YOURSELF BEFORE YOUR GOD, YOUR WORDS WERE HEARD, AND I HAVE COME IN RESPONSE TO THEM.

13

BUT THE PRINCE OF THE PERSIAN KINGDOM RESISTED ME TWENTYONE DAYS. THEN MICHAEL, ONE OF THE CHIEF

PRINCES, CAME TO HELP ME, BECAUSE I WAS DETAINED THERE WITH THE KING OF PERSIA.

14
NOW I HAVE COME TO EXPLAIN TO YOU WHAT WILL HAPPEN TO YOUR PEOPLE IN THE FUTURE, FOR THE VISION CONCERNS A TIME YET TO COME.

15
WHILE HE WAS SAYING THIS TO ME, I BOWED WITH MY FACE TOWARD THE GROUND AND WAS SPEECHLESS.

16
THEN ONE WHO LOOKED LIKE A MAN TOUCHED MY LIPS, AND I OPENED MY MOUTH AND BEGAN TO SPEAK. I SAID TO THE ONE STANDING BEFORE ME, I AM OVERCOME WITH ANGUISH BECAUSE OF THE VISION, MY LORD, AND I AM HELPLESS.

17
HOW CAN I, YOUR SERVANT, TALK WITH YOU, MY LORD? MY STRENGTH IS GONE AND I CAN HARDLY BREATHE.

18
AGAIN THE ONE WHO LOOKED LIKE A MAN TOUCHED ME AND GAVE ME STRENGTH.

Battling for our spiritual body also greatly affects our physical body.

That is why Paul mentions both the fact that our struggle is not against flesh and blood. We cannot, clearly, fight in the spiritual world with the physical body.

But the two have been merged by God and what happens to our spiritual body inevitably affects our physical body.

BATTLE
IN THE SPIRITUAL WORLD

Getting in the gap, it is a difficult concept to grasp because it is something that is totally out of our control and rarely perceived.

In Ezekiel 22, 30, God tells us that he sought and didn't find anyone to put in the gap, Jesus himself tells us that there is no better friend than that one who gives his life for his similar.

Paul clarifies us that our fight is not with flesh and blood but against principalities, against the authorities, against the rulers of this darkness, against spirits......

How can we fight against spirits in the heavenly regions?

If we perceive the concept of what our spirit is:

> ➢ **A PART LIVE AND ACTIVE.**
> ➢ **CAN TALK.**
> ➢ **CAN SING.**
> ➢ **CAN THINK.**
> ➢ **CAN PRAY.**

- CAN PRAISE THE LORD.
- AND FIGHT IN THE SPIRITUAL WORLD.

When we know this, many difficult Bible passages make sense:

How is it possible to comply with the following verses?

- 1 THESSALONIANS 2, 13
  WHICH ALSO US WITHOUT CEASING GIVE THANKS
  TO GOD,

- 1 THESSALONIANS 5, 17
  PRAY WITHOUT CEASING.

It is impossible that our mind may be praying and praising God without ceasing 24 hours a day, but what can our mind so may our spirit.

1 PETER 4, 6
"BUT LIVE ACCORDING TO GOD IN REGARD TO THE SPIRIT."

Note that "spirit" is written with lowercase because it refers to the human spirit. **How can we live in the spirit this way?**
Entrusting our spirit to God so that He can use it as He pleases;

Our spiritual body can:

- MOVE.
- THINK.
- AND SPEAKING.

As well as our physical body, but takes its character and way of thinking from our physical body and our soul.

As our physical body cannot fight the spirits in the spiritual world, our spiritual body is the one that has to fight.

That is why is so important to ask God every day that He put His armor and protect us and to cleanse us with the Holy Blood of his beloved Son Jesus Christ.

This battle is continuous and relentless and if we are not wearing the shield, armor of God and the blood of His son Jesus Christ in our spiritual body to the fight, we will receive terrible wounds of the **"fire darts"** from the evil.

EPHESIANS 6, 10 – 18
10
FINALLY, BE STRONG IN THE LORD AND IN HIS MIGHTY POWER.

11
PUT ON THE FULL ARMOR OF GOD SO THAT YOU CAN TAKE YOUR STAND AGAINST THE DEVIL'S SCHEMES.

12
FOR OUR STRUGGLE IS NOT AGAINST FLESH AND BLOOD, BUT AGAINST THE RULERS, AGAINST THE AUTHORITIES, AGAINST THE POWERS OF THIS DARK WORLD AND AGAINST THE SPIRITUAL FORCES OF EVIL IN THE HEAVENLY REALMS.

13
THEREFORE PUT ON THE FULL ARMOR OF GOD, SO THAT WHEN THE DAY OF EVIL COMES, YOU MAY BE ABLE TO STAND YOUR GROUND, AND AFTER YOU HAVE DONE EVERYTHING, TO STAND.

14

STAND FIRM THEN, WITH THE BELT OF TRUTH BUCKLED AROUND YOUR WAIST, WITH THE BREASTPLATE OF RIGHTEOUSNESS IN PLACE,

15

AND WITH YOUR FEET FITTED WITH THE READINESS THAT COMES FROM THE GOSPEL OF PEACE,

16

IN ADDITION TO ALL THIS, TAKE UP THE SHIELD OF FAITH, WITH WHICH YOU CAN EXTINGUISH ALL THE FLAMING ARROWS OF THE EVIL ONE.

17

TAKE THE HELMET OF SALVATION AND THE SWORD OF THE SPIRIT, WHICH IS THE WORD OF GOD.

18

AND PRAY IN THE SPIRIT ON ALL OCCASIONS WITH ALL KINDS OF PRAYERS AND REQUEST. WITH THIS IN MIND, BE ALERT AND ALWAYS KEEP ON PRAYING FOR ALL THE SAINTS.

By ourselves we can't enter the fight. Our spirit is entirely under the Dominion of our master, Jesus Christ.

We simply must tell the Lord that we want to use our spirit in this way if desired.

We must ask the Father to let us put ourselves in the gap and fight for a person in particular, but the decision is His.

We will soon recognize the symptoms:

> **FATIGUE.**
> **PAIN.**
> **DEPRESSION.**
> **AND OTHER DISEASES.**

In our physical body that are indications that our spiritual body is in strong battle.

The concept that our spirit can be separated and even geographically far from our physical body is strange and difficult to accept, There is a fascinating passage in which Paul describes this circumstance:

1 CORINTHIANS 5, 1 – 4
1
IT IS ACTUALLY REPORTED THAT THERE IS SEXUAL IM-MORALITY AMONG YOU, AND OF A KIND THAT DOES NOT OCCUR EVEN AMONG PAGANS: A MAN HAS HIS FATHER'S WIFE.

2
AND YOU ARE PROUD! SHOULDN'T YOU RATHER HAVE BEEN FILLED WITH GRIEF AND HAVE PUT OUT OF YOUR FELLOWSHIP THE MAN WHO DID THIS?

3
EVEN THOUGH I AM NOT PHYSICALLY PRESENT, I AM WITH YOU IN SPIRIT. AND I HAVE ALREADY PASSED JUDGMENT ON THE ONE WHO DID THIS, JUST AS IF I WERE PRESENT.

4
WHEN YOU ARE ASSEMBLED IN THE NAME OF OUR LORD JESUS AND I AM WITH YOU IN SPIRIT, AND THE POWER OF OUR LORD JESUS IS PRESENT,

Note that Paul puts spirit with lowercase (see the Bible) to denote his own spirit, not the Holy Spirit.

It is also of the utmost importance that the spirit of Paul is in **Corinth alone with the "Faculty"** of our Lord Jesus Christ.

The spirit of Paul was completely under the control of the Lord, not under his soul.

Normally the human spirit resides in the physical body. However, several passages show that the physical body can continue to live separated from the spirit.

ACTS 8, 39
WHEN THEY CAME UP OUT OF THE WATER, THE SPIRIT OF THE LORD SUDDENLY TOOK PHILIP AWAY, AND THE EUNUCH DID NOT SEE HIM AGAIN, BUT WENT ON HIS WAY REJOICING.

As for the soul, once the soul leaves the body, the body dies.

Why is it that many passages about physical death relate also to the soul? However, there is a peculiar depletion of the physical body when the spirit is not inside.

The Lord teaches us that the depletion of the physical body is peculiar in that it produces an acute lack of protein.

If we fail to take not enough proteins of high quality during the days of intense spiritual battle, we will be weakened. The Bible speaks quite widely on this subject.

Since the Covenant of God with Noah in which He asked Noah to eat meat, Satan and the demons have been trying to tell people not to eat meat.

GENESIS 9, 3
EVERYTHING THAT LIVES AND MOVES WILL BE FOOD FOR YOU. JUST AS I GAVE YOU THE GREEN PLANTS, I NOW GIVE YOU EVERYTHING.

It is interesting that Hindus and many other Eastern religions which believe that the success of a medium or an adept (whose powers originate from the demons that have possessed them) depends on the presence in their bodies of a mysterious fluid called **"akasa"**, it dries up quickly, and without which the demons cannot act, say Hindus, can regenerate only with a vegetarian diet and chastity.

Which led to the judgment of God in the form of flood, were sexual relations between humans and demons,

GENESIS 6, 2
THE SONS OF GOD SAW THAT THE DAUGHTERS OF MEN WERE BEAUTIFUL, AND THEY MARRIED ANY OF THEM THEY CHOSE.

I don't think it was coincidence that God ordered Noah to eat meat after the flood. God knew very well about the spiritual battle that they would have to hold, Noah and his sons to prevent the demons to dominate their lives.

When we study the Old Testament and the laws that God gave to the people of Israel, talking about the spiritual warriors of those days were the Levites of Israel. Their diet abounded in beef and lamb meat.

If beef is so harmful, why is it that Abraham prepared beef for the envoys from God when they came to visit him? Abraham undoubtedly would had like to prepare the best that he had.

GENESIS 18, 7 – 8

7

THEN HE RAN TO THE HERD AND SELECTED A CHOICE, TENDER CALF AND GAVE IT TO A SERVANT, WHO HURRIED TO PREPARE IT.

8

HE THEN BROUGHT SOME CURDS AND MILK AND THE CALF THAT HAD BEEN PREPARED, AND SET THESE BEFORE THEM. WHILE THEY ARE, HE STOOD NEAR THEM UNDER A TREE.

If we look at the different spiritual warriors of renown of the Old Testament, we will notice that every time they were preparing to fight a great battle, God prepared them with carnivorous food.

For example:
Elijah. Note the same menu God prepared during the period of preparation before the confrontation with the prophets of Baal.

1 KINGS 17, 2 – 6

2

THEM THE WORD OF THE LORD CAME TO ELIJAH:

3

LEAVE HERE, TURN EASTWARD AND HIDE IN THE KERITH RAVINE, EAST OF THE JORDAN.

4

YOU WILL DRINK FROM THE BROOK, AND I HAVE ORDERED THE RAVENS TO FEED YOU THERE.

5

SO HE DID WHAT THE LORD HAS TOLD HIM. HE WENT TO THE KERITH RAVINE, EAST OF THE JORDAN, AND STAYED THERE.

6

THE RAVENS BROUGHT HIM BREAD AND MEAT IN THE MORNING AND BREAD AND MEAT IN THE EVENING, AND HE DRANK FROM THE BROOK.

The Lord speaks very directly in this regard through Paul in the New Testament.

1 TIMOTHY 4, 1 – 5

1

THE SPIRIT CLEARY SAYS THAT IN LATER TIMES SOME WILL ABANDON THE FAITHE AND FOLLOW DECEIVING SPIRITS AND THINGS TAUGHT BY DEMONS.

2

SUCH TEACHINGS COME THROUGH HYPOCRITICAL LIARS, WHOSE CONSCIENCES HAVE BEEN SEARED AS WITH A HOT IRON.

3

THEY FORBID PEOPLE TO MARRY AND ORDER THEM TO ABSTAIN FORM CERTAIN FOODS, WHICH GOD CREATED TO BE RECEIVED WITH THANKSGIVING BY THOSE WHO BE-LIEVE AND WHO KNOW THE TRUTH.

4

FOR EVERYTHING GOD CREATED IS GOOD, AND NOTHING IS TO BE REJECTED IF IT IS RECEIVED WITH THANKSGIVING,

5

BECAUSE IT IS CONSECRATED BY THE WORD OF GOD AND PRAYER,

We want to clarify that we are referring to the lean meat, not fat, which the Lord, when given them the law, told the Israelites that they should not eat.

Are you suffering from?:

> **PAIN.**
> **DEPRESSION.**
> **EXHAUSTION.**

For being in the front line (or on any other occasion), don't forget one of the main weapons: **THE PRAISE.**

Satan and the demons do not support **the praise to the Lord**. I am sure that this was the reason why Paul wrote this much discussed verse from:

1 THESSALONIANS 5, 18
GIVE THANKS IN ALL CIRCUMSTANCES, FOR THIS IS GOD'S WILL FOR YOU IN CHRIST JESUS.

Note that says **everything**, not for something's.

If the circumstance worsens we can be sure and certain that Satan and the demons surround us.

When we praise the Lord, Satan, which is the cause of our problems, loses strength right away, and we receive many blessings.

When we fight in the spiritual field let's remember that any weapon and tactics that mentions the Bible is at our disposal.
The Psalms are especially useful. Don't forget to ask the Father to put our feet on **"The rock"** which is Jesus.

The Lord will show you and teach you step by step what you should know.

ARE YOU WILLING TO SERVE THE LORD THIS WAY?

PART III

THEME 1
ATTITUDE AND PERSPECTIVE
FOR THE LIBERATION

The process of expelling demon called liberation, which is part of the Ministry of healing.

The liberation is a not a cure for everything.

The demons can live in a person and we can say that **"they have evil spirits"** or is **"with unclean spirits"** or being **"possessed"** by demons:

- ➢ **LUKE 4, 33**
- ➢ **MARK 1, 23; 5, 2; 9, 17**
- ➢ **MATTHEW 4, 24**

The word that is used as a **"possessed"** is the Greek **"daimonizomai"** term;

Many authorities in the Greek language say that it is not an accurate translation and that it should have been translated **"this devilish"** or **"have a demon",** the **possessed** term suggests a **total possession**.

Total possession is when the demon takes control of the entire body of the human being.

But our body may be tormented by a demon, without having a total possession.

Our body and our mind belong to **God**. Our body is a **Temple of the Holy Spirit** and does not belong to us, we belong to **God** and we were purchased by price of blood of **Jesus**.

1 PETER 1, 18 – 19
18
FOR YOU KNOW THAT IT WAS NOT WITH PERISHABLE THINGS SUCH AS SILVER OR GOLD THAT YOU WERE RE-DEEMED FROM THE EMPTY WAY OF LIFE HANDED DOWN TO YOU FROM YOUR FOREFATHERS,

19
BUT WITH THE PRECIOUS BLOOD OF CHRIST, A LAMB WITHOUT BLEMISH OR DEFECT.

1 CORINTHIANS 6, 19 – 20
19
DO YOU NOT KNOW THAT YOUR BODY IS A TEMPLE OF THE HOLY SPIRIT, WHO IS IN YOU, WHOM YOU HAVE RECEIVED FROM GOD? YOU ARE NOT YOUR OWN;

20
YOU WERE BOUGHT AT A PRICE. THEREFORE HONOR GOD WITH YOUR BODY.

The Christian should consider the demons as their:

> **ENEMIES.**
> **INVADERS.**
> **UNDESIRABLE.**

The demons are invaders that illegally and on the sly take over the body of another person.

The devil has no legal right on the believer, and is for all of us to defend our rights.

No demon can stay when a Christian wants with all of his heart for the demon to leave.

JAMES 4, 7b
RESIST THE DEVIL, AND HE WILL COME NEAR TO YOU.

Demons believe the body of the person where they live as **"home"**.

MATTHEW 12, 43 – 44

43
WHEN AN EVIL SPIRIT COMES OUT OF A MAN, IT GOES THROUGH ARID PLACES SEEKING REST AND DOES NOW FIND IT.

44
THEN IT SAYS, I WILL RETURN TO THE HOUSE I LEFT. WHEN IT ARRIVES, IT FINDS THE HOUSE UNOCCUPIED, SWEPT CLEAN AND PUT IN ORDER.

No demon can sustain such claim. All demons are:

- ➤ **LIARS.**
- ➤ **DECEIVERS.**
- ➤ **MURDERERS.**

JOHN 8, 44
YOU BELONG TO YOUR FATHER, THE DEVIL, AND YOU WANT TO CARRY OUT YOUR FATHER'S DESIRE. HE WAS A MURDE-RER FROM THE BEGINNING; NOT HOLDING TO THE TRUTH, FOR THERE IS NO TRUTH IN HIM. WHEN HE LIES, HE

SPEAKS HIS NATIVE LANGUAGE, FOR HE IS LIAR AND THE FATHER OF LIES.

The demons have no right to the bodies redeemed by the blood of our Lord Jesus Christ.

OUR ATTITUDE AS TO DEMONS

THE ATTITUDE we should have towards the demonic spirits is:

> ➤ **AS SOON ARE CAUGHT, SHOULD BE EXPELLED IN THE NAME OF JESUS.**

Let's talk about **THE ATTITUDES** that we have with respect to **THE RELEASE**.

THE FIRST ATTITUDE

It relates to the people who tell us:

> ➤ **WELL, WE DON'T REALLY KNOW!**
> ➤ **THERE IS NO SUCH THING AS AN EVIL SPIRIT.**
> ➤ **THE DEVIL DOES NOT EXIST.**

Precisely this attitude and thoughts is what **SATAN** want us to believe fooling us all, but **THE BIBLE** tells us the opposite, from **GENESIS** to **REVELATION** speaks of **THE KINGDOM OF SATAN AND HIS DEMONS.**

GENESIS 3, 1
NOW THE SERPENT WAS MORE CRAFTY THAN ANY OT THE WILD ANIMALS THE LORD GOD HAD MADE. HE SAID TO THE WOMAN, DID GOD REALLY SAY, YOU MUST NOT EAT FROM ANY TREE IN THE GARDEN?

REVELATION 12, 9
THE GREAT DRAGON WAS HURLED DOWN– THAT ANCIENT SERPENT CALLED THE DEVIL, OR SATAN, WHO LEADS THE WHOLE WORLD ASTRAY. HE WAS HURLED TO THE EARTH, AND HIS ANGELS WITH HIM.

If you believe in **GOD**, let us see what **HE HIMSELF** says in the book of **JOB**.

JOB 1, 6 – 7
6
ONE DAY THE ANGELS CAME TO PRESENT THEMSELVES BEFORE THE LORD, AND SATAN ALSO CAME WITH THEM. THE LORD SAID TO SATAN, "WHERE HAVE YOU COME FROM?"

7
THE LORD SAID TO SATAN, "WHERE HAVE YOU COME FROM?" SATAN ANSWERED THE LORD, "FROM ROAMING THROUGH THE EARTH AND GOING BACK AND FORTH IN IT."

If **GOD** speaks with this character and reveals its existence in a conversation with **SATAN** how can anyone affirm demons do not exist? and that there is no such **Thing** called **DEMONS**.

DO YOU BELIEVE IN JESUS CHRIST?

Let's see what is written in **THE WORD OF GOD:**

MATTHEW 4, 1
THEN JESUS WAS LED BY THE SPIRIT INTO THE DESERT TO BE TEMPTED BY THE DEVIL.

JESUS spoke with the **DEVIL**, Brothers I believe that those who think that the **DEVIL** does not exist should change their attitude and reconsider its **position** thereon.

Many believe that the things that afflict us do not come from the devil, but that would be more or less:

> **MY OWN FEAR.**
> **MY OWN IRE.**

But it is more than that, we are referring to **ANOTHER ENTITY** to **AN EVIL SPIRIT** known as **SPIRIT OF FEAR** or **SPIRIT OF SCARE** that **TIE** one, and we know that this is very different.

Satan is much more than just an **"influence"** or a **"conduct disorder"** that affects the life of a Christian, although his efforts is that the church so creates it and continues in its state of ignorance or denial about the true presence of him in the life of many **"carnal Christians"**.

There is another **ENTITY** that is not oneself but **IS EVIL**:

> **OF DARKNESS.**
> **OF THE DEPTHS.**
> **OF HELL.**

And **THAT** is what keeps one **TIED** or **IN CAPTIVITY.**

EXAMPLE:

> **THE SPIRIT OF FEAR.**
> **THE SPIRIT OF ANGER.**
> **THE SPIRIT OF LUST.**
> **THE SPIRIT OF GLUTTONY.**
> **THE SPIRIT OF COMPULSION.**
> **THE SPIRIT OF SEX.**

THERE ARE EVIL SPIRITS and Saint Luke so it confirms;

LUKE 8, 2
AND ALSO SOME WOMEN WHO HAS BEEN CURED OF EVIL SPIRITS AND DISEASES: MARY (CALLED MAGDALENE) FROM WHOM SEVEN DEMONS HAD COME OUT;

If you don't believe, it is a shame, but **YES, THEY EXIST! THE WRONG** thing is **WHEN WE THINK THAT EVERYTHING THAT GOES BAD** in our lives is because of them, or **THAT EVERY PROBLEM** that come our way comes from them. As:

> ➤ **TIES (LINKS).**
> ➤ **SUFFERING.**
> ➤ **AND BURDENS.**

Not always is good to give the **DEVIL** all **THE CREDIT** for all **BAD THINGS** that afflicts the lives of so many people.

There are things that have nothing to do with **MALIGNANT SPIRITS:**

> ➤ **CONSCUPISCENCIA OF OUR OWN.**
> ➤ **PARANOIA.**
> ➤ **SCHIZOPHRENIA.**
> ➤ **OTHER MENTAL ILLNESS.**
> ➤ **EMOTIONAL INESTABILITY.**
> ➤ **DEPRESSIONS, ETC.**

These are other kinds of evils and it is not specifically from **MALIGNANT SPIRITS.**

Many people react negatively or are afraid of the **MINISTRY OF LIBERATION** and say:

> ➤ **I DO NOT WANT TO PRACTICE THIS HERE.**
> ➤ **DON'T WANT TO HAVE ANYTHING TO DO WITH THAT.**
> ➤ **KEEP IT AWAY FROM ME.**

Actually they are not reacting to **THE MINISTRY OF LIBERATION**, but **THE MISTAKES** that have been made in the practice and the kind of **MINISTRY** they have witnessed.

THE MINISTRY OF LIBERATION attracts people who want to be:

> * **AUTHORITARIAN.**
> * **GIVE ORDERS.**
> * **TO COMMAND.**
> * **AND USING TACTICS OF POWER.**

These people always wish to participate in **THE MINISTRY OF LIBERATION** and when they do it, they come to it with much of **THEIR OWN PERSONAL EMOTIONS.**

They confront the **MALIGNANT SPIRITS** and begin **TO CAST THEM OUT AND TIE** them in the **NAME OF JESUS** and enter **IN A BATTLE.** They are like military that gives orders out all the time, and all they are making is s A **BATTLE FULL OF**:

> * **SHOUTS.**
> * **SCREAMS.**
> * **PHYSICAL MANIFESTATIONS.**
> * **TORMENTS.**
> * **PEOPLE ON THE FLOOR.**
> * **VOMIT.**
> * **UNDRESS.**
> * **YOU CAN NOT CONTROL.**
> * **AND THE LIKE.**

Usually when this happens, in many cases persons:

> * **DO NOT RECEIVE HELP.**
> * **CAN GET HURT.**

The reaction of the people with all their reasons namely **"I DO NOT WANT THAT HERE"**

THE QUESTION IS:
IS THERE ANOTHER WAY OF DOING THIS?

It is precisely what we want to share with you in this book.

"THERE IS ANOTHER WAY TO DO IT"

   ➢ **A WAY OF APPROACHING THE RELEASE.**
   ➢ **DO THE RELEASE.**
   ➢ **AND BE IN THE RELEASE.**

Without going into **EXCESSIVE** or **INTEMPERATE BATTLE** without entering this kind of **THROW** and **PULLS, SHOUTS** and **SCREAMS**.

PROSPECTS FOR THE RELEASE:

THE RELEASE is part of the **HEALING; THE MINISTRY OF LIBERATION** is part of **THE MINISTRY OF HEALING.**

We say categorically, it is our foundation and our position and we keep it that way, simply DO **NOT EXIST** such a thing as **THE MINISTRY OF LIBERATION,** and is very disturbing to hear of certain people claiming they have this **MINISTRY OF LIBERATION**, we repeat IT DOES **NOT EXIST** such a thing.

On the other hand **EXIST THE MINISTRY OF HEALING,** in which **THE LIBERATION** plays a role, and if one **DIVORCED THE RELEASE OF THE HEALING "CREATES A MONSTER".**

If one removes **THE LIBERATION** in the context of **THE HEALING** has created a **"MONSTER"** that:

> ➢ **IT DESTROYS ONE.**
> ➢ **THE PERSON TO BE MINISTERED.**
> ➢ **AND YOUR MINISTRY.**

We must maintain **THE RELEASE** within the context of **THE HEALING** and the process of growth in **THE FULLNESS OF JESUS CHRIST.**

We see every day that few Christians which are instruments of Jesus to heal their brothers from spirits, ignore the mandate of Jesus.

JAMES 1, 23 – 25
23
ANYONE WHO LISTENS TO THE WORD BUT DOES NOT DO WHAT IT SAYS IS LIKE A MAN WHO LOOKS AT HIS FACE IN A MIRROR.

24
AND, AFTER LOOKING AT HIMSELF, GOES AWAY AND IMME-DIATELY FORGETS WHAT HE LOOKS LIKE

25
BUT THE MAN WHO LOOKS INTENTLY INTO THE PERFECT LAW THAT GIVES FREEDOM, AND CONTINUES TO DO THIS, NOT FORGETTING WHAT HE HAS HEARD, BUT DOING IT – HE WILL BE BLESSED IN WHAT HE DOES.

The demons are enemies of the gifts and fruits of the spirit.

They (demons) could prevent a Christian from give fruit in his lifetime, and therefore prevent the preparation of the believer for the coming of the Lord.

That is why the release is vital part in the preparation of the bride of Christ to be carried out today.

EPHESIANS 5, 25 – 27

25

HUSBANDS, LOVE YOUR WIVES, JUST AS CHRIST LOVED THE CHURCH AND GAVE HIMSELF UP FOR HER

26

TO MAKE HER HOLY, CLEANSING HER BY THE WASHING WITH WATER THROUGH THE WORD,

27

AND TO PRESENT HER TO HIMSELF AS A RADIANT CHURCH, WITHOUT STAIN OR WRINKLE OR ANY OTHER BLEMISH, BUT HOLY AND BLAMELESS.

THEME 2
PREPARATION
FOR
RELEASE

RECOMMENDATIONS.

BE VERY CAREFUL THOSE PEOPLE THAT READ:

- ➢ ABSTRACTS.
- ➢ NOTES.
- ➢ BOOKS.
- ➢ CASSETTES.
- ➢ VIDEOS.

IT IS OF SUM IMPORTANCE TO LEAD A LIFE OF:

- ➢ FAITH.
- ➢ OBEDIENCE TO THE LORD.
- ➢ ASK FORGIVENESS OF ALL OUR SINS.
- ➢ PURITY.
- ➢ FASTS.

- ➤ PRAYER.
- ➤ DAILY READING OF THE WORD OF GOD.
- ➤ LAST SUPPER (OFTEN COMMUNION) (IF ITS NOT RECEIVED FREQUENTLY IN YOUR CHURCH MAKE A SPIRITUAL COMMUNION).
- ➤ DO NOT SIN.

We previously said that the release is not a cure and we must be in obedience to be instruments of the love of God in Jesus Christ and to help our brothers and not make mistakes that we later may regret.

ACTS 19, 13 – 16

13

SOME JEWS WHO WENT AROUND DRIVING OUT EVIL SPIRITS TRIED TO INVOKE THE NAME OF THE LORD JESUS OVER THOSE WHO WERE DEMON-POSSESSED. THEY WOULD SAY, "IN THE NAME OF JESUS, WHOM PAUL PREACHES, I COMMAND YOU TO COME OUT."

14

SEVEN SONS OF SCEVA, A JEWISH CHIEF PRIEST, WERE DOING THIS.

15

ONE DAY THE EVIL SPIRIT ANSWERED THEM, "JESUS I KNOW, AND I KNOW ABOUT PAUL, BUT WHO ARE YOU?"

16

THEN THE MAN WHO HAD THE EVIL SPIRIT JUMPED ON THEM AND OVERPOWERED THEM ALL. HE GAVE THEM SUCH A BEATING THAT THEY RAN OUT OF THE HOUSE NAKED AND BLEEDING.

TESTIMONY:

One day in the St. Pius X church in Santo Domingo, Dominican Republic people were talking about a brother in Christ serving Jesus, who arrived in a Hall of the parish the previous day and there was a person with spiritual problems (A spirit Impure) he didn't want to pray for release of that person, because he had sinned and was not in spiritual conditions suitable to say the prayer of liberation.

Unfortunately the person was showing signs and malignant spirits manifestation, having no one dared to pray for the person, the brother in Christ decided to start the prayer of liberation.

As soon as he began when the devil took him and pushed him against a window breaking one of his legs.

We know that Jesus overcame the world and that the demons have to submit to Him, but for us to be instrument of Jesus, we must be in pure spiritual position to be able to combat the demons, as we say in a good Spanish, we cannot have tail to drag.

WE SHOULD START WITH CONTINUOS PRAYER, AND GET VERY DEEPLY IN THE PRESENCE OF JESUS:

> **HE IS THE LORD.**
> **THE JESUS VICTORIOUS.**
> **THE RISEN JESUS.**
> **JESUS THE EXALTED.**

PROCLAIM:

> **THE NAME OF JESUS AS OUR SAVIOR.**
> **THE GOSPEL OF THE "GOOD NEWS."**
> **RESURRECTION.**
> **"JESUS IS ALIVE."**

ACTS 4, 12

SALVATION IS FOUND IN NO ONE ELSE, FOR THERE IS NO OTHER NAME GIVEN TO MEN BY WHICH WE MUST BE SAVED.

WE MUST BE:

- ➤ **IN DEEP HUMILITY.**
- ➤ **IN THE HANDS OF GOD.**
- ➤ **IN THE PRESENCE OF JESUS.**
- ➤ **LED BY THE HOLY SPIRIT.**
- ➤ **AS A "TOOL" FOR HIM.**

LUKE 17, 10

SO YOU ALSO, WHEN YOU HAVE DONE EVERYTHING YOU WERE TOLD TO DO, SHOULD SAY, WE ARE UNWORTHY SERVANTS; WE HAVE ONLY DONE OUR DUTY.

Give **THANKS** to **GOD** because He has placed us in a condition of **SERVING HIM.**

COVER WITH THE BLOOD OF JESUS CHRIST:

- ➤ **MYSELF.**
- ➤ **MY FAMILY.**
- ➤ **MY HOME.**
- ➤ **INTERCEDE PEOPLE AND EQUIPMENT TO BE PRA-YING.**
- ➤ **YOUR PETS (IF ANY).**
- ➤ **SEAL THE SITE AND COVER IT WITH THE BLOOD OF JESUS FOR NOT INTERACTION OR COMMUNICA-TION OF THE DEMONS.**
- ➤ **COVER WITH THE BLOOD OF CHRIST ALL WIN-DOWS, DOORS, ROOF, SEALING THE PLACE, ETC.**

ASK THE HOLY SPIRIT:

> ➤ **FOR POWER FROM ABOVE.**
> ➤ **FOR GUIDANCE.**

SO NOTHING NOR NOBODY CAN CAUSE US ANY HARM OR DAMAGE.

MUST:

> ➤ **HAVE A LOT OF FAITH.**
> ➤ **TRUST IN GOD AND HIS SON JESUS CHRIST.**
> ➤ **PRAY CONTINUOSLY.**
> ➤ **FAST.**
> ➤ **ASK JESUS THE HELP OF ANGELS.**

HEBREWS 1, 14
ARE NOT ALL ANGELS MINISTERING SPIRITS SENT TO SERVE THOSE WHO WILL INHERIT SALVATION?

Jesus sent the twelve and when commissioned the seventies sent them two by two. Other teams are seen in the book of the acts:

> ➤ **PAUL, BARNABAS AND JOHN MARK.**
> ➤ **PAUL AND SILAS.**
> ➤ **BARNABAS AND JOHN MARK.**
> ➤ **AQUILA AND PRISCILLA.**

A team of six people would be ideal to pray for release, composed of men and women, and must not:

> ➤ **NEVER MINISTER ALONE.**
> ➤ **NOT A MAN TO MINISTER A WOMAN ALONE.**
> ➤ **NOT A WOMAN MINISTER A MAN ALONE.**

Only one person should be the one performing the release, a person who help you, while others are in prayer in silence and open to the action of the Holy Spirit to receive word of knowledge and guidance of the Holy Spirit.

If the person who is ministering gets tired, another person must take over, the rest should remained in silence, attentive to any information that can be received or provided.

As the **"imposition of hand"** can be used during the liberation it is preferable that there are witnesses of both sexes in the team.

OTHER RECOMMENDATIONS FOR THE TEAM:

> ➤ **ALL MEMBERS MUST ASK GOD THE FORGIVENESS OF THEIR SINS AND PRAY FOR ONE ANOTHER.**
> ➤ **UNIT IS ABSOLUTELY ESSENTIAL.**
> ➤ **SATAN LIKES IT WHEN THERE IS DISUNITY.**
> ➤ **YOU SHOULD BE ON GUARD STEADY AGAINST THESE TACTICS.**
> ➤ **ALL GROUPS WORKING TOGETHER MUST LEARN HOW TO FLOW IN THE SPIRIT.**
> ➤ **TRUST THE ONE ON THE OTHER.**
> ➤ **ASK JESUS TO CONFIRM ANY WORD OF KNOWLEDGE RECEIVED BY ANY MEMBER OF THE GROUP.**

When working in liberation, we have a path, which should not be rigid but flexible and allow the Holy Spirit to lead the liberation.

Each Member of the team must be sensitive and obedient to the direction of the Holy Spirit.

Only one person must give orders to the spirits, if this one tire gets must be relieved on the other, **they should not make the mistake** of wanting to all send the spirits because they do not obey, God is a God of order not disorder, even if you have the best of intentions, the spirits will not obey.

Other members must be in prayer, open to the action of the Holy Spirit, may be reading the Bible, about all the passages in which Jesus performed releases; pay attention if they have to grab or hold the person who is being released in case a demonic manifestation.

Some tend to play Christian songs:

> **OF FORGIVENESS.**
> **PRAISES.**
> **HEALING.**

This must be background music, which must not interfere with orders that are being given.

The purpose is to let the captive free from the clutches of Satan, give all the glory to Jesus, in a way that no matter who runs the fight, is an action of the team and each post is important as instruments of Christ's love.

All honor and glory is to God the Father and His son Jesus Christ and His Holy Spirit, we must finish giving thanks for choosing us as instruments of his love by saying:

LUKE 17, 10
SO YOU ALSO, WHEN YOU HAVE DONE EVERYTHING YOU WERE TOLD TODO, SHOULD SAY, WE ARE UNWORTHY SER-VANTS; WE HAVE ONLY DONE OUR DUTY.

For our joy Jesus Himself recognized what we do by telling us.

JOHN 15, 15
I NO LONGER CALL YOU SERVANTS, BECAUSE A SERVANT DOES NOT KNOW HIS MASTER'S BUSINESS. INSTEAD, I HAVE CALLED YOU FRIENDS, FOR EVERYTHING THAT I LEARNED FROM MY FATHER I HAVE MADE KNOWN TO YOU.

"IMPORTANT"

Check if the spirit or spirits have departed from the person, asking him or her to recognize (in words) that Jesus came into the world in flesh and was born of Mary and the Holy Spirit.

1 JOHN 4, 1 - 2
1
DEAR FRIENDS, DO NOT BELIEVE EVERY SPIRIT, BUT TEST THE SPIRITS TO SEE WHETHER THEY ARE FROM GOD, BE-CAUSE MANY FALSE PROPHETS HAVE GONE OUT INTO THE WORLD.

2
THIS IS HOW YOU CAN RECOGNIZE THE SPIRIT OF GOD: EVERY SPIRIT THAT ACKNOWLEDGES THAT JESUS CHRIST HAS COME IN THE FLESH IS FROM GOD,

After finishing the release you must:

> ➢ **GIVE THANKS TO GOD, TO HIS SON AND TO THE HOLY SPIRIT.**
> ➢ **TO THANK HIM FOR ALLOWING US TO SERVE HIM.**
> ➢ **DELIVER ALL OUR BURDENS TO OUR LORD JESUS.**

It is important to tie and give the demons to Jesus or his angels so they have them, is also important to give burdens we have received to our Lord Jesus, to keep those entities away from our homes.

1 TIMOTHY 5, 22
DO NOT BE HASTY IN THE LAYING ON OF HANDS, AND DO NOT SHARE IN THE SINS OF OTHERS. "KEEP YOURSELF PURE."

MATTHEW 11, 28
COME TO ME, ALL YOU WHO ARE WEARY AND BURDENED, AND I WILL GIVE YOU REST.

THEME 3
DISEASES
OF
THE SPIRIT

Our **SOUL** can also get **SICK**, and this is more serious than a cancer or a psychological trauma.

One Sabbath **JESUS** reached the pool of **BEEZATÁ** (which means "HOUSE OF MERCY"), saw a man who laid on his deathbed and ordered him to:

> ➢ STAND UP....... TAKE YOUR MAT AND WALK

That man, paralyzed for 38 years, found **GRACE** before **THE EYES OF GOD**, stood up and began walking.

Then the **MASTER** found him and warned him:

JOHN 5, 14
"SEE, YOU ARE WELL AGAIN. STOP SINNING OR SOMETHING WORSE MAY HAPPEN TO YOU."

JESUS did not say **THAT THE SINNER** would be paralyzed for more than 38 years, **THE SIN** would be worse than 38 years of paralysis.

Moreover, **THE SIN** is not only a disease but necessarily produces **DEATH**.

ROMANS 6, 23
FOR THE WAGES OF SIN IS DEATH,

Sin produces death that deprives us of the life of God; or rather God who is life.

JEREMIAH 2, 13
MY PEOPLE HAVE COMMITTED TWO SINS: THEY HAVE FORSAKEN ME, THE SPRING OF LIVING WATER, AND HAVE DUG THEIR OWN CISTERNS, BROKEN CISTERNS THAT CANNOT HOLD WATER.

THE SIN

It basically consists of a lack of **FAITH** to **GOD**; usually caused by an excess of confidence in ourselves.

It is believe more in ourselves than in **GOD**. He is the man who relies more on its own means towards the realization of his being, that in **THE WAY** proposed by **GOD**.

PROVERBS 8, 36; JEREMÍAS 26, 19
SIN HARMS MORE MEN THAN GOD HIMSELF.

JEREMIAH 7, 19
BUT AM I THE ONE THEY ARE PROVOKING? DECLARES THE LORD. ARE THEY NOT RATHER HARMING THEMSELVES, TO THEIR OWN SHAME?

GOD loves us so much that knowing the evil that produces sin in us, bans us from sin, forbids us to be slaves.

Complete healing consists in that we are freed from the law of sin which leads us to do evil that we do not want and prevents us from doing the good that we are proposing.

GOD not only **FORGIVES SIN** but **THAT STRENGTHENS** us to **NOT RETURN TO SIN.**

It further changes **OUR HEART** to **"WANT TO DO"** what **HE COMMANDS.**

There is no man like the one that has been liberated from **THE BONDAGE** of **SIN.**

NEHEMIAH 9, 17
BUT YOU ARE A FORGIVING GOD, GRACIOUS AND COMPA-SSIONATE,

PRECIOUS BLOOD OF CHRIST ON THE CROSS IS THE MEDI-CINE HEALER OF OUR SINS.

MICAH 7, 18 – 19
18
WHO IS A GOD LIKE YOU, WHO PARDON SIN AND FORGIVES THE TRANSGRESSION OF THE REMNANT OF HIS INHERI-TANCE? YOU DO NOT STAY ANGRY FOREVER BUT DELIGHT TO SHOW MERCY.

19
YOU WILL AGAIN HAVE COMPASSION ON US; YOU WILL TREAD OUR SINS UNDERFOOT AND HURL ALL OUR INI-QUITIES INTO THE DEPTHS OF THE SEA.

YOU THROW TO THE BOTTOM OF THE SEA ALL OUR SINS!

When **GOD** forgives, He forgives; who will be always reminding us our sins and wickedness is **Satan.**

For our part we should take and **OUR MEDICINE** that, through **THE FAITH AND RECONCILIATION.**

THE RECONCILIATION.

It plays a vital role; it is the encounter of joy because it is the return of the beloved **SON TO THE FATHER'S HOUSE.** (See Luke 15, 11-24)

1 JOHN 1, 9
IF WE CONFESS OUR SINS, HE IS FAITHFUL AND JUST AND WILL FORGIVE US OUR SINS AND PURIFY US FROM ALL UNRIGHTEOUSNESS.

JAMES 5, 16
THEREFORE CONFESS YOUR SINS TO EACH OTHER AND PRAY FOR EACH OTHER SO THAT YOU MAY BE HEALED. THE PRAYER OF A RIGHTEOUS MAN IS POWERFUL AND EFECTIVE.

MATTHEW 10, 8
JESUS SENT THE APOSTLES TO "RAISE THE DEAD".

And there are no more dead people than that whom has lost **THE LIFE OF GOD FOR THE SIN.**

We fear **THE CONFESSION** because we do not understand that thru it we have **RECONCILIATION** with **GOD.**

THE ACTION OF THE DEVIL IN THE WORLD

LUKE 11, 20
BUT IF I DRIVE OUT DEMONS BY THE FINGER OF GOD, THEN THE KINGDOM OF GOD HAS COME TO YOU.

ACTS 10, 38
HOW GOD ANOINTED JESUS OF NAZARETH WITH THE HOLY SPIRIT AND POWER, AND HOW HE WENT AROUND DOING GOOD AND HEALING ALL WHO WERE UNDER THE POWER OF THE DEVIL, BECAUSE GOS WAS WITH HIM.

PETER summarizes the Messianic work of JESUS in four points:

> ➢ ANOINTED WITH THE HOLY SPIRIT AND WITH PO-
>   WER.
> ➢ DOING GOOD DEEDS.
> ➢ HEALING.
> ➢ RELEASING ALL THE OPPRESSED BY THE DEVIL.

THE REGULAR OCCUPATION OF THE DEVIL, ALLOWED
BY GOD, IS THE TEMPTATION. THE DEVIL MAY HUNT
SOULS OF THREE FORMS:

> ➢ THE OPPRESSION OR SIEGE.
> ➢ THE OBSESSION.
> ➢ AND THE POSSESSION.

"The great victory of Satan" is that we don't believe in him, that way
he can act with complete freedom.

Many say "Is that you see Devil up in the soup", that is precisely what
he wants, so that he can act in people and the real thing is that **"YES,"**
THERE ARE DEVILS UP IN THE SOUP.

THE SIEGE OR OPPRESSION

Oppression or siege is the extraordinary action of **Satan** when looking
to terrorize through horrific appearances or by means of the things.

EXAMPLE:

> ➢ HORRIBLE APARITIONS.
> ➢ NOISES IN THE NIGHT.
> ➢ THINGS MOVING.
> ➢ LIGHTS GO OUT.
> ➢ VOICES.
> ➢ RARE DISEASES WITH NO MEDICAL EXPLANATION.

EXTERNAL ACTIONS

LUKE 13, 11
AND A WOMAN WAS THERE WHO HAS BEEN CRIPPLED BY A SPIRIT FOR EIGHTEEN YEARS. SHE WAS BENT OVER AND COULD NOT STRAIGHTEN UP AT ALL.

JESUS made a liberation when He said:

LUKE 13, 12
WHEN JESUS SAW HER, HE CALLED HER FORWARD AND SAID TO HER, "WOMAN, YOU ARE SET FREE FROM YOUR INFIRMITY."

AN OBSESSION

The influence and action of the enemy on **The Minds** of the people we call **Obsession.**

The obsession can be external when the devil acts in the external senses of the body or internal when influence imagination or memory.

There are people:

> - **TORMENTED WITH SEXUAL OBSESSIONS.**
> - **THOUGHTS OF SUICIDE.**
> - **SPIRIT OF BLASPHEMY.**
> - **SELF-DESTRUCTION.**
> - **CONTEMPT.**
> - **FEEL UNWORTHY OF GOD'S.**
> - **FORGIVENESS.**

The cause is not only physical or psychological but that they are tormented by an obsession that enslaves them, not having strength to come out victorious.

You could say the obsession resembles a temptation; but instead of being a temporary condition is permanent, as well as having a power and intensity that goes beyond our human capacities to overcome.

These people often are attacked by evil spirits.
In the New Testament we find different kinds of spirits that are worth knowing:

> **SPIRIT UNCLEAN OR IMPURE, WHICH IS THE MOST FREQUENT:**

  o **MATTHEW 12, 43**
  o **MARK 1, 23. 26. 27; 3,11; 5, 2. 8. 13; 7, 25**
  o **LUKE 4, 33.36; 6, 18; 8, 29; 9, 42; 11,24**

> **SPIRIT DUMB: MARK 9, 17**
> **DEAF AND DUMB SPIRIT: MARK 9, 25b**
> **BAD SPIRITS: LUKE 7, 21; ACTS: 19, 12**
> **EVIL SPIRITS: LUKE 8, 2**
> **SPIRITS SEER; ACTS 16, 16**
> **SPIRITS OF EVIL: EPHESIANS 6, 12**
> **DECEIVER SPIRITS: 1 TIMOTHY 4, 1**

THE POSSESSION

Possession is very rare and is the last thing we have to think of, even after other possibilities have been exhausted, is when the demon takes control of the entire body.

POSSESSION CAN BE ANY OF THE FOLLOWING:

> **BY PERMISSION OF GOD** (JUDE, SAUL).
> **WHEN SUFFERS A SPELL.**
> **STATE OF SIN AND HARDENING OF THE SAME.**

- ➢ **VISIT TO PLACES OR EVIL PEOPLE.**
- ➢ **SELLING SOUL TO THE DEVIL.**
- ➢ **SIGNING SATANIC PACTS WITH BLOOD.**
- ➢ **BELONGING TO DIABOLIC SECTS.**
- ➢ **PEOPLE WHO WERE CONSECRATED TO THE DEVIL BY PARENTS**

It is so strong this slavery that the person loses it willingly, being totally unable to break free of their chains.

Then you need a Superior outside power through an **EXORCISM.**

CATHOLIC CHURCHES

THE FORMAL OR LITURGICAL EXORCISM is done by the Bishop or a priest delegated by him in the case, who have received a specific license expressed, as established in Canon law (Can 1172)

The Formal or liturgical exorcism is a sacramental instituted by the Church to safeguard the faithful from tricksters and magicians.

The exorcism can never be exercised by laymen.

In the book Gabriele Amorth "Narratives of an Exorcist" relates the following:

- ➢ **Therefore only an authorized priest, as well as the exorcizing Bishop (I WISH THE WOULD!).**

The Church makes difference of the liberation of the exorcism prayer; the liberation prayer can be done by any layman, the exorcism according to the Sacramental Instituted to protect the faithful from tricksters and magicians. But this gives rise to some questions.

- ➤ ARE THE LAYMAN THAT CONDUCT PRAYERS OF LIBERATION LIARS OR MAGICIANS?
- ➤ IN THE BIBLE WHEN JESUS ORDERED TO EXPEL DEMONS, ARE THERE A DIFFERENCE BETWEEN PRAYER OF LIBERATION AND EXORCISM?
- ➤ WHO MUST WE OBEY, THE WORD OF GOD OR MEN?

Let us be clear, have you ever tried to find a priest who will say a prayer of liberation?

The Lord Jesus allowed me to work with a Bishop in Santo Domingo for several years and the majority of the bishops and priests sent their faithful to us for the prayer of liberation.

Does the ritual that contains prayers for the exorcism, is it a secret that may not be known or are they pleas and prayers to our God and His son Jesus Christ?

Often a sacramental is used for the sick, what is the difference between that and the sacramental of exorcism?

We understand that not just any crazy or insane would be authorized to practice exorcisms, but we are talking about proven people who just try to comply with the mandate of Jesus:

Thanks to God today at the Catholic University of Rome are organized courses specializing in exorcisms for students around the world. I am really glad for them for this great event.

MARK 16, 17 – 18
17
AND THESE SIGNS WILL ACCOMPANY THOSE WHO BELIEVE: IN MY NAME THEY WILL DRIVE OUT DEMONS; THEY WILL SPEAK IN NEW TONGUES;

18

THEY WILL PICK UP SNAKES WITH THEIR HANDS; AND WHEN THEY DRINK DEADLY POISON, IT WILL NOT HURT THEM AT ALL; THEY WILL PLACE THEIR HANDS ON SICK PEOPLE, AND THEY WILL GET WELL.

I wear lenses to correct my eyesight and I thank God that I can read, but in this passage of the Bible nowhere I found something that says:

IN MY NAME CAST OUT DEMONS, ONLY IN PRAYER OF RELEASE; IN EXORCISM CALL A BISHOP OR AN AUTHORIZED PRIEST, ETC.

Sorry, because my intention is not to be sarcastic to its standards, but it hurts me to see and hear every day more and more people in religions Afros, sorcerers, fortune-tellers, satanic cults and so many people in need and help of liberation and exorcisms are unable to find people who will pray for them, just because simple formalisms and have absolute control.

I really believe that the Church should organize a Ministry to train people, both priests and laity whom our Lord Jesus Christ has given them the wonderful gift of love and mercy.

We hope in God that the Catholic Church will change its attitude concerning the Exorcism.

OTHER CHURCHES

We have read many books by Christians writers with experience in the subject and I have found no differences between performing a release or an exorcism, thank God.

CAN A CHRISTIAN BE POSSESSED?

Some authors of Christian books read as follows:

No! A Christian can't be possessed because possession means owning, and Jesus Christ is the owner of every Christian, not the devil.

This assertion is based on the following biblical quote:

1 CORINTHIANS 6, 20
YOU WERE BOUGHT AT A PRICE. THEREFORE HONOR GOD WITH YOUR BODY.

I think there is a confusion or controversy of the translation of the word possession arises.

In the New Testament the word was not **"possession"** but:

> ➤ **BEING UNDER THE INFLUENCE OF A DEMON.**
> ➤ **HAVE A DEMON HURTS YOU.**

The demons are in the body of the Christian as any disease and not in its spirit.

And in this basis is that it believed that the Christian can't be possessed. For other authors of books the word "possession" means what is stated above; **is when the demon takes control of the body:**

This question can be contradictory and I started to investigate alleged possessions in saints of the Catholic Church and to them the rite of exorcism was practiced.

Such as:

- ➤ **DON BOSCO JOHN.**
- ➤ **JOHN VIANNEY (CURE OF ARS).**
- ➤ **MOTHER TERESA OF CALCUTTA.**
- ➤ **AND MANY MORE.**

Read the history of these exemplary people, according to accounts of history, none was found about a possession, what we could read was that the devil harassed these people, the majority of the saints of the Catholic Church have been sieges by demons.

Possession is very rare and is the last thing that we must think.

POSSESSION CAN BE GIVEN IN THE FOLLOWING CASES:

- ➤ **BY PERMISSION OF GOD.**
- ➤ **WHEN SUFFERS A SPELL.**
- ➤ **STATE OF SIN AND HARDENING OF THE SAME**
- ➤ **SELLING HIS SOUL TO THE DEVIL.**
- ➤ **SIGNING SATANIC PACTS WITH BLOOD.**
- ➤ **BELONGING TO DIABOLIC SECTS.**
- ➤ **PEOPLE WHO WERE CONSECRATED BY THEIR PARENTS TO THE DEVIL.**
- ➤ **BECOMING SERVER Ó WIFE OF SATAN.**

I wanted to ask this question to several people with much knowledge in the matter and that leads their respective ministries with great seriousness and filled with the Holy Spirit.

First Consultation:

Dear Sir
May God continue to bless you.....

I am writing you with a question and I would like to know your opinion:

"I am writing a book about healing, inner healing and Liberation, the question that arises is as follows:

Can a Christian be possessed?

I have read about this and really, some authors of books say not! And on the other hand in the Church in the lives of the saints they speak of that some have been practiced exorcisms to them.

I have read several lives of Saints and have discovered that what happened is they were besieged by demons, but not describing in their biography if there is something in relation to a possession:

Examples:

    Mother Teresa of Calcutta.
    Don John Bosco.
    John Vianney (Cure of Ars).

RESPONSE:

Yes, a Christian can be possessed............ YES....
But it is important not to conclude a possession, without first knowing if it really is.

Second Consultation:

Hello and May God continue to bless you.

I know that my name meant nothing to you, but I met you in Santo Domingo, Dominican Republic during a retreat.

I'm writing a book on inner healing and deliverance and would like to know your opinion about this:

Can a Christian be Possessed?

Many book authors say not!

ANSWERS:

Dear Luis
God Bless you

A Christian can deviate from the faith and fall into sin. It can then be possessed by the evil in some cases

At the moment I cannot say more because I am no expert in the field"

It may be that the translation of the word possession could be interpreted in a different way, and concepts and different views are identified.

I think that if Satan whom was an Angel of light, of intense beauty according to the Bible was condemned by his disobedience, I think that if a Christian disobeys is delivered to the tormentors and can reach the stage of being totally possessed.

In the writing of the Bible few cases are narrated in which the devil has entered a person:

1 SAMUEL 16, 14 – 15
14
NOW THE SPIRIT OF THE LORD HAD DEPARTED FROM SAUL, AND AN EVIL SPIRIT FROM THE LORD TORMENTED HIM.

15
SAUL'S ATTENDANTS SAID TO HIM, "SEE, AN EVIL SPIRIT FROM GOD IS TORMENTING YOU.

LUKE 22, 3
THEN SATAN ENTERED JUDAS, CALLED ISCARIOT, ONE OF THE TWELVE.

Sometimes God has allowed that people are infected by demons for his advancement spiritual, such as cases of religious people, also see the demonic attack to Job which was allowed by God.

THEME 4
HOW THE DEMONS
CAN ENTER IN PEOPLE
(ENTRY DOORS)

The demons are evil personalities. They are evil spirits; they are enemies of God and men.

OBJECTIVE:

Its objectives are:

- ➢ **ATTEMPTING TO HUMANS.**
- ➢ **CHEAT.**
- ➢ **ACCUSE.**
- ➢ **CONDEMN.**
- ➢ **MESS.**
- ➢ **RESIST.**
- ➢ **OPPOSE.**
- ➢ **CONTROL.**
- ➢ **STEAL.**
- ➢ **AFFLICT.**
- ➢ **PRESS.**

- ➢ HAUNT.
- ➢ PLACE THE POSITIVE.
- ➢ KILL AND DESTROY.

There are many ways that **THE DEMONS** can enter a person.

Now we must know first **WHAT IS A DOOR OF ENTRY?**

We are **TEMPLE OF THE HOLY SPIRIT** and when we **SIN** we profane **THE TEMPLE OF OUR BODY** and give **LEGAL RIGHT TO THE DEVIL** to enter our body, this is called **"ENTRANCE DOOR"**.

LEVITICUS 19, 31
DO NOT TURN TO MEDIUMS OR SEEK OUT SPIRITISTS, FOR YOU WILL BE DEFILED BY THEM. I AM THE LORD YOUR GOD.

1 CORINTHIANS 6, 19
DO YOU NOT KNOW THAT YOUR BODY IS A TEMPLE OF THE HOLY SPIRIT, WHO IS IN YOU, WHOM YOU HAVE RECEIVED FROM GOD?

In other words, you can't not receive a demon just by walking down the street and accidentally encounter one that is looking for a **"House"**.

These **Unclean Spirits** have access and enter lives through personal experiences that have been caused by **sin** and **disobedience**.
Many come during the **childhood** and **adolescence**, through **abuse** and **rejection** that some people were victims.

CAN A PERSON GIVE LEGAL RIGHT TO BE TORMENTED BY A DEMON?

The continuous practice of sin, the wounds and lack of forgiveness give you legal right to a demon to enter and haunt a person.

EPHESIANS 4, 27
... AND DO NOT GIVE THE DEVIL A FOOTHOLD.

ENTRY DOORS

There are countless **DOORS OF ENTRIES**, all what can relate man to sin falls into the following categories:

> - **LACK OF FORGIVENESS.**
> - **STATE OF SIN AND HARDENING OF THE SAME.**
> - **VISIT TO PLACES OR EVIL PEOPLE.**
> - **SELLING HIS SOUL TO THE DEVIL.**
> - **SIGNING SATANIC PACT WITH BLOOD.**
> - **BELONGING TO DIABOLIC SECTS.**
> - **PEOPLE WHO WERE CONSECRATED BY THEIR PARENTS TO THE DEVIL.**

HOW IS ENTERING ACHIEVED?

> - **LEGACY AND GENERATIONAL CURSES**
> - **SIN AND LACK OF FORGIVENESS**
> - **IN CIRCUMSTANCES OF LIFE**

LEGACY AND GENERATIONAL CURSES:

Found in many cases where the unclean spirits could inhabit people through the course of the inheritance.

If a child is told that it will be like his/her parents and can expect to inherit their weaknesses, then it becomes vulnerable.

If we allow the devil to do so, it will give us our inheritance, but the psalmist said of God:

PSALM 47, 4ª (47, 5 OTHER BIBLES)
HE CHOSE OUR INHERITANCE FOR US,

THEN GENERATIONAL CURSE also called ANCIENT CURSE OR FAMILY CURSE.

People not only inherit the sinful nature of their ancestors, they acquire the accumulated evil of his predecessors.

Not only God blame us for our sins, but also for the sins of our ancestors.

These generational sins give legal right to SATAN, resulting the persons in:

> - FAILURE.
> - VIOLENCE.
> - IMIMPOTENCE.
> - PROFANITY.
> - OBESITY.
> - POVERTY.
> - SHAME.
> - DISEASE.
> - GRIEF.
> - FEAR
> - DEPRESSION
> - AND EVEN DEATH

WE INHERIT FROM OUR ANCESTORS:

- ➢ SOLD TO DEMON.
- ➢ DEDICATION.
- ➢ CURSE.
- ➢ REJECTION.
- ➢ INHERITANCE OF OCCULT.

EXODUS 20, 4 – 5

4

YOU SHALL MAKE FOR YOURSELF AN IDOL IN THE FORM OF ANYTHING IN HEAVEN ABOVE OR ON THE EARTH BENEATH OR IN THE WATERS BELOW.

5

YOU SHALL NOT BOW DOWN TO THEM OR WORSHIP THEM; FOR I, THE LORD YOUR GOD, AM A JEALOUS GOD, PUNISHING THE CHILDREN FOR THE SIN OF THE FATHERS TO THE THIRD AND FOURTH GENERATION OF THOSE WHO HATE ME,

EXODUS 34, 6 – 7

6

AND HE PASSED IN FRONT OF MOSES, PROCLAMING, THE LORD, THE LORD, THE COMPASSIONATE AND GRACIOUS GOD, SLOW TO ANGER, ABOUNDING IN LOVE AND FAITHFULNESS,

7

MAINTAINING LOVE TO THOUSANDS, AND FORGIVING WICKEDNESS, REBELLION AND SIN; YET HE DOES NOT LEAVE THE GUILTY UNPUNISHED; HE PUNISHES THE CHILDREN AND THEIR CHILDREN FOR THE SIN OF THE FATHERS TO THE THIRD AND FOURTH GENERATION.

DEUTERONOMY 5, 9
YOU SHALL NOT BOW DOWN TO THEM OR WORSHIP THEM; FOR I, THE LORD YOU GOD, AM A JEALOUS GOD, PUNISHING THE CHILDREN FOR THE SIN OF THE FATHERS TO THE THIRD AND FOURTH GENERATION OF THOSE WHO HATE ME,

NUMBERS 14, 18
THE LORD IS SLOW TO ANGER, ABOUNDING IN LOVE AND FORGIVING SIN AND REBELLION. YET HE DOES NOT LEAVE THE GUILTY UNPUNISHED; HE PUNISHES THE CHILDREN FOR THE SIN OF THE FATHERS TO THE THIRD AND FOURTH GENERATION.

PROVERBS 3, 33
THE LORD'S CURSE IS ON THE HOUSE OF THE WICKED, BUT HE BLESSES THE HOME OF THE RIGHTEOUS.

We must reject and not accept inheritance proposed by the devil, in exchange, we must accept the sanity and health of our Lord Jesus Christ.

JOHN 10, 10
THE THIEF COMES ONLY TO STEAL AND KILL AND DESTROY; I HAVE COME THAT THEY MAY HAVE LIFE, AND HAVE IT TO THE FULL.

SINS AND DEMONS

SEXUAL SINS

THESE SEXUAL SINS WILL ALLOW THE DEMONS TO ENTER THE PERSON WHO COMMITS IT.

SEXUAL ABUSE AT EARLY AGE IS ONE OF THE GATES OF ENTERING MORE COMMON IN CHILDREN.

ACCORDING TO THE BOOK OF GALATIANS, THERE ARE FOUR SEXUAL SINS OF WHICH THE REST IS DERIVED FROM.

GALATIANS 5, 19
THE ACTS OF THE SINFUL NATURE ARE OVIOUS:

- ➢ ADULTERY.
- ➢ FORNICATION.
- ➢ FILTH.
- ➢ LASCIVIOUSNESS.

ADULTERY

VIOLATION OF CONJUGAL FAITH

SEXUAL RELATIONS WITH THE OPPOSITE SEX OUT OF WEDLOCK;

ADULTERY IN GREEK IS "MOIQUEIA" THAT DENOTES THE ACTION OF SEXUAL INTERCOURSE WITH ANOTHER PERSON OUTSIDE OF MARRIAGE.

IN THE BIBLE (GOD'S WORD), THIS SIN IS CALLED MARITAL INFIDELITY.

WHEN A PERSON OUT OF WEDLOCK JOINS ANOTHER BRINGS:

- ➢ LIGATURE PHYSICAL.
- ➢ EMOTIONAL TIE.
- ➢ SPIRITUAL LIGATION.

FURTHERMORE OCCURS A TRANSFER OF SPIRITS TO JOIN INTIMATELY, AND BECOME ONE FLESH.

JEREMIAH 23, 14

AND AMONG THE PROPHETS OF JERUSALEM I HAVE SEEN SOMETHING HORRIBLE: THEY COMMIT ADULTERY AND LIVE A LIE. THEY STREGTHEN THE HANDS OF EVILDOERS, SO THAT NO ONE TURNS FROM HIS WICKEDNESS; THEY ARE ALL LIKE SODOM TO ME; THE PEOPLE OF JERUSALEM ARE LIKE GOMORRAH.

1 CORINTIOS 6, 16 Y 18

16

DO YOU NOT KNOW THAT HE WHO UNITES HIMSELF WITH A PROSTITUTE IS ONE WITH HER IN BODY? FOR IT IS SAID, "THE TWO WILL BECOME ONE FLESH."

18

FLEE FROM SEXUAL IMMORALITY. ALL OTHER SINS A MAN COMMITS ARE OUTSIDE HIS BODY, BUT HE WHO SINS SEXUALLY SINS AGAINST HIS OWN BODY.

MATEO, 19, 6

SO THEY ARE NO LONGER TWO, BUT ONE. THEREFORE WHAT GOD HAS JOINED TOGETHER, LET MAN NOT SEPA-RATE.

IN WORDS OF LIBERATION, THAT IS CALLED:

> "LIGATURE OF THE SOUL"

PEOPLE WHO COMMIT ADULTERY ALWAYS HAVE AN ATTI-TUDE THAT **"NOBODY WILL SEE ME"**.

ALTHOUGH NO ONE WILL SEE THEM HERE ON EARTH, GOD FROM THE HEAVENS ALWAYS WILL.

JOB 24, 15

THE EYE OF THE ADULTERER WATCHES FOR DUSK; HE THINKS, NO EYES WILL SEE ME, AND HE KEEPS HIS FACE CONCEALED.

WHAT SHOULD WE DO WITH PEOPLE WHO ARE LIVING IN ADULTERY?

GET AWAY FROM THEM

1 CORINTHIANS 5, 9 – 11

9

I HAVE WRITTEN YOU IN MY LETTER NOT TO ASSOCIATE WITH SEXUALLY IMMORAL PEOPLE.

10

NO AT ALL MEANING THE PEOPLE OF THIS WORLD WHO ARE IMMORAL, OR THE GREEDY AND SWINLERS, OR IDO-LATRES. IN THAT CASE YOU WOULD HAVE TO LEAVE THIS WORLD.

11

BUT NOW I AM WRITING YOU THAT YOU MUST NOT ASSO-CIATE WITH ANYONE WHO CALLS HIMSELF A BROTHER BUT IS SEXUALLY IMMORAL OR GREEDY, AN IDOLATER OR A SLANDERER, A DRUNKARD OR A SWINDLER. WITH SUCH A MAN DO NOT EVEN EAT.

CONCLUSION

FORNICATION AND ADULTERY ARE SINS ABHORRENT IN THE EYES OF GOD, MUST THEREFORE MOVE AWAY FROM THEM.

TESTIMONY:

One day a lady came in to ask to be prayed for about a problem she was having for quite some time. She explained that sometimes, when she was walking, all of the sudden her legs became totally paralyzed.

In the prayer of healing, the Lord revealed to us thru a word of knowledge that she was having problems with her husband (she had requested the divorce) the lady told us that her husband was an engineer and was doing some work in the city of Puerto Plata, a city of Dominican Republic.

She lived with her two children in Santo Domingo about 4 hours from Puerto Plata; the husband was having sex with two prostitutes at the same time, and he wanted that she participated with them and have lesbian relationships.

She objected and that was the reason for the request for divorce, when he came back to Santo Domingo, he had relations with her and this motivated the spirits of sex to be introduced in her body the paralysis.

We pray for release and Jesus did His wonderful work.

Months later we were called again because the lady was paralyzed in bed.

When we arrived, immediately THE LORD revealed to us that she was having sexual relations with her ex-husband, they had already been divorced.

We explained to her that this could not continue happening because the demons would not go away and they would attacked more until she would be thinking about suicide; she confessed to us that she had been having depressions and that indeed, she had contemplated suicide.

We pray again for her with the promise of never again had relations with her ex-husband, the love of Christ and His immense mercy again made his work and the lady was released again.

Rightly the Bible tells us to keep away from adulterers and fornicators.

FORNICATION.

CARNAL UNION OUT OF WEDLOCK:
Any person without being married having intercourse sexual with another is certainly a fornicator.

There is **"A LIGATURE OF THE SOUL"**, as well as adultery, must flee from the fornicators as well as of the adulterer.

1 CORINTHIANS 6, 18
FLEE FROM SEXUAL IMMORALITY. ALL OTHER SINS A MAN COMMITS ARE OUTSIDE HIS BODY, BUT HE WHO SINS SEXUALLY SINS AGAINST HIS OWN BODY.

1 TESSALONIANS 4, 3
IS GOD'S WILL THAT YOU SHOULD BE SANCTIFIED: THAT YOU SHOULD AVOID SEXUAL IMMORALITY;

THE FILTH

FILTH, DIRT, RUBBISH, IMPURITY

WHAT IS THE FILTH?

IT IS A MORAL STAIN OF THE PEOPLE WHO ARE GIVEN TO:

> ➢ A LASCIVIOUSNESS.
> ➢ THE SEXUAL BINGE.

THE FILTH

IT IS A COMBINATION OF:

- **ADULTERY**
  VIOLATION OF CONJUGAL FAITH
  SEXUAL RELATIONS WITH THE OPPOSITE SEX OUT OF
  WEDLOCK

- **FORNICATION**
  CARNAL UNION OUT OF WEDLOCK

- **MASTURBATION**
  PRODUCE ORGASM BY EXCITATION OF THE GENITAL
  ORGANS WITH THE HAND.

- **HOMOSEXUALITY**
  SEX WITH THE SAME SEX (TWO MEN)

- **LESBIAN**
  SEX WITH THE SAME SEX (TWO WOMEN)

- **INCEST**
  SEXUAL INTERCOURSE BETWEEN RELATIVES THAT
  CAN NOT BE LEGALLY MARRIED

MATTHEW 23, 27
WOE TO YOU, TEACHERS OF THE LAW AND PHARISEES, YOU HYPOCRITES! YOU ARE LIKE WHITEWASHED TOMBS, WHICH LOOK BEAUTIFUL ON THE OUTSIDE BUT ON THE INSIDE ARE FULL OF DEAD MEN'S BONES AND EVERYTHING UNCLEAN.

LASCIVIOUSNESS
SUSCEPTIBILITY TO LUST

WHAT IS LASCIVIOUSNESS?

LEWDNESS COMES FROM THE GREEK WORD **"ASELGEIA"**;
THAT DENOTES:

- ➤ **EXCESS.**
- ➤ **NO BRAKE.**
- ➤ **INDECENCY.**
- ➤ **DISOLUTION.**

IT IS ONE OF THE EVILS THAT COME FROM THE HEART.

"ASELGEIA" IS:

- ➤ **LUST.**
- ➤ **ALL INDECENCY, SHAMELESS.**
- ➤ **DEPRAVED (ORGÍES).**
- ➤ **COMMIT SIN WITH ARROGANCE AND CONTEMPT.**

THE SERIOUSNESS OF THESE SINS IS PROGRESSIVE, IS
CALLED SIN OF LEWDNESS WHEN THE PERSON HAS COME
TO A BINGE, CAN NOT STOP THESE ACTS:

- ➤ **THERE IS A TOTAL ABSENCE OF CONTROL.**
- ➤ **LACK OF DECENCY.**
- ➤ **BECOMES DIRTY IN ALL ASPECTS.**

NOT ONLY COMMITS LEWDNESS IN THE SEXUAL AREA, BUT ALSO:

> EATING OUT OF CONTROL.
> BY USING DRUGS.
> ANY SIN IN GENERAL.

EPHESIANS 4, 19
HAVING LOST ALL SENSITIVITY, THEY HAVE GIVEN THEM-SELVES OVER TO SENSUALITY SO AS TO INDULGE IN EVERY KIND OF IMPURITY, WITH A CONTINUAL LUST FOR MORE.

THE HOMOSEXUALITY AND LESBIANISM.

SEX WITH THE SAME SEX.

ROMANS 1, 27
(HOMOSEXUALITY) *IN THE SAME WAY THE MEN ALSO ABANDONED NATURAL RELATIONS WITH WOMEN AND WE-RE INFLAMED WITH LUST FOR ONE ANOTHER. MEN COMMITTED INDECENT ACTS WITH OTHER MEN AND RE-CEIVED IN THEMSELVES THE DUE PENALTY FOR THEIR PERVERSION.*

1 CORINTHIANS 6, 9
DO YOU NOT KNOW THAT THE WICKED WILL NOT INHERIT THE KINGDOM OF GOD? DO NOT BE DECEIVED: NEITHER THE SEXUALLY IMMORAL NOR IDOLATERS NOR ADULTE-RERS NOR MALE PROSTITUTES NOR HOMOSEXUAL OFFEN-DERS.

ROMANS 1, 26 (LESBIANISM)
BECAUSE OF THIS, GOD GAVE THEM OVER TO SHAMEFUL LUSTS. EVEN THEIR WOMEN EXCHANGED NATURAL RELATIONS FOR UNNATURAL ONES.

OTHER BIBLE QUOTES

- ➤ **GENESIS 19, 5 – 8**
- ➤ **LEVITICUS 18, 22 ; 20, 13**
- ➤ **DEUTERONOMY 23, 17**
- ➤ **JUDGES 19, 22**
- ➤ **1 KINGS 14, 24 ; 15, 12 ; 22, 46**
- ➤ **TIMOTHY 1, 9 – 10**
- ➤ **2 PETER 2, 6 ; 2, 8**
- ➤ **JUDE 1, 7**
- ➤ **STORY OF DAVID AND JONATHAN**
- ➤ **1 SAMUEL 20, 41**
- ➤ **2 SAMUEL   1, 26**
- ➤ **1 SAMUEL 20, 30**

TRANSVESTISM.

A PERSON WHO DRESSES IN CLOTHES OF THE OPPOSITE SEX.

DEUTERONOMY 22, 5
A WOMAN MUST NOT WEAR MEN'S CLOTHING, NOR A MAN WEAR WOMEN'S CLOTHING; FOR THE LORD YOUR GOD DETESTS ANYONE WHO DOES THIS.

1 CORINTHIANS 11, 14

DOES NOT THE VERY NATURE OF THINGS TEACH YOU THAT IF A MAN HAS LONG HAIR, IT IS A DISGRACE TO HIM,

It is very alarming today that the majority of the media and tv shows portrays people who feel proud of their homosexuality or lesbianism.

Not only do not hide their sins but that they feel proud of them.

God loves all His creatures and God loves us all because we are and we were made in His image and likeness, but He hates sin and most He loathes those who feel proud and arrogant of his sin.

ISAIAH 3, 9
THE LOOK ON THEIR FACES TESTIFIES AGAINST THEM; THEY PARADE THEIR SIN LIKE SODOM; THEY DO NOT HIDE IT WOE TO THEM! THEY HAVE BROUGHT DISASTER UPON THEMSELVES.

ROMANS 1, 32
ALTHOUGH THEY KNOW GOD'S RIGHTEOUS DECREE THAT THOSE WHO DO SUCH THINGS DESERVE DEATH, THEY NOT ONLY CONTINUE TO DO THESE VERY THINGS BUT ALSO APROVE OF THOSE WHO PRACTICE THEM.

TESTIMONY

Being at the home of Monsignor Gómez we were approached by a young man of about 20 years, asking us with tears in his eyes that we pray for him.

His problem was that he was fighting inside, because a force and a voice fuelled in the homosexuality in him. He told us crying "I DO NOT LIKE MEN."

When we prayed for him, a manifestation of an unclean spirit of homosexuality came out, after healing his wounds the spirit was expelled in The Name of Jesus.

One of the Aspects = Forms of that particular demon was the transformation of the young man's face as a monster and a gesture to stick it's tongue out, I must confess, that I have never seen a tongue that big, it looked like a horse's.

148

God through His son Jesus Christ and the power of the Holy Spirit, did His work freeing this young man, everything is for His glory.

INCEST

SEXUAL INTERCOURSE BETWEEN RELATIVES WHO CAN NOT BE LEGALLY MARRIED;

SEXUAL RELATIONSHIP OF THE FATHER OR THE MOTHER WITH THE CHILDREN;

SEXUAL RELATIONSHIP OF BROTHERS, SISTERS; ETC.

GENESIS 19, 32 – 36
32
LET'S GET OUR FATHER TO DRINK WINE AND THEN LIE WITH HIM AND PRESERVE OUR FAMILY LINE THROUGH OUR FATHER.

33
THAT NIGHT THEY GOT THEIR FATHER TO DRINK WINE, AND THE OLDER DAUGHTER WENT IN AND LIE WITH HIM. HE WAS NOT AWARE OF IT WHEN SHE LIE DOWN OR WHEN SHE GOT UP.

34
THE NEXT DAY THE OLDER DAUGHTER SAID TO THE YOUN-GER, "LAST NIGHT I LAY WITH MY FATHER. LET'S GET HIM TO DRINK WINE AGAIN TONIGHT, AND YOU GO IN AND LIE WITH HIM SO WE CAN PRESERVE OUR FAMILY LINE THRO-UGH OUR FATHER."

35
SO THEY GOT THEIR FATHER TO DRINK WINE THAT NIGHT ALSO, AND THE YOUNGER DAUGHTER WENT AND LAY WITH HIM. AGAIN HE WAS NOT AWARE OF IT WHEN SHE LAY DOWN OR WHEN SHE GOT UP.

36

SO BOTH OF LOT'S DAUGHTERS BECAME PREGNANT BY THEIR FATHER;

LEVITICUS 18, 6 – 18

6

NO ONE IS TO APPROACH ANY CLOSE RELATIVE TO HAVE SEXUAL RELATIONS. I AM THE LORD.

7

DO NOT DISHONOR YOUR FATHER BY HAVING SEXUAL RELATIONS WITH YOUR MOTHER. SHE IS YOUR MOTHER; DO NOT HAVE RELATIONS WITH HER.

8

DO NOT HAVE SEXUAL RELATIONS WITH YOUR FATHER'S WIFE, THAT WOULD DISHONOR YOUR FATHER.

9

DO NOT HAVE SEXUAL RELATIONS WITH YOUR SISTER, EITHER YOUR FATHER'S DAUGHTER OR YOUR MOTHER'S DAUGHTER, WETHER SHE WAS BORN IN THE SAME HOME OR ELSEWHERE.

10

DO NOT HAVE SEXUAL RELATIONS WITH YOUR SON'S DAUGHTER OR YOUR DAUGHTER'S DAUGHTER; THAT WOULD DISHONOR YOU.

11

DO NOT HAVE SEXUAL RELATIONS WITH THE DAUGHTER OF YOUR FATHER'S WIFE, BORN TO YOUR FATHER; SHE IS YOUR SISTER.

12

DO NOT HAVE SEXUAL RELATIONS WITH YOUR FATHER'S SISTER; SHE IS YOUR FATHER'S CLOSE RELATIVE.

13
DO NOT HAVE SEXUAL RELATIONS WITH YOUR MOTHER'S SISTER, BECAUSE SHE IS YOUR MOTHER'S CLOSE RELATIVE.

14
DO NOT DISHONOR YOUR FATHER'S BROTHER BY APPROACHING HIS WIFE TO HAVE SEXUAL RELATIONS; SHE IS YOUR AUNT.

15
DO NOT HAVE SEXUAL RELATIONS WITH YOUR DAUGHTER-IN-LAW. SHE IS YOUR SON'S WIFE; DO NOT HAVE RELATIONS WITH HER.

16
DO NOT HAVE SEXUAL RELATIONS WITH YOUR BROTHER'S WIFE; THAT WOULD DISHONOR YOUR BROTHER.

17
DO NOT HAVE SEXUAL RELATIONS WITH BOTH A WOMAN AND HER DAUGHTER. DO NOT HAVE SEXUAL RELATIONS WITH EITHER HER SON'S DAUGHTER OR HER DAUGHTER'S DAUGHTER; THEY ARE HER CLOSE RELATIVES. THAT IS WICKEDNESS.

18
DO NOT TAKE YOUR WIFE'S SISTER AS A RIVAL WIFE AND HAVE SEXUAL RELATIONS WITH HER WHILE YOUR WIFE IS LIVING.

SEXUAL INTERCOURSE WITH ANIMALS OR BESTIALITY

LEVITICUS 20, 15 – 16

15
IF A MAN HAS SEXUAL RELATIONS WITH AN ANIMAL, HE MUST BE PUT TO DEATH, AND YOU MUST KILL THE ANIMAL.

16

IF A WOMAN APPROACHES AN ANIMAL TO HAVE SEXUAL RELATIONS WITH IT, KILL BOTH THE WOMAN AND THE ANIMAL. THEY MUST BE PUT TO DEATH; THEIR BLOOD WILL BE ON THEIR OWN HEADS

We have reached such depravity that Internet offer courses to train the animals to have sex with people, as they say: "May God have mercy on us".

SEXUAL INTERCOURSE WITH DEMONS

GENESIS 6, 2
THE SONS OF GOD SAW THAT THE DAUGHTERS OF MEN WERE BEAUTIFUL, AND THEY MARRIED ANY OT THEM THEY CHOSE.

There are many books that tell of wives of Satan here on earth, any book that talk about this, it will end up with sexual orgies between demons and people.

TESTIMONY:

While I lived in the city of Miami, I visited a dentist once for a regular checkup, the hygienist, a young lady, all of the sudden started to tell me that her boyfriend had died in a car accident a few days before their wedding.

She told me that her boyfriend's death affected her so much that she was in a constant depression.

Often inexplicably, people one does not know would start recounting intimate aspects of their life in minutes, things that normally is not told to everybody.

The Holy Spirit uses us as advocates to help these people.

She told me that she was very hurt by his death, but that at least she was communicating with her boyfriend and he came at night and had sexual relations with him.

I explained to her that this relationship was not with her boyfriend, that demons took advantage of her hurting and therefore. Door of entry had been open to the demon.

I advised her to go to a church in Miami called "The Servants of a Living Christ" and to tell them about this and ask for a prayer of liberation and inner healing.

Several months later I met her by chance in a charismatic retreat, she approached me smiling and told me about her release and liberation, she told me she had found peace and there was no signs of depression.

How great is our Lord that gives us the tools so in His name cast out demons and freed His people.

Unfortunately this experience is very common and there are many testimonies of people who have sexual intercourse with shadows or demon entities, these people should receive inner healing and deliverance and reject the devil and ask for protection with the blood of our Lord Jesus Christ.

THESE SHADOWS ARE TWO KINDS OF UNCLEAN SPIRITS:

> ➤ **INCUBI.**
> ➤ **SUCCUBI.**

INCUBI.
Demons that have appearance of male which stimulate and lead women to have sexual pleasure.

SUCCUBI.
Demons that have female appearance that stimulate men and take him to ejaculation.

SADOMASOCHISM

It is the Union of sadism and masochism in one person.

SADISM
An unhealthy pleasure at the view or make others suffer. It is considered as a sexual perversion.

MASOCHISM

Sexual perversion that it has to do with being abused by a person.

Many times we see in commercials, movies and what is worst , in comics (cartoons) the famous woman with a whip beating men up to provide sexual pleasure, this is not healthy but evil, they can also tie their partner in bed.

These sexual perversions are other ways to open doors to the demon.

PORNOGRAPHY

The **GREEK** word **"PORNOGRAPHOS"**, comes from the word **PORN**, meaning **PROSTITUTE**, and **GRAPHO**, which means **WRITING**.

Today THE MEANS OF COMMUNICATION IN THE WORLD AS:

- ➤ **TV.**
- ➤ **VIDEOS.**
- ➤ **MOVIES.**
- ➤ **NOVELS.**
- ➤ **MAGAZINES.**
- ➤ **BOOKS.**
- ➤ **INTERNET.**
- ➤ **LIVE SEX.**

They are sexual acts in all dimensions of the **LEWDNESS** by people who are engaged in prostitution and involved in these acts in exchange for money and some advertising.

WHAT CONSEQUENCE DOES PORNOGRAPHY BRING TO US?

➢ **INCREASE OF SEXUAL VIOLATIONS.**

➢ **CRIMES RELATED TO SEX.**

➢ **DIVORCES CAUSED BY MATERIALS PORNOGRAPHIC OR CONTACTS VIA THE INTERNET.**

➢ **IT INTRODUCES THE CHILDREN TO MASTURBATION AND BAD SEX UNFOUNDED PREMATURELY.**

➢ **DAMAGE OF THE MINDS OF THE PEOPLE CAUSED BY THE IMAGES THAT ATTACK THE MEMORIES CAUSING SHAME AND GUILT.**

➢ **BOTH MEN AND WOMEN THAT ARE USED FOR PHOTOS, VIDEOS AND PORN MOVIES END UP WITH UNCLEAN SPIRITS OF SEX AND NEED A RELEASE CONSIDERED TO BE ONE OF THE MOST DIFFICULT.**

THESE PEOPLE WHEN THEY HAVE RELATION-SHIPS TRANSFER THESE SPIRITS TO THE O-THER PERSON.

The people who produce these pictures, videos and movies such as persons who see them are exposed to demons.

If we read some stories of the Bible we see awful consequence brought to mankind for these practices:

➢ **GOD DESTROYED SODOM AND GOMORRAH.**
➢ **DESTROYED THE WORLD WITH THE FLOOD.**

- DESTROYED BABYLON.
- PUNISHMENT TO THE PEOPLE OF ISRAEL ON SEVERAL OCCASIONS.

Today some people say that these cities were virtually destroyed by phenomena of nature, but what a coincidence that the most promiscuous cities have been destroyed as:

- THE EARTHQUAKE IN SAN FRANCISCO.

- THE CITY OF NEW ORLEANS WITH HURRACANE KATRINA WAS FLOODED ALMOST COMPLETE.

WHAT CAN WE DO?

- REPENT BEFORE GOD.
- RELINQUISH EVERY UNCLEAN SPIRIT OF:

  - PORNOGRAPHY.
  - SEX.
  - LASCIVIOUSNESS.
  - SEXUAL FANTASIES MENTAL.
  - ADULTERY.
  - FORNICATION.
  - ADDICTION.
  - MASTURBATION
  - VOYERISM.
  - VIOLATION.
  - PROSTITUTION.
  - NYMPHOMANIA.
  - FRIGIDITY
  - FETISH.
  - LUSTFUL FANTASIES.

- ASK THE LORD TO DELETE ALL MEMORY OF THE VIEWED THINGS AND FOUND IN THE PORNOGRAPHY OF MIND.

> ➤ BURN AND THROW AWAY ALL PORNOGRAPHIC MA-
> TERIAL AND REMOVE THE PORNOGRAPHIC CHAN-
> NELS FROM TV.

TESTIMONY:

On one occasion a cousin of mine and his wife returned home sooner than expected and to their unpleasant surprise, found their 11 year old son in bed with two neighbor girls of the same age, completely naked, doing the same thing than they were watching in a porno video he had forgot in his bedroom.

As the word of God says the devil is like a roaring lion seeking someone to devour

One of the most frequent ways to open doors to the demon is pornography and we must be very careful not to have any material of this kind in our homes and also with the TV channels that we have on the Cable.

1 PETER 5, 8
BE SELF-CONTROLLED AND ALERT. YOUR ENEMY THE DEVIL PROWLS AROUND LIKE A ROARING LION LOOKING FOR SOMEONE TO DEVOUR.

MASTURBATION.

WHAT IS MASTURBATION?

It is to excite the genital organs in order to obtain sexual pleasure.

A person can become dependent or create this habit to the point of turning the person into a sexual ill and not be able to control it.

Many come to prefer masturbation that to have a relationship with their partner.

Stimulation usually begins during puberty:

> **THE DESIRE TO STIMULATE A SELF.**
> **SEXUAL ABUSE.**

Both the man and the woman may be dominated by this spirit of lust, opening doors for the spirit to enter the individual. This sin is lust and is associated with sexual fantasies.

MASTURBATION COMES IN TWO SOURCES:

> **HERITAGE.**
> **ELECTIVE.**

TO SOLVE THIS SIN YOU SHOULD:

> **SEEK PRAYER OF RELEASE.**
> **RESIGN VOLUNTARILY TO THAT ACT.**
> **DO NOT WATCH ANY PORNOGRAPHY.**
> **AVOID IMPURE THOUGHTS.**
> **TRANSFORM YOUR THOUGHTS TO GOD.**

IMMORALITY AND SEXUAL FANTASIES.

Fill the mind of man, God's Word tells us:

MATTHEW 5, 28
BUT I TELL YOU THAT ANYONE WHO LOOKS AT A WOMAN LUSTFULLY HAS ALREADY COMMITTED ADULTERY WITH HER IN HIS HEART.

These sexual fantasies and promiscuous thoughts lead us to sin.

Many times we want to seem naive:

> ➢ **WHEN A WOMAN WEARS TIGHT PANTS, DOES NOT SHE WEAR IT TO TEMPT A MAN?**

> ➢ **WHEN A WOMAN OR MAN MAKES A SEXUAL COMMENT ABOUT CERTAIN LOOKS ON ANOTHER PERSON:**

"LOOK AT HIM OR HER! REFERRING TO THEIR LOOKS OR CERTAIN PARTS OF THEIR BODY."

ARE THEY TALKING ABOUT AN ICE CREAM, OR IS NOT REALLY REFERRING TO HOW GOOD WOULD BE TO HAVE RELATIONS WITH HIM OR HER?

RAPE AND ABUSE.

2 SAMUEL 13, 11 – 14
11
BUT WHEN SHE TOOK IT TO HIM TO EAT, HE GRABBED HER AND SAID, "COME TO BED WITH ME, MY SISTER."

12

"DON'T MY BROTHER!" SHE SAID TO HIM. "DON'T FORCE ME. SUCH A THING SHOULD NOT BE DONE IN ISRAEL! DON'T DO THIS WICKED THING.

13

WHAT ABOUT ME? WHERE COULD I GET RID OF MY DISGRACE? AND WHAT ABOUT YOU? YOU WOULD BE LIKE ONE OF THE WICKED FOOLS IN ISRAEL.

PLEASE SPEAK TO THE KING; HE WILL NOT KEEP ME FROM BEING MARRIED TO YOU.

14

BUT HE REFUSED TO LISTEN TO HER, AND SINCE HE WAS STRONGER THAN SHE, HE RAPED HER.

TESTIMONY:

One day I was with a friend named Renzo praying for some people when two ladies came in who were professors at a meditation course, one of them told us that she was having many problems with her 15 year old son, and that she did not feel love for her son and that the young man had decided to suddenly go to live with his father, the couple was divorced.

Again the son returned to live with her and began to rebel toward both his parents, she continued to feel rejection towards her son, she is talking with my friend, Renzo, meanwhile, I'm praying in silence, when thru a word of knowledge the word "rape" comes to my mind.

I interrupt them very subtly and I ask her, does the word "rape" mean something to you? The woman breaks down crying, and crying and crying over for about 10 to 15 minutes and sobbing tells us; that she was "raped" by the father of that child, and that as a result of this "violation" this son was son born.

We prayed for her and for inner healing so that the Lord would heal those wounds of this "violation" and as it was expected, the Lord made His wonderful work. After that she forgave the boy's father and his son and forgave herself. It was wonderful to see her face transformed after this healing; many people don't realize the damage that produces an abuse or a violation and all trace of bitterness that it carries. If you could compare this lady's face when she first came in and her face after the healing, you couldn't believe it was the same person.

TESTIMONY:

At the beginning I started to pray for people and not having experience in release, we went to pray for a 14 year old girl who has come from Miami with her mother. The mother told us that the girl's father, while under the influence of drugs had raped her repeatedly, when she found out, she called the Miami police and he was arrested and prosecuted, sentenced to 10 years in prison.

We prayed for both, the mother and daughter. Sometime later, we learned that the father had written a letter to his daughter asking forgiveness because he had accepted Christ in his heart while in prison.

On this occasion we didn't have any experience about liberation and there was unfortunately no prayer of release for this girl.

Sadly, after returning to Miami, this girl turned into prostitution. Rape is such a great damage and it is worse when accompanied by incest. May God have mercy on her.!

THE PROMISCUITY

Confusing mixture, heterogeneous coexistence of people of different sexes
Ambiguous, double meaning.

- ➢ **FORNICATION.**
- ➢ **ADULTERY.**
- ➢ **ORAL SEX.**
- ➢ **SEXUAL MASOCHISM.**
- ➢ **THE SEXUAL FANTASIES.**
- ➢ **PORNOGRAPHY.**
- ➢ **HOMOSEXUALITY AND LESBIANISM.**
- ➢ **BESTIALITY.**
- ➢ **ABORTIONS.**

Promiscuous people are those who practice these sexual aberrations.

ANAL SEX.

Having anal relations is an act against nature; the majority of persons who practice it do it to avoid the risk of getting pregnant or to retain her virginity.

This can lead man to homosexuality, also can open doors to the demons of:

> - LASCIVIOUSNESS.
> - HOMOSEXUALITY.
> - DEGRADATION.
> - DEPRAVITY.
> - PERVERSION.

They can also produce trauma in women as:

> - SHAME.
> - GUILT.
> - LOW SELF ESTEEM.
> - PHYSICAL.

ABORTIONS.

Abortion is voluntarily caused the termination of pregnancy.

Abortion is murder of a defenseless creature that is in a woman's uterus

Women who undergo elective abortions don't realize the damage spiritual, emotional and physical they caused themselves, it is one of the ways to open doors to demons, especially to the murders spirits, spirits of fear, depression of spirits which can lead a person to suicide.

TESTIMONY:

A woman came one afternoon asking for prayer, and almost immediately after arriving, some evil spirits manifested in her, Monsignor Gómez and I prayed for release or liberation of this lady, which was received through the mercy of God and His son Jesus Christ.

A few weeks later she came back with the same problem and once again we prayed for her and Jesus again performed His wonderful work in her.

A month later she returned with the same problem, was about noon and Monsignor Gómez did not feel well, then I told him:

Monsignor, let me talk with her before praying and the Lord to reveal why those demons keep on returning.

The lady and I sat down and I started to pray and ask Jesus to reveal me the root of the problem, suddenly I see on my mind a vision of 7 babies faces, I kept praying and asking the Lord for confirmation of my vision, that vision again returned, and a word of knowledge "Abortion" and then I asked the woman:" Have you had seven abortions? I had not finished the last word when she started crying and sobbing and telling me that her husband had forced her to have seven abortions.

We asked God and His son Jesus to heal these deep wounds and stop the legal right to be in that body and cast out those demons in the name of Jesus.

Then deliver those creatures to Jesus and named them and we blessed them in the name of the Father, and of the Son and of the Holy Spirit, Jesus returned her dignity and her face shone with peace and quiet after that, she forgave her husband and herself.

Once again proves that the release is part of the Ministry of healing and that it cannot be separated.

OTHER SINS.

All sin open doors to demons to enter:

GALATIANS 5, 20 - 21

20

IDOLATRY AND WITCHCRAFT; HATRED, DISCORD, JEA-
LOUSY, FITS OF RAGE, SELFISH AMBITION, DISSENSIONS,
FACTIONS;

21

AND ENVY; DRUNKENNESS, ORGIES, AND THE LIKE. I WARN
YOU, AS I DID BEFORE, THAT THOSE WHO LIVE LIKE THIS
WILL NOT INHERIT THE KINGDOM OF GOD.

THE LACK OF FORGIVENESS (SIN OF OMISSION).

When a person suffer in his/her heart for something that another person did and have a resentment and does not forgive, that is one of the mechanisms most used by Satan so that the person is hurt and does not forgive ,that way it gives legal right to introduce his demons.

When we prayed to GOD the prayer taught to us by Our Lord JESUS CHRIST we ask GOD to forgive us as well as we forgive our debtors, we are promising conditional forgiveness to God, promising that we will forgive.

What happens if we do not forgive and have already pledged to God that we are going to forgive? He always fulfills His promises....... But if we don't forgive He will not forgive us either!

PETER asked JESUS how many times we should forgive and He replied as follows:

MATTHEW 18, 22
JESUS ANSWERED, I TELL YOU, NOT SEVEN TIMES, BUT
SEVENTY-SEVEN TIMES.

It means "ALWAYS", also tells us:

MATTHEW 5, 23 – 24
23
THEREFORE, IF YOU ARE OFFERING YOUR GIFT AT THE ALTAR AND THERE REMEMBER THAT YOUR BROTHER HAS SOMETHING AGAINST YOU,

24

LEAVE YOU GIFT THERE IN FRONT OF THE ALTAR. FIRST GO AND BE RECONCILED TO YOUR BROTHER; THEN COME AND OFFER YOUR GIFT.

MATTHEW 5, 44
BUT I TELL YOU: LOVE YOUR ENEMIES AND PRAY FOR THOSE WHO PERSECUTE YOU,

JESUS and His word teach us how important it is to forgive.

We must ask God not only to forgive, but also to forget He will make our memories of hurt to disappear and we will have peace and love for the people who have hurt us.

PRIDE, SUPERB AND ARROGANCE.

These sins led Satan to rebelled against God.

THE PRIDE.

Too good opinion which one has of its own self, high sense of personal dignity:

- ➢ **COCKY.**
- ➢ **HAUGHTY.**
- ➢ **PROUD.**
- ➢ **DISDAINFUL.**

- ➢ INSOLENT.
- ➢ SUPERB.
- ➢ VAIN.

He lives for oneself believing is better than others.

THE SUPERB.

Pride excessive:

- ➢ IRE.
- ➢ CHOLERA.
- ➢ RABIES.
- ➢ ANGER.

This is a person that usually depend on his/her skills, what they know and what they has learned.

THE ARROGANCE.

The person who has a high esteem of himself and despises others, also boasts of its present achievements and the past, always believed that he achieved everything with their own efforts:

- ➢ HAUGHTY.
- ➢ SUPERB.
- ➢ INSOLENT.
- ➢ BRAVE.
- ➢ AIRY.

PROVERBS 8, 13
TO FEAR THE LORD IS TO HATE EVIL; I HATE PRIDE AND ARROGANCE, EVIL BEHAVIOR AND PERVERSE SPEECH.

PROVERBS 6, 16 – 19
16

THERE ARE SIX THINGS THE LORD HATES, SEVEN THAT ARE DETESTABLE TO HIM;

17

HAUGHTY EYES, A LYING TONGUE, HANDS THAT SHED INNOCENT BLOOD,

18

A HEART THAT DEVISES WICKED SCHEMES, FEET THAT ARE QUICK TO RUSH INTO EVIL,

19
A FALSE WITNESS WHO POURS OUR LIES AND MAN WHO STIRS UP DISSENSION AMONG BROTHERS.

CHARACTERISTICS OF PERSONS:

PRIDE, SUPERB AND ARROGANCE:

> SELF.
> PERFECTIONIST.
> SELFISH.
> COMPETITIVE.
> SPITEFUL.
> WILLFUL.
> AMBITIOUS.
> CONTENTIOUS.
> DO NOT BELIEVE IN THE WORD OF GOD.

AFRAID AND FEAR.

Many people feel afraid of death; Jesus defeated the devil and destroyed death with His resurrection.

The death is the main root of fear, to overcome this fear we must receive the new life that Jesus promised us.

Jesus broke the chains of slavery that kept us tied to fear of death.

Whoever does not depart their thoughts from Jesus and stays in constant communion with Him don't have to fear anything.

Renounce to all fear spirit in the name of Jesus.

WITCHCRAFT, OCCULTISM, SECTS, AND SORCERY:

- ➤ ACUPUNCTURE.
- ➤ ALTERNATIVE MEDICINE.
- ➤ DIVINATION
- ➤ ASTROLOGY.
- ➤ CHART.
- ➤ HOROSCOPE.
- ➤ WITCHCRAFT.
- ➤ SORCERY.
- ➤ CONSULTATIONS TO MEDIUMS OR SPI-RITS.
- ➤ MAGIC.
- ➤ SPIRITUALISM.
- ➤ OCCULT.
- ➤ THE OUIJA.
- ➤ SATANIC SECTS AND CULTS.
- ➤ TAROT.
- ➤ TELEPATHY
- ➤ HYPNOTISM.
- ➤ MIND CONTROL.
- ➤ MEDITATIONS OF ANY KIND, INCLUDING LOSS OF CONSCIOUSNESS OR LEAVE BLANK MIND.
- ➤ USE WATER OR MINERAL OILS IN WHAT HAS BEEN A ROD OR A PENDULUM.
- ➤ LEVITATION.

- ➤ METAPHYSICS.
- ➤ PARAPSYCHOLOGY.
- ➤ PERCEPTION EXTRASENSORY.
- ➤ NEW ERA.
- ➤ ASTRAL PROJECTION.
- ➤ REINCARNATION.
- ➤ BUDDHISM.
- ➤ ISLAMISMO.
- ➤ HINDUISM.
- ➤ YOGA.
- ➤ MARTIAL ARTS.
- ➤ THE HAREKRISNA.
- ➤ ROSICRUCIAN.
- ➤ FREEMASONRY.
- ➤ CHAKRAS.
- ➤ CULTS
- ➤ AFRO-CUBAN RELIGION, ANY OF THEIR PRACTI-CES.

ANY OF THESE PRACTICES **OPEN DOORS** TO THE INFLUENCE OF THE SATANIC AND DEMONIC POWERS.

WE CONCLUDE THAT **EVERY SIN** CAN OPEN A DOOR TO SATAN AND HIS SPIRITS MALIGNANT.

IN CIRCUMSTANCES OF LIFE.

The evil spirits do not have the sense of fair play. They never hesitate to completely seize the moments of weakness in the person's life.

One of the first questions asked during the internal healing is:

- ➤ **HOW WAS YOUR RELATION WITH YOUR PARENTS WHEN YOU WERE A CHILD?**

In the majority of cases this question opens the door for a list of complaints for which the parents are to be blamed. How often I have heard answers like:

- ➢ MY FATHER NEGLECT ME (OR MY MOTHER).
- ➢ MY FATHER ABUSED ME.
- ➢ MY FATHER WAS ALCOHOLIC OR DRUG ADDICT.
- ➢ MY PARENTS DID NOT WANT ME TO BE BORN.

Other circumstances that open doors is when a loved one dies:

- ➢ PARENT.
- ➢ CHILD.
- ➢ BOY FRIEND OR GIRLFRIEND.
- ➢ HUSBAND OR WIFE.

Any use or abuse of:

- ➢ DRUGS HEROIC.
- ➢ REPEATED DRUNKENNESS.
- ➢ ANY INCIDENT THAT PRODUCE SEVERE PHYSICAL OR EMOTIONAL TRAUMA.

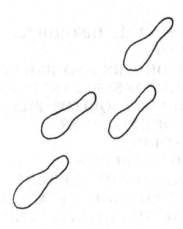

THEME 5
STEPS
IN THE RELEASE

WE HAVE DISCERNMENT AND MUST NOT SEE DEMONS EVERYWHERE.

We must investigate the person, with an account of their lives and their activities and ask **GOD, JESUS** and **HIS HOLY SPIRIT** to reveal through **THE GIFT OF DISCERNMENT OF SPIRIT WHICH IS THE ROOT OF THE PROBLEM.**

IMPORTANCE OF COMPLETION OF THE QUESTIONNAIRE.

It is of utmost importance to obtain much information of the person that we will be praying for release. (Completing the questionnaire).

After **THE PREPARATION** we must ensure that **THE PERSON** really has a spiritual problem and not of other kinds such as:

MENTAL DISEASES:

> ORGANIC MENTAL DISORDERS, INCLUDING THE SYMPTOMATIC.
> MENTAL DISORDERS AND BEHAVIOR DUE TO THE CONSUMPTION OF SUBSTANCES PSICOTROPAS.
> ESQUIZOFRENÍA, ESQUIZOTIPICOS DISORDERS AND DISORDERS OF DELUSIONS.
> MENTAL DISORDERS.
> NEUROTIC DISORDERS, SECONDARY TO STRESSFUL SITUATIONS AND SOMATOFORM.
> ASSOCIATED PHYSIOLOGICAL DYSFUNCTION AND SOMATIC FACTORS BEHAVIOR DISORDERS.
> DISORDERS OF PERSONALITY AND BEHAVIOR OF THE ADULT.
> MENTAL RETARDATION.
> DISORDERS OF PSYCHOLOGICAL DEVELOPMENT
> DISORDERS OF BEHAVIOR AND EMOTIONS OF THE USUAL BEGINNING IN CHILDHOOD AND ADOLESCENCE.

It is advisable to get a psychological evaluation or psychiatric, depending on these results it can be determined if **THE PERSON** needs a **PRAYER OF PHYSICAL HEALING OR OF RELEASE.**

THE FORM
MINISTRY OF HEALING

1. This is only a healing Ministry, in which we pray for physical, inner and spiritual healing (Liberation).

2. There is no charge for the time (for free you receive give for free).

3. The process could take hours or more, the team is willing to spend the time which is required and necessary

4. You must sign this document as consent that the session or sessions is an application volunteer of prayer and a promise not to sue the parties involved who are praying for healing.

5. Requires full participation and sincerity.

6. Be prepared to forgive people from the present or the past that have wronged you.

7. Before giving an appointment, you must promise to stop sinning intentionally and leave bad habits, and that you want to really heal and if necessary pray for release of the demonic oppression.

8. It is suggested that you fast the day before the appointment; or if some friends or relatives have suggested that you attend this Ministry, that they also pray and to pray for those who come to participate in the meeting.

9. Before any meeting you could be asked to read aloud the next plea:

LORD.

I CONFESS WITH MY MOUTH THAT JESUS IS LORD, AND BELIEVE IN MY HEART THAT GOD HAS RAISED FROM THE DEAD.

I MUST ALSO CONFESS THAT JESUS CHRIST IS MY PERSONAL SAVIOR.

I RENOUNCE TO ANY OPPRESSION OF THE DEVIL IN MY LIFE BY REASON OF INIQUITY, TRANSGRESSION AND SINS OF MY PARENTS, ANCESTORS AND MYSELF, AND I HUMBLY ASK GOD THAT I BE RELEASED AND CLEANED AND I PROTECT MYSELF THROUGH THE BLOOD OF HIS SON JESUS CHRIST.

I REGRET ANY ATTITUDE, ACTION OR HABIT SINFUL ON MY PART NOT GLORIFYING JESUS CHRIST, AND ASK FORGIVENESS, HEALING PHYSICAL, INNER HEALING, LIBERATION, CLEANING AND INTEGRITY.

RESIGNED TO THE DEVIL AND ALL INFLUENCES, SHAC-KLES, DOMAINS AND DEMONICS DISEASES IN MY LIFE;

I ASK YOU, LORD, FOR THE LIBERATION AND FREEDOM PROMISED BY JESUS CHRIST SO THAT HE CAN BE THE LORD OF MY LIFE AND THAT HE MAY BE GLORIFIED IN EVERYTHING I SAY AND DO IN BODY, SOUL AND SPIRIT.

I PRAY IN YOUR PRECIOUS NAME, AMEN.

SAY AN OUR FATHER (EXPLAIN THIS SENTENCE).

10. As part of the completion of this form, identify the person or persons this document will be sent.

You need to complete the questionnaire at least 10 days before the assigned appointment.

All cancellation must be announced at least with twenty-four hours in advance.

QUESTIONNAIRE

Name:

Date of Birth:

Place of Birth:

Address:

City:

State: **Zip Code:**

Social No:

Driver License:

Marital: Status:

Profession or Occupation:

Phones: **Res:**

Cell.

Ofc.

E-Mail [   ]

In emergency which person calls:

Person: [   ]

Kinship: [   ]

Phones:
    Res: [   ]

    Cell: [   ]

    Ofc: [   ]

Date: [   ]

Signature: [   ]

Note: [   ]

LEGAL STATEMENT

VOLUNTARY RELEASE, ASSUMPTION OF RISK AND IN-DEMNITY AGREEMENT.

Into account to allow me to participate in the voluntary ministering of prayer, which here referred to as **"Healing Ministry"**, the below signed,

Name:

Social No:

Date of Birth:

Drive License: State:

Which here referred to as the "resigning" accepts the following:

1.- RELEASE, WAIVER, DISPENSES AND MAKES COVE-NANT NOT TO SUE.

Both the person to be liberated as well as their personal representatives, assignees, insurers, heirs, executors, administrators, spouse and relatives close by the present document release, waive and dispense and make an agreement not to bring action against the Ministry:

Address at:

And their directors, officers, employees, agents, volunteers, and heirs, assignees, affiliates, subordinate, subsidiary, which here referred to as the **"Liberators"**, by any liability to the person to be liberated as to their personal representatives, assignees, insurers, heirs, executors, administrators, spouse and relatives nearby for any damage, loss or cost due to injury to the person or property or as a result of the death of the person, whether is caused by negligence of the liberators or while the person is participating in the "Ministry of healing." and any other activity related to the Ministry of healing

2.- ASSUMPTION OF RISK.

The person understands, is aware of, and assumes all risks inherent to its participation in the Ministry of healing. These risks include physical and emotional reactions and responses, but are not limited to them, as a result of this ministering.

3.- COMPENSATION.

The person agrees to compensate the liberators of any liability, loss, damage or costs that the liberators may incur due to the participation of the person in the Ministry of healing, since it is caused by the negligence of the liberators or anything else. The person assumes full responsibility and risk of bodily injury, death or damage to property due to negligence of the liberators or while participating in the Ministry of healing.

The person explicitly accepts this voluntary release, risk-taking and agreement of compensation, here referred to as **"Agreement"**, whose intention is as broad and inclusive as permitting the laws of country _____ and that if any portion of this agreement is invalid, accepts a counterweight to continue in full force and effect.

This agreement contains the agreement between the parties in relation to the Ministry of healing.

THE RENOUNCER AFFIRMS THAT:

I HAVE READ WITH CARE THIS AGREEMENT, WHAT I UNDERSTAND IS A RELEASE OF ALL CLAIMS, INCLUDING IN CASE OF NEGLIGENCE OF THE LIBERATORS.

I UNDERSTAND THAT I ASSUME ALL RISKS INHERENT TO THE MINISTRY OF HEALING SET FORTH IN THIS AGREE-MENT.

I UNDERSTAND THAT I AM TO COMPENSATE THE LIBERA-TORS.

VOLUNTARILY SIGNED AS EVIDENCE OF MY UNDERS-TANDING AND ACCEPTANCE OF THE PROVISIONS OF THIS AGREEMENT:

DATE:

**SIGNATURE
OF THE RESINGNING**

(blank box)

**SIGNATURE
OF WITNESS**

SOCIAL: _(blank box)_

NOTE:
This Legal document should be adapted to their country of origin, would be prudent to consult with a lawyer in your country and adapt it to laws.

QUESTIONNIRE
PART I

1. Ecclesial Experience:
   What church do you belong to?:

   Evangelical
   Christian: ☐

   Protestant
   Christian: ☐

   Catholic: ☐

   Adventist: ☐

   Mormons: ☐

   Jehovah's
   Witnesses: ☐

   Other: ☐

   Any: ☐

   Explain:

   ┌───┐
   │   │
   │   │
   │   │
   └───┘

2. Briefly explain your conversion experience:

   ┌───┐
   │   │
   │   │
   │   │
   └───┘

3. Did it really change your life, whether you came to Christ as a teenager or adult?

   ┌───┐
   │   │
   │   │
   │   │
   └───┘

4. Were you baptized as a child?

    Yes ☐ No ☐ Don't know ☐

5. Who is Jesus Christ for you?

    ┌───┐
    │   │
    │   │
    │   │
    │   │
    └───┘

6. Is repentance part of your life?

    ┌───┐
    │   │
    │   │
    │   │
    │   │
    └───┘

7. What does the blood of Jesus Christ on Calvary means to you?

    ┌───┐
    │   │
    │   │
    │   │
    │   │
    └───┘

8. How is your prayer life?

    ┌───┐
    │   │
    │   │
    │   │
    │   │
    └───┘

9. Do you have the security of salvation?

    ┌───┐
    │   │
    │   │
    │   │
    │   │
    └───┘

10. Are you satisfied with your walk in your religion?

RELATIONSHIP WITH FAMILY.

1. How was the relationship with your parents?

Good ☐ Bad ☐ Indifferent ☐

Explain:

    A. How was the relationship with your parents?
    B. With your mother?
    C. With your brothers or sisters?

2. Information about your parents.

    A. Are your parents Christians?

Father   Yes ☐ No ☐ Don't know ☐
Mother   Yes ☐ No ☐ Don't know ☐

B. Are your parents married?

By the Church?   Yes ☐ No ☐ Don't know ☐

Civil?   Yes ☐ No ☐ Don't know ☐

Do they live together? Yes ☐ No ☐ Don't know ☐

Divorced?   Yes ☐ No ☐ Don't know ☐

If they were divorced, how old were you?

Age ☐

Have your parents re-married?

Father   Yes ☐ No ☐ Don't know ☐

Mother   Yes ☐ No ☐ Don't know ☐

3. About your childhood?

A. Were you a wanted child?

Yes ☐ No ☐ Don't know ☐

B. Were you the expected sex?

Yes ☐ No ☐ Don't know ☐

C. Were you conceived out of wedlock?

Yes ☐ No ☐ Don't know ☐

D. Were you adopted?

Yes ☐ No ☐ Don't know ☐

4. If you were adopted, do you know everything about your biological parents?

Yes ☐ No ☐ Don't know ☐

5. Do you have stepparent?

Stepfather   Yes ☐ No ☐ Don't know ☐

Stepmother   Yes ☐ No ☐ Don't know ☐

How is your relationship with them?

Stepfather:

Stepmother:

6. How was your father?

Passive ☐ Firm ☐ Neither one nor the other ☐

Manipulator?   Yes ☐ No ☐

Were you Friends?   Yes ☐ No ☐

Briefly describe your relationship with your father:

7. How was your mother?

Passive ☐ Firm ☐ Neither one nor the other ☐

Firm?   Yes ☐ No ☐

Were you friends?   Yes ☐ No ☐

Your relationship with your mother describe briefly:

```
┌─────────────────────────────────────────────────────┐
│                                                       │
│                                                       │
│                                                       │
│                                                       │
└─────────────────────────────────────────────────────┘
```

8. Did you have a happy home during childhood?

Yes ☐ No ☐ Don't know ☐

Describe briefly:

```
┌─────────────────────────────────────────────────────┐
│                                                       │
│                                                       │
│                                                       │
└─────────────────────────────────────────────────────┘
```

9. How would you describe the economic situation of your family when you were a child?

Poor ☐
Moderate Income ☐
Mild Financial Struggles ☐
Good ☐
Rich ☐

10. Did you suffer injustice as a child, teenager or in your adult life with your parents?

Yes ☐ No ☐ Fair ☐

What were they? Who committed them?

```



```

11. Do you know if your mother suffered some trauma during her pregnancy with you?

Yes ☐ No ☐ Don't know ☐

Explain:

```



```

12. Do you know if the birth was difficult or complicated??

Yes ☐ No ☐ Don't know ☐

Explain:

```



```

13. Did you receive some trauma during childbirth?

Yes ☐   No ☐   Don't know ☐

Were you breastfed by your mother?

Yes ☐   No ☐   Don't know ☐

14. Do you have brothers and sisters?

Name: _____

Age: _____

Name: _____

Age: _____

Name: _____

Age: _____

Name: _____

Age: _____

What number are you between siblings?

_____

How was your relationship with them as you grew up?

_____

How is it now?

(blank box)

Are there any special problems?

(blank box)

15. Are your parents alive?

Father   Yes ☐   No ☐

Mother   Yes ☐   No ☐

16. Were your parents perfectionists?

                         Yes ☐   No ☐

17. Have you, your parents or grandparents participated in any of these organizations:?

Christian Science	Yes ☐	No ☐
Rosacrutians	Yes ☐	No ☐
Bajai	Yes ☐	No ☐
Jehovah's Witnesses	Yes ☐	No ☐
Yoga, Gurús	Yes ☐	No ☐
Native religions	Yes ☐	No ☐
Unitarianism	Yes ☐	No ☐
United Church	Yes ☐	No ☐
Spiritualist Churches	Yes ☐	No ☐
Moonies	Yes ☐	No ☐

Children of Love	Yes	☐	No	☐
Cristadelphians	Yes	☐	No	☐
Scientology	Yes	☐	No	☐
Theosophy	Yes	☐	No	☐
Religions Common	Yes	☐	No	☐
Mormons	Yes	☐	No	☐
Islam	Yes	☐	No	☐
New Age	Yes	☐	No	☐
Hinduism	Yes	☐	No	☐
Buddhism	Yes	☐	No	☐
Zen, Tibetan, Etc.	Yes	☐	No	☐
Eastern	Yes	☐	No	☐
Daughter of the Nile	Yes	☐	No	☐
Sanctuary of Molay	Yes	☐	No	☐
Other	Yes	☐	No	☐

Explain:

```


```

18. Do you know if a close family member has participated in?:

Franco-Masonry	Yes	☐	No	☐
Secret Societies	Yes	☐	No	☐
The Girl of the Rainbow	Yes	☐	No	☐
Star of the East	Yes	☐	No	☐
Daughter of Job	Yes	☐	No	☐
Elk Worshipers	Yes	☐	No	☐

Do you have in your possessions garments or objects of Masonic interest?

Yes ☐ No ☐ Don't know ☐

Are you ready to renounce it?

Yes ☐ No ☐

19. **Do you know if some curses have been launched on you or your family?**

Yes ☐ No ☐ Don't know ☐

Who did it?

┌─────────────────────────────────────┐
│   │
│   │
│   │
│   │
│   │
│   │
└─────────────────────────────────────┘

Why?

┌─────────────────────────────────────┐
│   │
│   │
│   │
│   │
│   │
│   │
│   │
└─────────────────────────────────────┘

Explain:

20. Do you have knowledge that there was evidence of lust in your Father, grandparents or siblings?

Yes ☐ No ☐ Don't know ☐

Explain:

21. Where was your father born? (City, State and Nation).

22. Where was your mother born? (City, State and Nation).

23. Where were your grandparents born? (City, State and Country).

Maternal grandfather?
Maternal grandmother?

```

```

Paternal grandfather?
Paternal grandmother?

```

```

24. Does any of your parents suffer from depression ?

Father   Yes ☐ No ☐
Mother   Yes ☐ No ☐

25. Does any of your relatives suffer from any nervous or mental Problems?

Parents   Yes ☐ No ☐
Brothers   Yes ☐ No ☐
Sisters   Yes ☐ No ☐
Grandparents   Yes ☐ No ☐

26. Do you know if any member of your family have addictions of some sort?

Yes ☐ No ☐

Explain:

```

```

27. Do you know if your parents or even a distant relative, has been involved in occultism or witchcraft?

Yes ☐ No ☐ Don't know ☐

Who and what was done?

To what extent?

PART II

INFORMATION ABOUT YOU

Answer the following questions:

1. What is your country of birth?

2. Have you lived in other countries?

Yes ☐ No ☐

In which ones?

3. Talk about yourself image:

Low image of myself	Yes ☐	No ☐
I feel insecure	Yes ☐	No ☐
I condemn myself	Yes ☐	No ☐
I hate myself	Yes ☐	No ☐
I feel unworthy	Yes ☐	No ☐
I think I'm a looser	Yes ☐	No ☐
I feel inferior	Yes ☐	No ☐
I question my identity	Yes ☐	No ☐
I punish myself	Yes ☐	No ☐

(If you answered Yes to any of the above, explain

```




```

4. **What is your higher level of education?**

   College ☐ **High School** ☐

   Explain levels, grades or/and if any what kind of studies

```




```

5. **Were you lonely as a teenager?**

   Yes ☐   **No** ☐   **Sometime** ☐   **Never** ☐

6. **Do you have problems with giving or receiving love?**

   Yes ☐   **No** ☐   **Sometime** ☐   **Never** ☐

7. **Was it difficult to communicate with people close to you?**

   I have real difficulty ☐
   Not willing to ☐
   Sometimes I have trouble ☐
   It is easy ☐

8. Are you a perfectionist?

Yes ☐ No ☐

9. Were your parents perfectionists?

Yes ☐ No ☐

10. Do you come from a proud family?

Yes ☐ No ☐

11. Do you have problems of pride?

Yes ☐ No ☐

12. Have you had or still have any problem with?:

Impatience	Yes ☐	No ☐
Character	Yes ☐	No ☐
Depression	Yes ☐	No ☐
Rebellion	Yes ☐	No ☐
Violence	Yes ☐	No ☐
Anger	Yes ☐	No ☐
Irritability	Yes ☐	No ☐
Obstinacy	Yes ☐	No ☐
Racial prejudice	Yes ☐	No ☐
Desire to kill	Yes ☐	No ☐

13. Are you a person who criticizes?
Yes ☐ No ☐ Perhaps ☐

14. Do you feel emotionally immature?
Yes ☐ No ☐ Not Necessarily ☐

15. Have you had any problems with lies and theft?

Yes ☐ No ☐ Not Necessarily ☐

Are still today?

Yes ☐ No ☐ Not Necessarily ☐

Explain:

```



```

16. Any inclination to?:

Oaths	Yes	☐	No	☐
Blasphemy	Yes	☐	No	☐
Smut	Yes	☐	No	☐
Swear	Yes	☐	No	☐
Use profanity	Yes	☐	No	☐

17. Do you have toward someone the following feelings?

Lack of forgiveness? Who and why?

```



```

Resentment? Who and why?

```


```

Bitterness? Who and why?

```


```

Hate? Who and why?

```


```

18. Have you ever had psychiatric counseling?

Hospitalization	Yes ☐	No ☐
Electroshock	Yes ☐	No ☐
Psychoanalysis	Yes ☐	No ☐
Other	Yes ☐	No ☐

19. Have you ever been hypnotized?

Yes ☐   No ☐

If the answer Yes, when and why?

```


```

20. Do you suffer from?:

Apathy of Emotions	Yes ☐	No ☐
Confusion	Yes ☐	No ☐
Hardness	Yes ☐	No ☐
Questions	Yes ☐	No ☐
Immature	Yes ☐	No ☐
Skepticism	Yes ☐	No ☐
Financial Disaster	Yes ☐	No ☐
Allergies	Yes ☐	No ☐
Frequent Difficulty	Yes ☐	No ☐
Difficulty Understanding	Yes ☐	No ☐
Discomforts	Yes ☐	No ☐
Disease	Yes ☐	No ☐
Suffer From Nightmares	Yes ☐	No ☐
Tried to Commit Suicide	Yes ☐	No ☐
Dying Wishes spoke out loud	Yes ☐	No ☐

Explain:

21. Have you ever had strong and prolonged fear of something in the following list:

Failure	Yes ☐	No ☐
Inability to Compete	Yes ☐	No ☐
Ineptitude	Yes ☐	No ☐
Authority	Yes ☐	No ☐
Darkness	Yes ☐	No ☐
Figures or images of dead	Yes ☐	No ☐
Violation	Yes ☐	No ☐
Violence	Yes ☐	No ☐

To Be Alone	Yes	☐	No	☐
Future	Yes	☐	No	☐
Satan and Evil Spirits	Yes	☐	No	☐
Women	Yes	☐	No	☐
Crowds	Yes	☐	No	☐
Men	Yes	☐	No	☐
Heights	Yes	☐	No	☐
Madness	Yes	☐	No	☐
Public Speaking	Yes	☐	No	☐
Accidents	Yes	☐	No	☐
Getting Old	Yes	☐	No	☐
Opinion of Others	Yes	☐	No	☐
Closed Places	Yes	☐	No	☐
Terminal Illness	Yes	☐	No	☐
Divorce or Separation	Yes	☐	No	☐
Marriage	Yes	☐	No	☐
Insects	Yes	☐	No	☐
Spiders	Yes	☐	No	☐
Dogs	Yes	☐	No	☐
Snakes	Yes	☐	No	☐
Other Animals	Yes	☐	No	☐
Water	Yes	☐	No	☐
Suffering	Yes	☐	No	☐
Strong Noise	Yes	☐	No	☐
Open Space	Yes	☐	No	☐
Death of Injury of a loved one	Yes	☐	No	☐
Grocery Stores	Yes	☐	No	☐
Air Travel	Yes	☐	No	☐

Does any of the above fears still trapped in you since you became a Christian.

Yes ☐ No ☐

If so, which ones?

☐

22. Are you an anxious person?

	Yes	No
	☐	☐
Worried?	Yes ☐	No ☐
Depressed?	Yes ☐	No ☐

23. Feels mentally confused.

	Yes	No
	☐	☐
Do you have blackouts?	Yes ☐	No ☐

24. Do you daydream?

	Yes	No
	☐	☐
You have mental fantasies?	Yes ☐	No ☐

25. Do you suffer continually of nightmares?

	Yes	No
	☐	☐
Insomnio?	Yes ☐	No ☐

26. Have you ever made a pact with the devil?

Yes ☐   No ☐

If yes, was it a covenant of blood ?

What was it?

When?

| |
| |

Why?

| |
| |

27. **Are you willing to renounce it?**

                    Yes ☐ No ☐

28. **Do you know if some curse has been launched on you and your family?**

                    Yes ☐ No ☐

Who He did it?:

| |
| |

Why?

| |
| |

Explain:

[ ]

29. Have you ever participated in the following?:

Quíja Board	Yes [ ]	No [ ]
Tarot Cards	Yes [ ]	No [ ]
Mediums	Yes [ ]	No [ ]
Seances	Yes [ ]	No [ ]
Diviners	Yes [ ]	No [ ]
Palmistry	Yes [ ]	No [ ]
Occultism and Witchcraft	Yes [ ]	No [ ]
Consult a Babalawo	Yes [ ]	No [ ]
Hypnotism	Yes [ ]	No [ ]
Astrology	Yes [ ]	No [ ]
Color Therapy	Yes [ ]	No [ ]
Levitation	Yes [ ]	No [ ]
Astral Travel	Yes [ ]	No [ ]
Horoscopes	Yes [ ]	No [ ]
Feet	Yes [ ]	No [ ]
Clairvoyance	Yes [ ]	No [ ]
Black Magic	Yes [ ]	No [ ]
Worship Demons	Yes [ ]	No [ ]
Crystals	Yes [ ]	No [ ]
Automatic Writing	Yes [ ]	No [ ]
New Age Movement	Yes [ ]	No [ ]
Seeing a Healer	Yes [ ]	No [ ]
Request a Spirit Guide	Yes [ ]	No [ ]

30. Have you ever been in any other activity of witchcraft, demonic or satanic?

Yes ☐ No ☐

If yes, explain.

```



```

31. Have you ever read books on occultism or witchcraft?

Yes ☐ No ☐

Why?

```



```

32. Have you ever participated in games such as dungeons and Dragons demonic?

Yes ☐ No ☐

Have you watch demonic/evil movies ?

Yes ☐ No ☐

Do you still now?

Yes ☐ No ☐

33. Have you been involved in transcendental meditation?

Yes ☐ No ☐

Do you have a mantra?   Yes ☐ No ☐

If yes, what is it?

☐

34. Have you participated in Eastern religions?

Yes ☐ No ☐

Did you follow the gurus?   Yes ☐ No ☐

35. Have you visited pagan temples?

Yes ☐ No ☐

When?

☐

Did offerings?

Yes ☐ No ☐

What kind?

☐

Did you take part in a ceremony?
Explain:

36. **Have you ever done any kind of yoga?**

Yes ☐ No ☐

Meditation? Yes ☐ No ☐

Exercises? Yes ☐ No ☐

37. **Have you learned or ever use any kind of communication or mind control?**

Yes ☐ No ☐

Explain:

38. **Have you ever used talismans, fetishes, amulets or signs of the Zodiac?**

Yes ☐ No ☐

Do you have any among your possessions?

Yes ☐ No ☐

208

39. Do you have symbols of idols or worship of spirits at home? Such as:

Buddhas	Yes	☐	No	☐
Totems	Yes	☐	No	☐
Painted Face Masks	Yes	☐	No	☐
Painted	Yes	☐	No	☐
Fetishes	Yes	☐	No	☐
Carved Ídolos	Yes	☐	No	☐
Pagan Symbols	Yes	☐	No	☐
Plumes of Feathers	Yes	☐	No	☐
Tikis Native Folklore	Yes	☐	No	☐
Kachina Dolls (What Class)	Yes	☐	No	☐
Others?	Yes	☐	No	☐

Where did they come from and how did you get them?

```
┌─────────────────────────────────────────────┐
│                                             │
│                                             │
│                                             │
│                                             │
│                                             │
│                                             │
└─────────────────────────────────────────────┘
```

40. Do you have any adornment of sorcery as the Witch of good luck in your home or in your kitchen?

Yes ☐ No ☐

41. Are you "In wave" with some of the following music?:

Rock and Roll	Yes	☐	No	☐
Punk Rock	Yes	☐	No	☐
Rap	Yes	☐	No	☐
Heavy metal	Yes	☐	No	☐
Reggeton	Yes	☐	No	☐
Other (Related)	Yes	☐	No	☐

How much time you spend listening to it?

Hours:
Days a week:

42. Have you practiced martial arts?

Yes ☐   No ☐

If yes, of what kind?

Do you the practice it now?

43. Have you ever had any premonitions ?

	Yes ☐	No ☐
Deja Vu?	Yes ☐	No ☐
Psychic Vision?	Yes ☐	No ☐

44. Have you walked on fire ?

	Yes ☐	No ☐
Have you practiced voodoo?	Yes ☐	No ☐

45. Do you have tattoos?

Yes ☐   No ☐

If so, what kind?

PART III
MORALITY INFORMATION

1. **What is your marital status?**

Married	☐
Divorced	☐
Separate	☐
Living together	☐
Widower	☐
Engaged	☐
Single	☐

2. **How would you describe your sexual relationship with your spouse?**

3. **Have you ever committed fornication (being single)?**

    Yes ☐ No ☐

    How many partners?
    First names, and When?

With Prostitutes?

Yes ☐ No ☐

How many?, When?

```



```

Have you committed adultery while (at least one of the partners being married)?

Yes ☐ No ☐

First Name, and When?

```



```

Are you currently involved in unlawful sexual relationship?

Yes ☐ No ☐

Names:

```



```

Are you willing to stop?

Yes ☐ No ☐

4. Do you have thoughts of lust?

Yes ☐ No ☐

What kind and how often?

```



```

5. Have ever been involved in oral sex?

Yes ☐ No ☐

With Whom?

```



```

Have you ever participated in anal sex?

Yes ☐ No ☐

With Whom?

```



```

6. Do you masturbate often?

Yes ☐ No ☐

How often? Do you know why?

┌──┐
│   │
│   │
│   │
│   │
└──┘

Do you feel that it has become a compulsive problem?

┌──┐
│   │
│   │
│   │
│   │
└──┘

7. Have you ever been assaulted sexually by someone from your family or another person as a child or teenager?

Yes ☐ No ☐

By whom?, More than once?
Explain:

┌──┐
│   │
│   │
│   │
│   │
└──┘

Were you actually raped?
By whom?, More than once?
Explain:

┌──┐
│   │
│   │
│   │
│   │
└──┘

8. Have you been victim of incest by a member of your family?

Yes ☐ No ☐

By whom?, Often?, How long?

```


```

9. Men: Have you assaulted or raped someone?

Yes ☐ No ☐

Names:

```


```

Did you commit incest?   Yes ☐ No ☐
Explain:

```


```

10. WOMEN:

Were you raped?   Yes ☐ No ☐

Names: "Explain"

```
┌─────────────────────────────────────────────────────────┐
│                                                           │
│                                                           │
│                                                           │
│                                                           │
│                                                           │
└─────────────────────────────────────────────────────────┘
```

Are you frigid?   Yes ☐ No ☐

Explain:

```
┌─────────────────────────────────────────────────────────┐
│                                                           │
│                                                           │
│                                                           │
│                                                           │
│                                                           │
│                                                           │
└─────────────────────────────────────────────────────────┘
```

11. Have you ever had gay or lesbians thoughts?

                                        Yes ☐ No ☐

Do you have them now?   Yes ☐ No ☐
Experience?   Yes ☐ No ☐

With whom and when?

```
┌─────────────────────────────────────────────────────────┐
│                                                           │
│                                                           │
│                                                           │
│                                                           │
│                                                           │
└─────────────────────────────────────────────────────────┘
```

12. Have you ever had sexual fantasies with animals?

                                        Yes ☐ No ☐

Have you committed sexual act of bestiality? With an animal.

Yes ☐ No ☐

List all animals involved:

```
```

13. Has pornography ever attracted you?

Yes ☐ No ☐

How did you get involved?
Name of people involved:

```
```

To what degree?

```
```

Is it still a problem?	Yes ☐	No ☐
Have you watched porn movies?	Yes ☐	No ☐
Videos?	Yes ☐	No ☐
Have you seen live sex shows?	Yes ☐	No ☐

14. Do you buy or rent pornographic material or have those channels on television in your home?

Yes ☐ No ☐

Watch pornography on the internet?

Yes ☐ No ☐

15. Have you ever wish of having sex with a child (pedophilia)?

Yes ☐ No ☐

Have you ever done it?

Yes ☐ No ☐

16. Have you ever had internal stimulation and climax beyond your control, especially at night?

This means:
You may have dreams in which someone approached you and ask you to have sex with, and you "feel" a presence beside you on the bed, then wake-up with a sexual climax (this is very different from a normal nocturnal emission).

Yes ☐ No ☐

17. Have you ever gone to a massage parlor where you have been sexually stimulated?

Yes ☐ No ☐

PART I V
ACCIDENT AND HEALTH QUESTIONNAIRE

1. Do you suffer from diseases or chronic allergies?

Yes ☐ No ☐

What?

```
┌─────────────────────────────────────────────────┐
│                                                   │
│                                                   │
│                                                   │
│                                                   │
└─────────────────────────────────────────────────┘
```

Are they hereditary?

```
┌─────────────────────────────────────────────────┐
│                                                   │
│                                                   │
│                                                   │
└─────────────────────────────────────────────────┘
```

2. Did you ever had accidents or severe trauma that still vivid in your mind (other than those mentioned above)?

Explain:

```
┌─────────────────────────────────────────────────┐
│                                                   │
│                                                   │
│                                                   │
│                                                   │
│                                                   │
│                                                   │
└─────────────────────────────────────────────────┘
```

3. **Do you have other problems not found in this questionnaire?**
    (Tell them as much as possible.) Try to see when they started and if
    they are connected to some trauma, if you were victimized or if you
    caused the problem).

```
┌─────────────────────────────────────────────────────────┐
│                                                           │
│                                                           │
│                                                           │
│                                                           │
│                                                           │
│                                                           │
│                                                           │
│                                                           │
└─────────────────────────────────────────────────────────┘
```

4. **Do you have addiction of some kind?**

    Yes ☐ No ☐

5. **Are you or have been addicted to any of these things?**

Alcohol	Yes ☐	No ☐
Cigarette	Yes ☐	No ☐
Food	Yes ☐	No ☐
Game	Yes ☐	No ☐
Compulsive Exercise	Yes ☐	No ☐
Waste of Money	Yes ☐	No ☐
Watch TV	Yes ☐	No ☐
Coffee	Yes ☐	No ☐
Drugs	Yes ☐	No ☐
Internet	Yes ☐	No ☐

Drugs (Prescribed or Hallucinogenic).
What?

```
┌─────────────────────────────────────────────────┐
│                                                   │
│                                                   │
│                                                   │
│                                                   │
│                                                   │
└─────────────────────────────────────────────────┘
```

Are they a current problem any of the above?

```
┌─────────────────────────────────────────────────┐
│                                                   │
│                                                   │
│                                                   │
│                                                   │
│                                                   │
└─────────────────────────────────────────────────┘
```

6. **MEN:**
Have you ever conceived a baby that was aborted?

Yes ☐   No ☐

How many? ☐

When? Give dates and names of the mothers.

```
┌─────────────────────────────────────────────────┐
│                                                   │
│                                                   │
│                                                   │
│                                                   │
│                                                   │
│                                                   │
└─────────────────────────────────────────────────┘
```

7. **WOMEN:**
   Have you had any abortions?

   Yes ☐ **No** ☐

   How many? ☐

   Dates and names of fathers.

   ```



   ```

8. **Any other important information?**

   ```




   ```

QUESTIONNAIRE
SUGGESTIONS

PART I

1. CHURCH EXPERIENCE:
   What church do you belong to?:

2. BRIEFLY EXPLAIN THE EXPERIENCE OF YOUR CONVERSION;

3. HAS IT REALLY CHANGED YOUR LIFE, WETHER YOU CAME TO CHRIST AS A TEENAGER OR ADULT?

4. WERE YOU BAPTIZED AS A CHILD?

5. WHO IS JESUS TO YOU?

6. IS IT REPENTANCE PART OF YOUR LIFE?

7. WHAT DOES THE BLOOD OF JESUS CHRIST ON CALVARY MEANS TO YOU?

8. HOW IS YOUR PRAYER LIFE?

9. DO YOU HAVE THE SECURITY OF SALVATION?

10. ARE YOU SATISFIED WITH YOUR WALK IN YOUR RELIGION?

RELATIONSHIP WITH YOUR FAMILY

1. HOW WAS YOUR RELATIONSHIP WITH YOUR PARENTS?

2. INFORMATION ABOUT YOUR PARENTS

3. HOW DID YOU BEHAVE AS A CHILD?

A Were you a planned child?

> Unplanned children may suffer rejection from the womb.
> If the news of the pregnancy was received with regret.
> Such expressions as "I do not want to have this baby now, or "I can't be pregnant now" or "It comes at a bad time."

B Were you of the "expected" sex?

> Many parents are disappointed by the sex of the child at birth.
> In these cases, the forgiveness must extend to the parents by their insensitivity.
> You must cast out:

- A spirit of rejection.

C Did you conceived out of wedlock?

> Those who were conceived in lust often struggle with lust throughout their life.

> They can suffer from:

- Spirit of lust.
- Spirit of violence.
- Spirit of anger.
- And a variety of fears.

D Were you adopted?

> Adopted children can become rebels and difficult to handle, it should be cast out:

- Spirit of abandonment that resides in adopted children.

> They must pray to forgive their biological parents for the rejection.

> Pray to God so they can be grateful to their adoptive parents.

> Pray against the hereditary rejection since we do not know the past of those parents, generally need:

- Remove the fear of rejection.
- The perceived rejection.
- And their own origins of rejection.

4. IF YOU WERE ADOPTED, DO YOU KNOW ALL ABOUT YOUR NATURAL PARENTS?

> There are often good reasons to explain why a child is given in adoption:

- There may be strong rejection.
- And ties that must be deal with.

5. DO YOU HAVE A STEPFATHER OR STEPMOTHER?

> Did you parents get remarried?
> If yes, what is your relationship with your stepfather or stepmother?
> Any of your stepparents or stepsiblings are Christian?
> Do you have half-brother or stepsister?

➢ How was the relationship with them as you grew up?
➢ How is your relationship with them now?

Perhaps we should forgive someone for his hurtful behavior and rejection.

6. HOW WAS YOUR FATHER?

Was it passive or strong and manipulative father?

- Pray against a spirit of manipulation and control.

7. HOW WAS YOUR MOTHER?

Was she a passive mother or strong and manipulative?

- Pray against a spirit of manipulation and control.

8. DID YOU HAVE A HAPPY HOME DURING YOUR CHILD-HOOD?

9. HOW WILL YOU DESCRIBED THE ECONOMIC SITUATION OF YOUR FAMILY WHEN YOU WERE A CHILD?

➢ Poor?, With few economic problems?, Regular income?, Thriving?, Rich?

- Pray for spirits of misery.
- Spirit of shame.
- Spirit of greed and materialism.

10. DID YOU SUFFER UNFAIRNESS BY YOUR PARENTS AS A CHILD OR AS AN ADULT?

Children may have FEARS because of injustices, such as insults, theft or some kind of hoax, seemingly insignificant.

HOWEVER, THEY COULD HAVE BEEN CONTAMINATED WITH SPIRITS SUCH AS:

- Spirits of anger.
- Spirits of rejection.
- Spirits of shame.
- Spirits of pain.
- Spirits of bitterness.
- Spirits of resentment.
- Spirits of lack of forgiveness, etc.

11. DO YOU KNOW IF YOUR MOTHER SUFFERED SOME TRAUMA WHEN SHE WAS PREGNANT WITH YOU?

➢ During pregnancy some of the following spirits can enter a woman:

- Spirits of trauma.
- Spirits of violence.
- To spirits of death.

➢ Especially if the mother was an abused wife.

➢ The child feels guilty somehow by the problems.

- The result is rejection.

12. DO YOU KNOW IF THE BIRTH WAS DIFFICULT OR COMPLICATED?

➢ Spirits often take advantage of the situation, when certain instruments are used to help with the birth or when the umbilical cord entangled the neck, etc.

CAST OUT A:

- Spirits of trauma.
- Spirits of violence.
- Panic and other spirits.

13. DID THEY BOND WITH YOU WHEN YOU WERE BORN?

➢ Were you breastfed?

CAST OUT A:

- Spirits of trauma.
- Spirits of violence.
- Panic and other spirits

14. DO YOU HAVE BROTHERS AND SISTERS?

➢ Which number of child are you?

➢ How was your relationship with them while growing up?
   Is there a special problem?

We try to find out if there were family factors that could be the origin of a rejection.

- Such as a child with favoritism over another.

CAST OUT A:

- Spirits of trauma.
- Spirits of violence.
- Spirits of rejection.

15. ARE YOUR PARENTS ALIVE?

> Are your parents alive?

- If one of your parents or both had died or a sibling, It may be the cause of a rejection or a lack of forgiveness to God.
- The person must tell the Lord that is willing to forgive, even though the relative has died.

16. WERE YOUR PARENTS OR YOU PERFECTIONISTS?

- Hereditary spirits of perfectionism.
- Spirits of rejection.
- Spirits of stress.

17. HAVE YOU OR YOUR PARENTS OR GRANDPARENTS PARTICIPATED IN ANY OF THESE ORGANIZATIONS?

- Christian Science.
- Rosicrucian's.
- Jehovah's Witnesses.
- Mormons.
- Unification Church (Moonies).
- Unitarianism.
- Churches Spiritualists.
- Children of Love.
- Scientology.
- Christadelphians
- Bajai.
- Common religions.
- Theosophy.
- Native Religions (United States or other countries).
- Gurus.

Eastern religions such as:

- Hinduism.
- Buddhism.
- Zen.
- Tibetan.
- Islamism's, Etc.
- Others?

These sects and creeds can be transmitted:

- Spirits of false religion. Call the spirit by the name of the sect.

18. DO YOU KNOW IF ANY CLOSE MEMBER OF YOUR FAMILY HAS BEEN INVOLVED IN?:

- Masonry.
- Communitarianism.
- Rainbow Girls.
- Mormonism.
- Star of the East.
- Shrines Daughters of the Nile.
- Job's Daughters.
- Elk or In Milay.

Do you suffer from apathy, emotional hardness, confusion, economic disaster, skepticism, doubt, disbelief, difficulty to understand diseases, frequent ailments, allergies and teasing?

ALL OF THE ABOVE CAN BE SYMPTOMS OF MASONIC CURSE.

- To take this spirit, call it "The spirit of Freemasonry and doctrine Lucifer".

OTHER SPIRITS MAY BE:

- Spirits of sorcery.
- Spirits of Antichrist.
- Spirits of confusion.
- Spirits of mockery.
- Spirits of false religion.

Pray and break the generational chain by their descendants.

Is there among your possessions objects or clothing of the masons? All objects of interest and clothing must be destroyed. (Put it in the fire). If it is a piece of jewelry, such as a gold ring, you must melt it or throw it into the sea, lake or river. Renounce any Ligature and throw it away in the name of Jesus.

19. DO YOU KNOW IF IT HAS BEEN LAUNCHED SOME CURSE ON YOU OR YOUR FAMILY?

Here the person should pray asking for forgiveness for whom launched the curse and asking for God's mercy.

Break the curse and pray more or less like this:

In the name of Jesus I break the power of the curse. And through the blood of Jesus Christ I cancel all curse on (name), in the glorious name of Jesus.

20. DO YOU HAVE KNOWLEDGE THAT THERE WAS EVIDENCE OF LUST IN YOUR PARENTS, GRANDPARENTS OR SIBLINGS?

We are trying to discover if there are generational spirits of lust loitering. These are very common.

IT IS USEFUL TO CUT OFF GENERATIONAL SPIRIT OF LUST:

- And now, spirit of lust, in the name of Jesus I bind, destroyed your power and ordered you to release this brother (his name) and let go "Right now" in the name of Jesus... out!

21. WHERE WAS YOUR FATHER BORN? (CITY, STATE AND NATION).

22. WHERE WAS YOUR MOTHER BORN? (CITY, STATE AND NATION).

23. WHERE WERE YOUR GRANDPARENTS BORN? (CITY, STATE AND NATION).

21, 22 and 23
Attempts to gather information of parents and ancestors and the cultural heritage of the person, which sometimes is very useful.

I personally know and understand many cultures, and this gives plenty of light and it has proved to be practical on several occasions, especially in the Hispanic culture.

Certain cultures have a tendency towards specific ties.

24. DOES ANY OF YOUR PARENTS SUFFER FROM DEPRESSION?
   - Generational spirits of depression.
   - Spirits of nervous disorder.

25. DOES ANY OF YOUR PARENTS, GRANDPARENTS OR SIBLINGS HAS SUFFERED FROM NERVOUS OR MENTAL PROBLEMS?

Some mental problems could be related to evil spirits.

Other perhaps not, but may be caused by certain physical problems such as chemical imbalance, deformities, injuries, among others.

IF YOU THINK THAT IT IS RELATED TO SOME SPIRITS, SEEK:

- Spirits of schizophrenia.
- Spirits of manic depression.
- Spirits of mental illness.
- Spirits of confusion, etc.

Always in these cases is recommended to pray for physical and spiritual healing (see Matthew 10, 8).

MATTHEW 10, 8
HEAL THE SICK, RAISE THE DEAD CLEANSE THOSE WHO HAVE LEPROSY, DRIVE OUT DEMONS. FREELY YOU HAVE RECEIVE, FREELY GIVE..

26. AS FAR AS YOU KNOW, DOES ANY MEMBER OF YOUR FAMILY HAVE ADDICTIONS OF ANY KIND?

The spirit of addiction can manifest in different ways.

Often occurs a generational spirit of addiction, which should be treated.

It is important to tell the spirit of addiction that its work in this family line is done, and will forbid this generational spirit to pass on to the children of the person for whom I am praying (mention the name of the person).

Then pray on every spirit that causes addiction and problems faced by the person and ordered to leave.

27. DO YOU KNOW IF YOUR PARENTS OR A RELATIVE, HAS BEEN INVOLVED IN OCCULTISM OR SORCERY?

> If witchcraft has been in the family ancestors, the person must forgive who left that door open in the family line.

  • Then we cast out a generational witchcraft spirit.

PART II
INFORMATION ABOUT YOU

1. **WHAT IS YOUR COUNTRY OF BIRTH?**

   Attempts to gather information of your country and of your cultural heritage, which sometimes is very useful.

   I personally know and understand many cultures, and this gives plenty of light, and it has become practical on several occasions, especially in the Hispanic culture.

2. **HAVE YOU LIVE IN OTHER COUNTRIES?**

   It is important to know the cultures experienced by you.

3. **TALK ABOUT YOUR OWN IMAGE:**

   Described yourself personally; give a few expressions of one or two words that are possible.

   This is a useful reflection of the person's image of itself.

   Here may appear specific problems that went unnoticed.

   FOR EXAMPLE:

   - If you type the word "Sloth", pray against a spirit of laziness.

   I use this part to make a final prayer for the opposite of negative perceptions that the person has of itself.

Also ask God to help you in these perceived problems, especially if it has to do with self-discipline or misconduct.

4. HAVE YOU HAD A COLLEGE EDUCATION?

The person can educate itself toward unbelief.

THE PROBLEMS MAY BE:

- Spirits of Skepticism.
- Spirits of Disbelief.
- Discussion spirits.
- Spirits of Pride and Arrogance.

5. WERE YOU A LONELY TEENAGER?

- Spirits of Solitude.
- Spirits of Pain.
- Spirits of Abandonment.

6. DO YOU HAVE PROBLEMS WITH GIVING OR RECEIVING LOVE?

- Spirits of emotional coldness.

BREAK THE SHACKLES ON THE EMOTIONS.

7. IS IT HARD FOR YOU TO COMMUNICATE WITH PEOPLE CLOSE TO YOU?

✓

8. ARE YOU A PERFECTIONIST?

SEE QUESTION 9

9. **WERE YOUR PARENTS PERFECTIONISTS?**
   QUESTIONS 8 and 9:

   - Ancestral spirits of perfectionism.
   - Spirits of rejection.
   - Spirits of stress.

10. **DO YOU COME FROM A PROUD FAMILY?**

    - A generational spirit of pride.

11. **DO YOU HAVE PROBLEMS OF PRIDE?**

    - Spirits of pride.
    - Spirits of arrogance.
    - Spirits of self-sufficient.

12. **DO YOU HAVE TROUBLE WITH?:**

    This is a group of symptoms of rejection, with other aggregates.

    It helps to see if the self-rejection and the aggressive rejection are problems.

    - Pray for each one,
    - And if needed add then the self-rejection and aggression.

13. **ARE YOU A PERSON WHO CRITICIZES?**

    - Find a generational spirit of criticism.

14. **DO YOU FEEL EMOTIONALLY IMMATURE?**

    - If so, pray against a spirit of emotional immaturity.

15. HAVE YOU HAD PROBLEMS WITH LIES AND THEFT?

- Lying Spirits.
- Spirits of Deception.
- Spirits of Kleptomania.
- Spirits of Theft.
- Spirits of Unforgiveness, etc.

16. DO YOU HAVE A TENDENCY TO?:

THESE ARE REJECTION:

- Rebellion.
- And Aggression.

17. DO YOU FEEL TOWARD SOMEONE THE FOLLOWING FEELINGS?

Here it is necessary that you forgive people.

- They must break soul ties and throw out those spirits.

WE MUST PRAY TO END AND FOR THE HEALING OF WOUNDED MEMORIES.

18. HAVE YOU EVER RECEIVED PSYCHIATRIC COUNSELING ANY TIME?

There are times that patients are abused and mistreated in hospitals, nursing homes and this open up the possibilities of:

- Spirits of Trauma.
- Spirits of Rage.
- Spirits of Victimization.
- Deception and Related Spirits.

19. HAVE YOU EVER BEEN HYPNOTIZED?

Hypnosis can be an open door of which evil spirits, take advantage of when the person is not in control of their mind.

Often it worsens the mental illness after the hypnosis.

IF THIS IS THE CASE, PRAY THIS WAY:

- I am now addressing to any spirit that takes advantage of the hypnotic state of (name) and that had entered that person I tie the spirit altogether, break it's power and order to release of (name) in the name of Jesus, etc.

  There could also be spirits of mental control and confusion.

20. DO YOU SUFFER FROM?

- Pray for the name of the spirit which suffers.

21. DO YOU HAVE STRONG FEAR TO ANY THING IN THE FOLLOWING LIST?

Since you became a Christian, are you still prisoner of any of the above mentioned fears?

Pray above all fear that the person expresses feeling after becoming Christian, calling him by his name, in this way:

- Spirit of fear (spiders) or "whatever", in the name of Jesus I bind and break your power, I command that you let go of (name of person) and (a) free now, in the name of Jesus.

AFTER PRAYING ABOUT EVERY FEAR, I AM ADDRE-
SING TO THE:

- Generational spirit of fear which has manifested itself in the listed fears.

THE SENTENCE IS THE SAME, EXCEPT THAT I ORDERED: "YOU, GENERATIONAL SPIRIT OF FEAR..."

22. ARE YOU AN ANXIOUS PERSON?
"Worries a lot or are depressed"

- Spirits of Anxiety.
- Spirits of Concern.
- Spirits of Depression.

23. DO YOU FEEL MENTALLY CONFUSED?

Do you have mental blocks?

- Spirits of Confusion.

24. DO YOU HAVE FANTASIES WHILE AWAKE?

Do you dream while awake? Do you have mental fantasies?

- Spirits of Mental Fantasies.
- Spirits of Mental Escapism.

25. DO YOU HAVE CONTINUOUS NIGHTMARES? FROM INSOMNIA?

- Spirits of Death.
- Spirits of Violence.
- Spirits of Fear or Lust (depending on the subject of dreams).

26. HAVE YOU EVER MADE A PACT WITH THE DEVIL?

27. ARE YOU WILLING TO RENOUNCE TO IT?

ANSWER 26 AND 27

It was a Covenant of blood? Are you willing to renounce?

"A pact with the devil" is simply a deal that an individual makes with the devil, exchanging his soul for a favor, often money, power or love.

It is sometimes accompanied by the extraction of drops of blood from the body.

When expressed curses or made votes in magical meetings of witchcraft, or worship of adoration Satanic, these accompany the libation of portions of blood of a sacrifice, it can range from human to animal, may be another matter as you urinate or another substance.

These pacts when they are accompanied by blood are very strong.

But the blood of Jesus Christ is much more powerful and first thing you should do is to renounce the Covenant, meaning to "Renounce" the words spoken.

THEN DECLARE:

- Now, through the blood of Jesus, which is more powerful than the blood used in this Covenant, I declare null and invalid this Pact; It has no more power on (name of person).

I would like to express that the curse on (name of person) is broken and no longer has effect in their lives, in the name of Jesus.

241

Pray in the name of Jesus for total cleaning of your body and complete purity from the contamination caused by the potion drank or spells that were made.

28. DO YOU KNOW IF IT HAS BEEN RELEASED SOME CURSE ON YOU AND YOUR FAMILY?

"See Question 19" Part 1.

Here the person pray asking for forgiveness for who launched the curse and asking for God's mercy on whom did it.

Break the curse and pray more or less like this:

In the name of Jesus I break the power of the curse. And through the blood of Jesus Christ I cancel all curse on (name), in the glorious name of Jesus.

29. HAVE YOU EVER PARTICIPATED IN THE FOLLOWING?

These activities may be open to:

- Spirits of Witchcraft.
- Spirits of Fear.
- Spirits of Death.

Quijas boards are very common entrances for entry:

- Spirits of Fear
- Spirits of Witchcraft

Over 7 million of Quijas boards have been sold in the United States in 1997. These boards are instruments of communication with demons! United States and Europe have sold more than 25 million.

If the person has participated in some of these activities:

- You must pray and ask forgiveness for their participation in (name of the activity) and miss out to spirit of witchcraft, and often death, fear, and some others that may come to mind.

30. HAVE YOU EVER BEEN IN ANY ACTIVITY OF WITCH-CRAFT, DEMONIC OR SATANIC?

If there have been witchcraft it should stop this practice immediately.

- Then we cast out the spirit of witchcraft.

31. HAVE YOU READ ANY BOOKS ON OCCULTISM OR WITCHCRAFT?

If you had read them to learn how to throw curses on someone to worship Satan, or something similar.

The person must repent. The books or items should be destroyed (burned), such as a Bible Satanic as it has been used in idolatrous worship.

Before reading any books on occultism, with the sole purpose of obtaining the knowledge of who they are (demons) before reading it, please pray for protection on your mind and body.

All material in this context should be cremated (burnt).

32. HAVE YOU PARTICIPATED IN DEMONIC AS DUNGEONS AND DRAGONS GAMES?

Have you watched demonic movies? Do you now?
Destroy all materials.

OFTEN SUCH THINGS ACCOMPANY:

- Spirits of Fear.
- Spirits of Death.
- Spirits of Suicide.

33. HAVE YOU PARTICIPATED IN TRANSCENDENTAL MEDITATION?

Do you have a mantra? If yes, what?

Praying for a college student that had taken a course in transcendental meditation and been given a mantra, he was asked what it was and said that there were only two syllables that you should repeat over and over again when meditate.

The Lord guide me to ask him to write it down on a piece of paper, I then took it to a friend from India and asked the meaning of the word; She look terrified and said it was the name of a disgusting sexual goddess of Hinduism. While the young man meditated, he was calling this demon lecherous.

It is not surprising that he was struggling with lust! At his invitation the demon had put a haunting foothold on his life.

I asked him to pray asking for forgiveness to God for practicing transcendental meditation.

Once he rejected the mantra, we cast out the spirit of lust.

We all have concerns in our walk and our Lord in His immense goodness allowed me to walk in different religions before finding the truth in Him.

I was on those roads, a mantra is a word you are provided with, they never tell you the meaning of.

When one gets to meditate must begin to repeat that word (Mantra) repeatedly, this must be used with the guru or a spirit guide. The reason is that the person, by repeating the mantra removes the spirit from his body and enter at levels which are prohibited by the word of God as we have explained previously.

The reason that you can't repeat the word or mantra on your own is that you can enter in a level where there are evil spirits or demons, this is very dangerous and in my walk I have met people affected mentally as well as physically.

I came to such a high degree that the guru gave me a list of mantras so that I distribute them to the people; It sells you the idea that you can stay in your religion, to be gradually introduced in theirs.

Thank God that He gave me the opportunity to renounce and re-pent me with all my heart of all of that.

34. HAVE YOU PARTICIPATED IN EASTERN RELIGIONS?

Have you followed a guru?

Once again, quit the participation, being as specific as possible and promise loyalty to God the Father, Jesus Christ the Son, our Savior, and the Holy Spirit.

35. HAVE YOU VISITED PAGANS TEMPLES?

Have you made offerings in which you consented? Have you taken part in a ceremony?

If after visiting a temple you have had negative symptoms such as:
- Fears.
- Nightmares.
- Or something similar.

Pray for cleansing.

Many times as tourists people visits these temples, before entering it is recommended to pray for protection and cleaning as leaving.

While this request there God mercy on those who are worshiping demons or idols that they find the truth in Crist.

Never take part in any ceremony, offering, dances etc.

36. HAVE YOU EVER TAKEN ANY YOGA CLASS?

Meditation? Exercises?

Renounce these religious exercises, meditation and worship time.

- Cast out the religious spirits of yoga.

37. HAVE YOU EVER LEARNED OR USED ANY KIND OF COMMUNICATION OR MIND CONTROL?

Repent and:

- Expelled demons of mental control.
- Demons of extrasensory perception.
- Demons of mental dynamics and confusion.

38. HAVE YOU EVER USE TALISMANS, AMULETS, FETISHES OR SIGNS OF THE ZODIAC?

Do you have any?

Such objects should be burned or destroyed completely, many are cursed objects and they can carry demons with them or receive influence from them.

You must be repentant, renunciation, and cleaning.

- Cast out the spirits of sorcery.

39. DO YOU HAVE AT HOME ANY SYMBOLS OF IDOLS OR WORSHIP SPIRITS?

Such as:

Where are they or how they got into your hands?

You should break the curses on all these articles and then destroy them, preferably by burning them or throwing them to the sea.

It could be that these figures are not yours, but of a relative who lives with you and therefore you are not able to destroy them.

You could point out you to the owner that you are Christian and do not want to have communion with idols.

You must pray for cleansing of your home or whatever place you live in and anoint with oil the doors, windows, bed, etc.:

- You must pray for protection for yourself
- Instruct the unclean spirits to go.
- And instruct the demons to leave.

Ask the Lord to surround you spiritually, to fill you with the presence of the Holy Spirit, and do not allow the entry to evil spirits.

40. DO YOU HAVE ANY ADORNMENT OF WITCHCRAFT AS THE WITCH OF GOOD LUCK IN YOUR HOUSE OR IN YOUR KITCHEN?

No which is good, they represent the devil, and they have no place in the home of a believer in Christ.

41. ARE YOU "IN WAVE" WITH SOME OF THE FOLLOWING MUSIC?

It is very wise to destroy any music with lyrics which incite to sin, or perverse sexual behavior, violence, suicide, and profanity.

42. HAVE YOU PRACTICED MARTIAL ARTS?

Do you practice it today?

Martial arts are linked to the Buddhism.

They are often a door open for:

- Spirits of Rage.
- Spirits of Violence
- Spirits of Vengeance.
- Spirits of Murder.

This practice should be abandoned.

43. HAVE YOU EVER HAD ANY PREMONITIONS ?

DEJA VU? PSYCHIC VISION?

I don't worry about Deja Vu that possibly happen once or twice a few years ago.

Deja Vu or Reduplicative experience is the feeling that a person has witnessed or been previously experienced the same situation.

This term was coined by the French psychic researcher, Émile Boirac (1851-1917).

The experience of Déjà Vu is usually accompanied by a compelling sense of familiarity and also a sense of AWE, surprise or rarity.

Previous experience is often attributed to a dream, although some cases are given a strong sense that the experience truly occurred in the past.

However, we need to pray when the psychic visions, premonitions and Deja Vu appear more often.

- **Search for spirits of deceit, psychic visions.**
- **Déja Vu, sorcery and witchcraft.**

44. HAVE YOU EVER WALKED ON FIRE?

Have you participated in Voodoo, walking on coals or any other form of pagan religious ceremony?

This requires:

- **Repentance.**
- **Disclaimer.**
- **And breaking curses.**

45. DO YOU HAVE TATTOOS?

I am sure that you have seen tattoos very demonic in the bodies of men and women of all ages.

It is not a good thing for a Christian to have a demonic symbolism or Satanic in their body. It is recommended to have them removed with laser surgery.

These tattoos can create a slavery to the symbolism that represents and can obstruct the path of total freedom in Christ.

It is interesting to read:

LEVITICUS 19, 28
AND IF YOU DEFILE THE LAND, IT WILL VOMIT YOU OUT AS IT VOMITED OUT THE NATIONS THAT WERE BEFORE YOU.

In the new international version says:

DO NOT CUT YOUR BODIES FOR THE DEAD OR PUT TATTOO MARKS ON YOURSELVES. I AM THE LORD.

This verse is in the middle of a passage that teaches against sorcery, divinations, omens, mediums and familiar spirits, all of this is related to the devil, Hmm...! Perhaps there could be some connection.

PART III
PERSONAL INFORMATION

1. WHAT IS YOUR MARITAL STATUS?

✓

2. HOW COULD YOU DESCRIBE YOUR SEXUAL RELATION-SHIP WITH YOUR SPOUSE?

I believe God created sexual relationship so that couples can enjoy it fully.

If there is not a satisfying sexual relation among the spouses, I try to find spiritual causes of the problems and pray for them.

I find that women are often guilty of using sex as a weapon, to deny it for their personal purposes.

I see that this is wrong and I want to remind them what the Scriptures say.

1 CORINTHIANS 7, 3 – 5
3
THE HUSBAND SHOULD FULFILL HIS MARITAL DUTY TO HIS WIFE, AND LIKEWISE THE WIFE TO HER HUSBAND.

4
THE WIFE'S BODY DOES NOT BELONG TO HER ALONE BUT ALSO TO HER HUSBAND. IN THE SAME WAY, THE HUSBAND'S BODY DOES NOT BELONG TO HIM ALONE BUT ALSO TO HIS WIFE.

5

DO NOT DEPRIVE EACH OTHER EXCEPT BY MUTUAL CONSENT AND FOR A TIME, SO THAT YOU MAY DEVOTE YOURSELVES TO PRAYER. THEN COME TOGETHER AGAIN SO THAT SATAN WILL NOT TEMPT YOU BECAUSE OF YOUR LACK OF SELF-CONTROL.

Some men are rude and some are cruel, demanding and not careful, some are rough.

They do not have the slightest idea when it comes to romantic skills.

A huge problem is that they confuse the relationship of love with sex, and we see frequently use these words interchangeably.

Not it is surprising that they are totally confused!
It is common to both men and women to fail to understand the love of God for humanity. Because its definition of "Love" is not clear;

When these problems occur, I would suggest giving a little time once it has been prayed for both spouses.

If there are still problems to establish a matrimonial pleasurable sexual experience, the couple should be referred to a good Christian marriage counselor.

3. HAVE YOU EVER FORNICATED WHILE BEING SINGLE?

How many partners? Names and dates, with prostitutes? How? When? Have you committed adultery (at least one of the spouses married)? Names and when.

Are you currently in an illicit sexual relationship? Are willing to end it?

4. ¿ ARE YOU THINKING OF LUST?

- Spirits of lust.

Pray for cleansing and sanity.

5. HAVE YOU EVER BEEN INVOLVED IN ORAL SEX?

WITH WHOM?

Oral sex out of wedlock is an open door for the spirits of sexual perversion to create a binding.

These must be cast out and you must pray for cleansing of parts of the body involved.

There are differences of views on whether occasional and mutually accepted oral stimulation is well within marriage.

I would say that what is wrong is to require from a spouse to the other something offensive or repulsive, which she or he does not want to do, this stimulation should be abandoned.

The feelings of the wife are very important and must be respected.

If oral sex within the marriage is required by the husband to replace the normal sex, it could be there is an evil spirit, which should be expelled.

HAVE YOU PARTICIPATED IN ANAL SEX?

WITH WHOM?

Sodomy is condemned in the Scriptures, forgiveness should be extended when necessary and you must pray for cleansing of the body.

ALL OF THESE SHOULD BE CAST OUT:

- Spirits of homosexuality.
- Spirits of sodomy.
- Spirits of degradation.
- Spirits of rejection.

6. DO YOU MASTURBATE OFTEN?

DO YOU KNOW WHY? DO YOU FEEL THAT IT IS A COMPULSIVE PROBLEM?

Occasional masturbation is often a part of the growth. If it becomes a habit, perhaps a demonic spirit is attached .

Compulsive masturbation may be an addiction that interferes with the marriage and produces guilt and shame.

There are people who have a habit of masturbating several times a day.

- We cast out a spirit of masturbation and lustful fantasies.

- Find also a spirit of addiction in severe cases and eject the guilt and the shame.

7. WERE YOU SEXUALLY ASSAULTED BY SOMEONE FROM YOUR FAMILY OR ANOTHER PERSON WHEN YOU WERE A CHILD OR TEENAGER?

BY WHOM? MORE THAN ONE TIME? WERE YOU RAPED?

8. HAVE YOU BEEN VICTIM OF INCEST BY A MEMBER OF YOUR FAMILY?

SEARCH:

- Generational spirits.
- Spirits of sexual harassment.
- Spirits of lust.
- Spirits of incest, etc.

9. MEN?

Have you raped someone?

Name of the raped victim. Have you committed incest?
Women: were you ever raped? Names.

Many sexual bonds are rooted "at that time", at the time of a sexual harassment. Questions 4, 5 and 6 seek to collect information about those unfortunate events.

The person must forgive the guilty party, or forgive themselves for hurting the other.

Attackers are often in turn attacked, that is why. LOOK FOR:

- Generational spirits.
- Spirits of sexual harassment.
- Spirits of Lust.
- Spirits of Incest, Etc.

The victim should forgive God if they believed He abandoned them at the time of the assault.

We find:

- Spirits of lust.
- Spirits of debasement.
- Spirits of hate.
- Spirits of incest.
- Spirits of anger.
- Spirits of guilt.
- Spirits of shame.
- Spirits of un-forgiveness
- Spirits of bitterness.
- Evil spirits.
- Spirits of hatred towards the man and the like.

10. WOMEN: (See also answer 9)

Were you raped?
Are you frigid?

SEARCH:

- Spirits of Resentment.
- Spirits of Bitterness.
- Spirits of Frigidity.
- Spirits of Emotional Coldness.

11. HAVE YOU EVER HAD ANY GAY OR LESBIAN THOUGHTS?

Do you have them now?

Sins and sexual assault are different from the other sins.

1 CORINTHIANS 6, 13 – 20

13b
THE BODY IS NOT MEANT FOR SEXUAL IMMORALITY, BUT FOR THE LORD, AND THE LORD FOR THE BODY.

14
BY HIS POWER GOD RAISED THE LORD FROM THE DEAD, AND HE WILL RAISE US ALSO.

15
DO YOU NOT KNOW THAT YOUR BODIES ARE MEMBERS OF CHRIST HIMSELF? SHALL I THEN TAKE THE MEMBERS OF CHRIST AND UNITE THEM WITH A PROSTITUTE? NEVER!

16
DO YOU NOT KNOW THAT HE WHO UNITES HIMSELF WITH A PROSTITUTE IS ONE WITH HER IN BODY? FOR IT IS SAID, "THE TWO WILL BECOME ONE FLESH."

17
BUT HE WHO UNITES HIMSELF WITH THE LORD IS ONE WITH HIM IN SPIRIT.

18
FLEE FORM SEXUAL IMMORALITY. ALL OTHER SINS A MAN COMMITS ARE OUTSIDE HIS BODY, BUT HE WHO SINS SEXUALLY SINS AGAINST HIS OWN BODY.

19
DO YOU NOT KNOW THAT YOUR BODY IS A TEMPLE OF THE HOLY SPIRIT, WHO IS IN YOU, WHOM YOU HAVE RECEIVED FROM GOD? YOU ARE NOT YOUR OWN;

20
YOU WERE BOUGHT AT A PRICE. THEREFORE HONOR GOD WITH YOUR BODY.

The physical body of the person is "Not" to Sin

It should be cleaned in order to enjoy a proper marriage relationship.

I ask the names of those involved with incidents:

- Fornication.
- Prostitution.
- Adultery.
- Gay or lesbian relations.
- As well as incestuous facts and victimization.

We do not enjoy collecting this information. The purpose is to break ties ungodly in each of those individuals.

Through a prayer like this, is ordered the destruction of the ties of the soul:

PRAYER:

And now, in the name of Jesus, break all ungodly ties to the body, soul and spirit among you (name) and (insert name). I ask God to take each part that was commissioning tie back to (insert another name).

I am now writing to every unclean spirit who took advantage of this unholy soul tie and order it to leave in the name of Jesus and that you do not return more. I forbid you to haunt (name)

When it comes to homosexuality, I often hear the expression:

- "But I was born this way."
- "I was born in the wrong body."
- "I was born man but I am a woman trapped in a man's body."

MY ANSWER IS:

- "Maybe it was so"

MY QUESTION FOR YOU IS:

- Do you want to continue that way or want to get rid of it and be normal?

I'm going after a generational spirit of homosexuality, then after his own spirit of homosexuality or, in the case of a woman after the corresponding spirit of lesbianism.

The shackles of the soul must be broken.

We must take into account any object or gift with each other, any link of the soul must be broken with these gifts such as:

- Rings.
- Clothing of any kind.
- Objects, ornaments, stuffed animals, etc.
- Clothing, Etc.
- Photos.

They must be destroyed or burn, or return to the other person pray and break any link of the soul.

When cleaning the sexual problems should be cleaning prayers by which it has been downgraded:

- Skin.
- Sex organs.
- Eyes.
- Ears.
- Mouth, Etc.

Also with a prayer dedicate to the Lord those parts of the body, so that they are used appropriately and it is usually good to pray so that each assumes the appropriate roles of male and female, that men are completely male, as God wants it, and that in the same way women are totally female.

12. DO YOU HAVE SEXUAL FANTASIES WITH ANIMALS?

Have you had (bestiality) sexual acts with an animal?
List all animals involved:

- Cast out the Spirit of (name of the animal).
- Spirits of Bestiality.
- Spirits of Guilt.
- Spirits of Shame.

13. HAVE YOU BEEN ATTRACTED BY PORNOGRAPHY?

Has pornography attracted you ever? How were you involved? Have you seen pornographic films? Videos? Live sex shows? Buy or rent pornography, or have in your home one of these channels on television?

Pornography is extremely addictive.

The images are marked in the mind and seem impossible to delete; they always return. If this was a sin is intentional on the part of the person who is praying, please pray something like:

PRAYER

"Lord" forgive me for getting involved in pornography. I regret it and I ask you to cleanse me of their pollution and release me from this slavery.

If the person became a victim by finding pornography in his/her home, or was invited to watch a video by a teenage neighbor or friend, must then forgive those who put him/her in that trap, before making a prayer similar to the previous paragraph.

SEARCH FOR:

- Spirits of pornography.
- Spirits of Sexual Fantasies.
- Spirits of Addiction.

In prayer, ask for cleaning of images marked in the memory. Ask God to remove them from their minds.

Destroy all materials such as books, magazines, photos, videos, films, etc.

Also you should cancel TV channels, should block or delete any pornographic activity on your computer.

14. DO YOU PURCHASE OR RENT CURRENTLY PORNO-GRAPHY OR HAVE ANY PORN CHANNELS IN YOUR HOME?

(See answer 13)

15. HAVE YOU EVER WISHED TO HAVE SEX WITH CHILDREN (PHEDOPHILIA)?

HAVE YOU EVER DONE THIS?

Must cast out:

- Spirits of Pedophilia.

A person with this spirit probably received it:

- By Inheritance.
- By Viewing Pornography.
- Or for having been assaulted sexually as a child.

16. HAVE YOU EVER HAD ANY INTERNAL STIMULATION OR CLIMAX BEYOND YOUR CONTROL, SPECIALLY AT NIGHT?

What I mean is this:

Have you ever dreamed that a figure comes to you and asks you to have sex, or do you simply "feel a presence at your side of the bed, and then wake up with sexual climax?" (This is different from a normal broadcast).

This problem is caused by lusty spirits that dealt with a person in a dream and cause sexual stimulation after having asked for permission.

Once given permission, they can return freely.

They enjoy especially working in darkness, but often they are so bold that also during the day, they cause problems.

- If the spirit is female in nature, its name is SUCCUBUS.
- If it acts like a boy, his name is INCUBUS.

Call it by its name to expel him.

Many times these spirits have been in family lines for several generations.

These spirits come many times:

- Through witchcraft ceremonies.
- Satanic worship.
- Emotional hurt by the death of a loved one, as a husband or boyfriend.

ALSO FIND:

- Spirits of Lust.
- Spirits of Guilt.
- Spirits of Demonic Mind Control.

They frequently startled the body when they are called by his name. It seems that you impressed them by calling them by their legitimate names.

17. HAVE YOU EVER VISITED A MASSAGE ROOM WHERE YOU WERE SEXUALLY STIMULATED?

SEARCH:

- Spirits of Pornography.
- Spirits of Sexual Fantasies.
- Spirits of Lust.

PART I V
ACCIDENT AND HEALTH QUESTIONNAIRE

1. DO YOU SUFFER FROM CHRONIC DISEASES OR ALLER-GIES?

   LOOK FOR:

   - Hereditary disease spirits.
   - Also a specific spirit of disease.

   Always pray against a spirit of disease if there are allergies or chronic ills, and pray also asking for physical health.

2. HAVE YOU EVER HAD ANY ACCIDENTS OR SEVERE TRAUMA THAT STAYS FIRM IN YOUR MIND (OTHER THAN THOSE MENTIONED ABOVE)?

   If during the time of prayer, a spirit of trauma has not manifested,

   - But appears here, now is the time to pray against it.

3. DO YOU HAVE OTHER PROBLEMS NOT FOUND IN THIS QUESTIONNAIRE?

   Explain as fully as you can.

   Try to specify when they started and if they were connected with some kind of trauma, if you were victimized, or if you invite the problem to enter.

4. DO YOU HAVE ANY ADDICTION?

   Are any addictions a current problem?

5. HAVE YOU BEEN ADDICTED TO ANY OF THESE?

Have you once been addicted to?:

ALCOHOL, TOBACCO, FOOD, GAMES, COMPULSIVE EXERCISE, SPENDING, TV, COFFEE, DRUGS (PRESCRIPTION OR HALLUCINOGENIC)?

Is any of this a current problem?

The spirit of addiction can manifest itself in different ways.

Often occurs a generational spirit of addiction, which should be treated.

It is important to tell the spirit of addiction that its work has ended in this family line, and will forbid the generational spirit of addiction to continue through the children of the person who is been prayed for.

Then pray on each spirit of addiction causing problems and afflicting the person and ordered it out in the name of Jesus.

6. MEN:

Have you ever conceived a baby which was aborted? How many? Dates and name of the mother.

The emotional damage caused by having an abortion can last for a lifetime.

It must extend forgiveness to himself and the mother prior to pray asking for cleanliness and integrity.

TO LOOK FOR:

- Spirits of Murder.
- Spirits of Death.
- Spirits of Pain.
- Spirits of Un-forgiveness.
- Spirits of Bitterness.
- Spirits of Hatred towards Humanity.
- Spirits of Self-hate.
- Spirits of Rejection.
- Spirits of Selfishness

Always pray for the health of the womb once there a murder has been committed in it.

Sometimes the frigidity in marriage can be traced to an abortion.

We must tell the woman that the baby is with the Lord, that one day they will see each other and that God has forgiven this sin.

Men who have insisted on the abortion of a child are in fact an accomplice to murder.

They must repent and ask for forgiveness.

SEARCH:

- Spirits of Lust.
- Spirits of Abandonment.
- Spirits of murder.
- Spirits of emotional cruelty.
- Spirits of selfishness.
- Spirits of violation (if applicable).

7. **WOMEN**

    Have you ever had an abortion?

    How many? GIVE THE NAME OF THE FATHER.

    (See Reply 6).

8. **ANY OTHER INFORMATION IMPORTANT?**

    ✓

STEP I
PLACE, MINISTER
AND
THE RELEASE TEAM

PLACE

The place can be:

> ➤ THE CHURCH.
> ➤ A PRIVATE ROOM.
> ➤ THE HOUSE OF THE INFECTED, IF DULY REVISED.

AS WELL AS ON THE NIGHT OF PASSOVER, THE LINTELS OF THE HEBREWS, PROTECTED BY THE BLOOD OF THE PASCHAL LAMB, WERE RESPECTED BY THE ANGEL EXTERMINATOR; **WELL AS THE BLOOD OF THE LAMB OF GOD US COVERS, PROTECTS AND FREES FROM ANY INFLUENCE OF THE BAD.** WITH THIS PROTECTION PREVENTS:

> ➤ COMMUNICATION BETWEEN SPIRITS.

> ➤ DO NOT ALLOW INTERACTION SO THAT THE DEMONS CAN NOT TAKE STRENGTH AND POWER FROM EACH OTHER.

We must protect all premises where the release will take place with "**The blood of Jesus Christ**":

> **PROTECT ALL THE DOORS AND LINTELS WITH THE BLOOD OF JESUS.**
> WE ENVISION THAT WE ARE SMEARING WITH AN AESOP THE BLOOD OF JESUS TO THOSE DOORS AND THESE LINTELS AND ALL HOLES IN THE PLACE.

> **PROTECTS ALL WINDOWS AND HOLES IF THE THERE ARE ANY WITH THE BLOOD OF JESUS.**

> **WE BLESS THE PLACE AND ASK THE HOLY SPIRIT TO COME TO THIS PLACE.**
> BLESSED OIL OR WATER BLESSED THAT IT EMANATES FROM THE SIDE OF CHRIST, CAN BE USED THERE ARE CHURCHES THAT DO NOT USE WATER, MAKE A SMALL CROSS WITH THE OIL AT EVERY DOOR AND WINDOW IF YOU WISH TO.

> **WE ASK JESUS TO SEND HIS ANGELS TO SURROUND THE PLACE.**

> **SO THEY CAN NOT BRING MORE DEMONS.** THUS WE AVOID THAT THEY CAN ATTACK US AND THAT KEEP COMMUNICATIONS AND INTERACTIONS OF ONE DEMON WITH OTHERS AND AVOID TO TAKE FORCE AND POWER ONE OF OTHERS.

ALL THIS IS DONE IN A PRAYER OF PETITION:

> **ASK THE FATHER IN THE NAME OF JESUS.**
> **WE ASK JESUS TO INTERCEDE WITH THE FATHER.**

THE MINISTER.

The Minister or person who will lead the liberation must be only one who speaks and who has the authority of Jesus Christ:

> ➢ FULL OF GOD AND HIS HOLY SPIRIT.
> ➢ HAD PREVIOUS EXPERIENCE IN THE MINISTRY OF HEALING.
> ➢ HAVE COMPASSION AND MERCY FOR HIS BRO-THERS.
> ➢ GET THE AUTHORITY THE POWER AND STRENGTH OF THE HOLY SPIRIT.
> ➢ FOLLOW THE STEPS IN THE TOPIC 2 PREPARATION FOR RELEASE.

We must protect ourselves with:

> ➢ THE ARMOR OF GOD.
> ➢ WITH THE COAT OF ARMS OF GOD.
> ➢ THE BLOOD OF THE LAMB (JESUS).
> ➢ BY YOUR HOLY WOUNDS.
> ➢ WITH HIS CROWN OF THORNS.

We can say a prayer as follows:

"I CLAIM FOR ME AND FOR ALL WHOM ARE HERE, THE BLOOD OF THE LAMB OF GOD WHO TAKES AWAY THE SIN OF THE WORLD TO PURIFY US FROM ALL SIN AND TO PROTECT US AGAINST ALL EVIL INFLUENCE."

WE ALSO PROTECT:

> ➢ OUR FAMILIES.
> ➢ PROPERTY AND THINGS, ANIMALS.
> ➢ THE PLACE WHERE THEY MAKE THE RELEASE.

THE RELEASE TEAM.

THE TEAM MUST BE INTEGRATED BY PEOPLE:

- ➤ **MATURE IN THE LORD.**
- ➤ **WISE ENOUGH TO KNOW HOW TO DISCERN PRE-SENCE AND DEMONIC INFLUENCE.**
- ➤ **THE TEAM MAY BE MADE PREFERABLY FROM 6 PERSONS, COMPOSED OF MEN AND WOMEN.**

One person should be the releaser, another person to help, while the other, preferably 6 in total are in prayer in silence and open to the action of the Holy Spirit to receive word of knowledge and guidance from the Holy Spirit and be able to restrain the infected if necessary.

- ➤ **MINISTER SHOULD NEVER BE ALONE. .**
- ➤ **NOT SHOULD A MAN MINISTER ALONE TO A WO-MAN.**
- ➤ **NOT SHOULD A WOMAN MINISTER ALONE TO A MAN.**

OTHER RECOMMENDATIONS FOR THE TEAM:

- ➤ **ALL MEMBERS SHOULD ASK GOD FORGIVENESS FOR THEIR SINS AND PRAY FOR THE OTHER.**
- ➤ **THE UNIT IS ABSOLUTELY ESSENTIAL.**
- ➤ **SATAN WILL CAPITALIZE ON ANY DISUNITY.**
- ➤ **YOU NEED TO BE ON GUARD AGAINST THIS TAC-TICS.**
- ➤ **THE ENTIRE GROUP THAT WORKS TOGETHER, MUST LEARN TO FLOW IN THE SPIRIT.**
- ➤ **YOU HAVE CONFIDENCE IN THE OTHER.**

> ASK JESUS TO CONFIRM ANY WORD OF KNOW-
> LEDGE RECEIVED BY ANY OF THE MEMBERS OF
> THE GROUP.

The purpose of the team is to leave the captive free from the clutches of
Satan, give all the glory to Jesus, in a way that no matter who directs the
fight; is a joint action of the team and each position (the body of Christ)
is important.

STEP 2
THE FIGHT
AGAINST
THE DEMONS

The demons are spiritual enemies and we Christians must face them.

EPHESIANS 6, 10 – 12

10
FINALLY BE STRONG IN THE LORD AND IN HIS MIGHTY PO-WER.

11
PUT ON THE FULL ARMOR OF GOD SO THAT YOU CAN TAKE YOUR STAND AGAINST THE DEVIL'S SCHEMES.

12
FOR OUR STRUGGLE IS NOT AGAINST FLESH AND BLOOD, BUT AGAINST THE RULERS, AGAINST THE AUTHORITIES, AGAINST THE POWER OF THIS DARK WORLD AND AGAINST THE SPIRITUAL FORCES OF EVIL IN THE HEAVENLY RE-ALMS.

2 CORINTHIANS 10, 3 – 4

3

FOR THOUGH WE LIVE IN THE WORLD, WE DO NOT WAGE WAR AS THE WORLD DOES.

4

THE WEAPONS WE FIGHT WITH ARE NOT THE WEAPONS OF THE WORLD. ON THE CONTRARY, THEY HAVE DIVINE POWER TO DEMOLISH STRONGHOLDS.

The enemy is a spiritual enemy. Weapons are spiritual.

The term fight also suggests pressure tactics.
Speaks of the tactics that Satan uses to push us.

It does so in the areas of our:

- ➢ **THOUGHT.**
- ➢ **EMOTIONS.**
- ➢ **DECISIONS.**
- ➢ **IN OUR BODY.**

Many times we ignore the trickery and lies of Satan and try to find relief in:

- ➢ **TRANQUILIZERS.**
- ➢ **SLEEPING PILLS.**
- ➢ **PSYCHOLOGISTS OR PSYCHIATRISTS.**
- ➢ **VISIT TO A WITCH.**

But the remedy of God to defeat the demonic oppression is the spiritual struggle.

Ephesians 6, 12 expresses four important things about our spiritual enemies.

- ➤ PRINCIPALITY.
- ➤ AUTHORITIES.
- ➤ RULERS OF DARKNESS.
- ➤ THE FIGHT AGAINST SPIRITUAL HOSTS OF WICKED-NESS IN BLUE REGIONS.

PRINCIPALITY.

The term Greek for principalities is **"archas"**.
This word is used to describe:

- ➤ RULERS.
- ➤ LEADERS.
- ➤ JUDGES.

This would describe his rank and organization. Therefore the word **"Principality"** tells us that Satan's Kingdom is very well structured and organized.

The term **"Principality"** is defined as:

- ➤ THE TERRITORY OF A PRINCE.
- ➤ THE JURISDICTION OF A PRINCE.
- ➤ THE REGION THAT GIVES TITLE TO A PRINCE.

These Governors spirits are assigned to areas such as Cities and Nations.

DANIEL 10, 13
BUT THE PRINCE OF THE PERSIAN KINGDOM RESISTED ME TWENTY-ONE DAYS. THEN MICHAEL, ONE OF THE CHIEF PRINCES, CAME TO HELP ME, BECAUSE I WAS DETAINED THERE WITH THE KING OF PERSIA.

AUTHORITIES.

The Greek word for **"Authorithy"** is **"Exousias."**

This term also translates as:

> ➤ **AUTHORITHY.**

Who believes in Jesus receives an authority and power, even more.
It is vested with the authority of the name of Jesus.

MARK 16, 17
AND THESE SIGNS WILL ACCOMPANY THOSE WHO BELIEVE:
IN MY NAME THEY WILL DRIVE OUT DEMONS; THEY WILL
SPEAK IN NEW TONGUES;

The demons are obliged to submit to the authority of the name of Jesus.

Scripture reveals that the demons have:

> ➤ **AUTHORITHY.**
> ➤ **POWER.**

LUKE 10, 19
HAVE GIVEN YOU AUTHORITY TO TRAMPLE ON SNAKES
AND SCORPIONS AND TO OVERCOME ALL THE POWER OF
THE ENEMY; NOTHING WILL HARM YOU.

The Word **"Power"** in Greek is **"Dunamis"**.

In the word of God we have received the promise that we can have more
power than our enemies and demons.

ACTS 1, 8
BUT YOU WILL RECEIVE POWER WHEN THE HOLY SPIRIT COMES ON YOU;

THE POWER of the believer arrives with **the Baptism in the Holy Spirit.**

Jesus knows that his followers needed both **The Authority** and **The Power** to engage the enemy.

Jesus sent the twelve to release and heal the sick.

LUKE 9, 1
WHEN JESUS HAS CALLED THE TWELVE TOGETHER, HE GAVE THEM POWER AND AUTHORITY TO DRIVE OUT ALL DEMONS AND TO CURE DISEASES,

Then Jesus sent seventy disciples (other versions 72) two by two:

LUKE 10, 17 – 18
17
THE SEVENTY-TWO RETURNED WITH JOY AND SAID, "LORD, EVEN THE DEMONS SUBMIT TO US IN YOUR NAME."

18
HE REPLIED: I SAW SATAN FALL LIKE LIGHTNING FROM HEAVEN.

The Commission that Jesus gave his Church gives us the same power and the same authority.

In Mark 16, 17 we are told that believers can expel demons in the name of Jesus. The Commission that appears in Matthew 28, 18-20, begins with this statement:

> ALL POWER IS GIVEN TO ME IN HEAVEN AND ON EARTH. THEREFORE GO.......

It would be very foolish to go against the demonic spirits without this power and authority.

> THE AUTHORITY COMES TO US BY MEANS OF SAL-VATION.
> THE POWER COMES THROUGH THE BAPTISM IN THE HOLY SPIRIT.

This power is evident through the operation of the gifts of the spirit (see 1 Corinthians 12, 7-11)

The gift of discernment of the spirit and the word of knowledge, are indispensable in **The Fight** against the demons.

THE GOVERNORS.

We know that the fight is against **The Governors of the Darkness of this century.** The Greek word: **"The Governors of the World"** is **"kosmokratoras".**

This Word can be translated as **"Gentlemen of the World"** or **"Princes of this time".**

This designation of the enemy emphasizes its intention to control. Satan is referred to in writing as **"god of this world"** or **"god of this century".**

2 CORINTHIANS 4, 4
THE god OF THIS AGE HAS BLINDED THE MINDS OF UNBE-LIEVERS, SO THAT THEY CANNOT SEE THE LIGHT OF THE GOSPEL OF THE GLORY OF CHRIST, WHO IS THE IMAGE OF GOD.

When Adam fell into sin, Satan got domain on this world.

Jesus Himself did not refute this claim of the devil, during the temptations in the wilderness.

MATTHEW 4, 8 – 9
8
AGAIN, THE DEVIL TOOK HIM TO A VERY HIGH MOUNTAIN AND SHOWED HIM ALL THE KINGDOMS OF THE WORLD AND THEIR SPLENDOR.

9
ALL THIS I WILL GIVE YOU, HE SAID, "IF YOU WILL BOW DOWN AND WORSHIP ME."

It is of utmost importance to know that Satan is a defeated foe. He has been stripped of his power and his kingdom, and we have every right to treat him as an invader.

Jesus explained its competence to expel demons with these words:

LUKE 11, 20
BUT IF I DRIVE OUT DEMONS BY THE FINGER OF GOD, THEN THE KINGDOM OF GOD HAS COME TO YOU.

In Ephesians 6, 11 the Christian is called to **"wear full armor of God"**.

Thus the Christian is not vulnerable to any point; on the other hand the devil is in every point.

Satan still seeks to rule the world and we must agree that considerable progress has been made.

WHY?

Because the Church is not lifted with the power and authority given to us

THE FIGHT IS AGAINST HOSTS SPIRITUAL OF EVIL IN THE CELESTIAL REGIONS.

The key word is **"evil"**.
This term suggests everything that is highly harmful or destructive by nature.

These malignant powers only have one goal:

> ➤ **THE EVIL.**

They may appear as angels and their deception lead many to their networks of destruction.

Jesus exposed the purposes of evil with these words:

JOHN 10, 10ª
THE THIEF COMES ONLY TO STEAL AND KILL AND DESTROY;

In Ephesians 6, 12 give us a clear idea of the kingdom of Satan:

> ➤ **IS HIGHLY ORGANIZED, TO FULLFIL ITS PURPOSES.**
> ➤ **POWERS DEMONIC ARE POSTS IN ORDER OF FIGHT.**
> ➤ **THE DEMONS HAVE RECEIVED AUTHORITY OF SATAN TO CONTROL EVERYONE AND FILL IT WITH THE MORE HARMFUL EVIL.**

The vast majority of Christians have not been compromised in the spiritual struggle because they have never received education on its importance, nor on the way and it should carry out.

Now Satan holds his power through:

- ➤ **THE SPIRITUALISM.**
- ➤ **THE OCCULT.**
- ➤ **FALSE RELIGIONS.**
- ➤ **OF CULTS.**
- ➤ **PORNOGRAPHY AND SEX.**

Never before in the history of humanity.

A newspaper quoted Billy Graham when he said:

We are fighting with forces and supernatural powers... It is perfectly obvious to all of us in the spiritual work that the demons can possess people, harass them and control them. More and more Christians must learn to use the power of God to liberate the people of these terrible possessions of the devil.

HOW MANY CHRISTIANS HAVE BEEN TRAINED "TO TOPPLE FORTRESSES"?

2 CORINTHIANS 10, 4
THE WEAPONS WE FIGHT WITH ARE NOT THE WEAPONS OF THE WORLD. ON THE CONTRARY, THEY HAVE DIVINE POWER TO DEMOLISH STRONGHOLDS.

HOW MANY KNOW HOW TO RESIST THE DEVIL?

JAMES 4, 7
SUBMIT YOURSELVES, THEN, TO GOD. RESIST THE DEVIL, AND HE WILL FLEE FROM YOU.

LIKE FIGHTING AGAINST, PRINCIPALITIES, POWERS, THE GOVERNORS OF THE DARKNESS, THE FIGHT AGAINST SPIRITUAL HOSTS OF WICKEDNESS IN BLUE REGIONS?

As soldiers of Christ we must acquire practical knowledge. It is imperative to learn today, how to be good Christian soldiers.

1 TIMOTHY 1, 18

TIMOTHY, MY SON, I GIVE YOU THIS INSTRUCTION IN KEEPING WITH THE PROPHECIES ONCE MADE ABOUT YOU, SO THAT BY FOLLOWING THEM YOU MAY FIGHT THE GOOD FIGHT,

We are exhorted to wear full armor of God to stay and stand against **"the snares of the devil"**

The word that is translated as ambush is **"methodeia"** which means to follow such as method and established plan, the use of:

- ➢ **SCAMS.**
- ➢ **FALSE.**
- ➢ **TRICKS.**
- ➢ **BAD HABITS.**

ASPECTS AND ATTRIBUTES OF DEMONS.

When we entered in the release of a person, several spirits can manifest but each spirit can have several **Aspects** or **Forms**, these can confuse a Minister and make him believe that there are more spirits; with the experience and the gift of discernment we can discover the reality.

MARK 5, 13

HE GAVE THEM PERMISSION, AND THE EVIL SPIRITS CAME OUT AND WENT INTO THE PIGS. THE HERD, ABOUT TWO THOUSAND IN NUMBER, RUSHED DOWN THE STEEP BANK INTO THE LAKE AND WERE DROWNED.

THE ASPECTS = FORMS.

An evil spirit has:

- ➢ **A PERSONALITY.**
- ➢ **INSIDE IF IT HAS CERTAIN DIMENSIONS OF PERSO-NALITY.**
- ➢ **HAVE A NATURE.**
- ➢ **HAVE SOMETHING INSIDE.**

EXAMPLE:

Many say and believe that what we need in a **SPIRIT OF FEAR** is **FEAR** nothing more and you can do nothing more than that.

But that is not true, there is a minimum of **SIX THINGS** or more in a spirit of fear that can be done, and those **SIX THINGS** are called **ASPECTS OR FORMS OF THE DEVIL.**

What kind of fear there is in the spirit of fear, in the majority of the spirits have **DECEPTION** within them.

It is a spirit of deceitful fear:

- ➢ **ITS NATURE.**
- ➢ **PERSONALITY.**
- ➢ **PART OF ITS CONSTITUTION.**

HIS APPEARANCE IS LOOKING TO DECEIVE.

Sometimes there are:

- ➢ **TERROR.**
- ➢ **REJECTION.**
- ➢ **PARALYSIS.**

If we ask what **KIND OF SPIRIT IS THAT?**

It is a **SPIRIT OF PARALYZING FEAR** that is the **KIND OF FEATURE INTERIOR**, which has.

THERE ARE TWO CLASSES:

ASPECT = FORMS.

THE FIRST.

One can usually find one, four or maybe six aspects in a spirit of fear.

The Mission of the aspect is to avoid that the spirit be removed from the person:

> ➤ **IT COULD BE DESOBEDIENCE.**
> ➤ **WHEN ONE SAY THAT YOU GO, IS CHALLENGING.**

He sits there and challenge one, it can be also deceitful.

One of the worst spirits against which one can work are of playful aspect, which made any kind of possible game:

> ➤ **THEY DO THINGS.**
> ➤ **THEY SAY THINGS.**
> ➤ **AND CAN SHOW YOU ANYTHING.**

If you think working in the Ministry of healing in the part of release with the idea that every spirit comes vomiting, then these playful spirits will laugh at us and we'll see them vomiting, because they know that is what you are looking for.

There are certain elements in the spirit, especially for its own projection to avoid being released:

> - MAKE FUN OF YOU.
> - LIE TO ONE.
> - CHALLENGE ONE.
> - DISOBEY ONE.
> - REBEL AGAINST ONE.

So what do you do?

TIE,

> - YOUR ANTICS IN THE NAME OF JESUS.
> - YOUR REBELLION IN THE NAME OF JESUS.
> - YOUR DISOBEDIENCE IN THE NAME OF JESUS.
> - YOUR CHALLENGES IN THE NAME OF JESUS, ETC., ETC.

Until the spirit is completely **TIED** up (see step 3)

As we go alone we will understand how the spirit works, see who is **HOSTING** and is like a **CLAW.**

If we want, we can make an image of that spirit and create a visual image of where this **GRIP** is, where is **NAILED**, then say:

> - TIE YOUR DECEPTION.
> - TAKE YOUR DECEPTION AND REMOVED IT.
> - OR I TELL, TIE YOUR REBELLION.
> - YOUR DISOBEDIENCE.
> - YOUR CHALLENGE.
> - YOUR GAME.

And I remain so until there is nothing left **UNTIED** and continue **IN THE NAME OF JESUS.**

Then there is nothing that protects it, thus the spirit is **RETRACTING TOWARDS ITSELF AND DO NOT HOLD.**

The spirit is weakened because you can't get more **POWER or FORCE** of another spirit, not be strengthened.

THE SECOND.

Perhaps the most important are the ways in which **the spirit is stuck** in **THE EMOTIONAL WOUNDS** of people.

All series of aspects indicate as the spirit of fear **AFFECTS** a person.

If we have before us a spirit of paralyzing fear and when activated it is affecting the person so that they may not:

> ➤ **BREATHE.**
> ➤ **OR MOVE.**
> ➤ **IS PARALYZED.**

Because the spirit is **DOING** something, **THIS IS AN ASPECT.**

One says:

> ➤ **TIE YOUR PARALYSIS IN THE NAME OF JESUS.**
> ➤ **FEAR CAN CAUSE TERROR.**
> ➤ **OR FEAR OF REJECTION.**

One becomes aware of a number of things, from wounds that that spirit is reacting and keeps nailed on that person.

All this is extremely important, because it gives us **THE CLUES** in how to make **THE HEALING OF THE PERSON.**

THE INNER HEALING has to be carried out where the spirit is or in **THE FEAR OF REJECTION** of the person.

Therefore the aspects are **very, very, very** important because they say to one:

- ➤ **FEATURES OR GENERAL ASPECTS OF THE SPIRIT.**
- ➤ **THE DIMENSIONS IN THE SPIRIT.**
- ➤ **WHAT THE SPIRIT IS AND WHAT IT DOES.**
- ➤ **AS THIS IS NAILED AND WORK IN PERSON.**

THE ATTRIBUTE.

There is something greater than THE ASPECT, is called ATTRIBUTE.

NOT ALL SPIRITS HAVE ATTRIBUTES.

An attribute is when the spirit has:

- ➤ **INTELLIGENCE.**
- ➤ **KNOWLEDGE.**
- ➤ **COMMUNICATION.**
- ➤ **POWER.**
- ➤ **AUTHORITY.**
- ➤ **AND ANYTHING LIKE.**

It has an intelligence far more great than ours, and can read all **THE INTERACTION** that is there in the room.

They know more than us, so one has to **TIE** their intelligence. (See step 3)

THE ASPECTS

Aspects are important for this reason:

The number of aspects tells us what kinds of hierarchy are working with:

> - **MORE THAN 10 ASPECTS, IS A HIERARCHY.**
> - **MORE THAN 12 ASPECTS, IS A THRONE.**
> - **MORE THAN 13 ASPECTS, IS THE GUARD.**
> - **MORE THAN 14 ASPECTS, IS A DOMINATION.**
> - **MORE THAN 15 ASPECTS, IS THE COUNCIL.**
> - **MORE THAN 16 ASPECTS, IS A DEMON.**
> - **MORE THAN 24 ASPECTS, IS A PRINCE.**
> - **MORE THAN 36 ASPECTS, IS A PRINCIPALITY.**

The quantities of aspects will tell us with whom we are working.

STEP 3
TIE, TIE AND TIE

Different situations may occur to a person:

> ➤ THAT A SPIRIT IS BEING MANIFESTING IN THE PER-
> SON, THEN MAKE THE RELEASE AND EXPULSION OF
> DEMONS AND AFTER FINISHED MAKE THE INNER
> HEALING.

> ➤ THAT THE PERSON IS MANIFESTING A SPIRIT, BIND
> THE SPIRITS AND ASPECTS, STOP THE RELEASE TO
> MAKE THE INTERNAL HEALING AND THEN WHEN
> FINISHED EXPELLING DEMONS.

> ➤ PROCEED WITH THE INTERNAL HEALING AND
> THEN RELEASE.

The Bible declares that Jesus gave us power to **TIE** and **UNTIE** with
reference to **SATAN** and **HIS MINIONS**.

289

MATTHEW 16, 18 – 19

18

*AND I TELL YOU THAT YOU ARE PETER, AND ON THIS ROCK
I WILL BUILD MY CHURCH, AND THE GATES OF HADES WILL
NOT OVERCOME IT.*

19

*WILL GIVE YOU THE KEYS OF THE KINGDOM OF HEAVEN;
WHATEVER YOU BIND ON EARTH WILL BE BOUND IN HEA-
VEN; WHATEVER YOU BIND ON EARTH WILL BE BOUND IN
HEAVEN AND WHATEVER YOU LOOSE ON EARTH WILL BE
LOOSED IN HEAVEN.*

See also John 20, 23; Matthew 18, 18

This passage has caused many disagreements, but gives us light with
respect to the authority which the Christian has over demons.

**WHAT THE IMMEDIATE TEXT TO TIE AND UNTIE AUTHO-
RITY?**

**IS "....AND THE GATES OF HELL CANNOT PREVAIL
AGAINST IT."**

The expanded Bible translate this, "The gates of Hades (the powers of
the infernal region)."

The power to **Bind** and **Unleash** on **Satan** is described as **"The keys of
the Kingdom of heaven"**.

The Greek word for **"Kingdom"** is **Basileia** which means **"Rule"**. It is
the promise of the word of God to those who will inherit the Kingdom of
God and govern with Christ.

ROMANS 5, 17
*FOR IF, BY THE TRESPASS OF THE ONE MAN, DEATH REIG-
NED THROUGH THAT ONE MAN,   HOW MUCH MORE WILL*

THOSE WHO RECEIVE GOD'S ABUNDANT PROVISION OF GRACE AND OF THE GIFT OF RIGHTEOUSNESS REIGN IN LIFE THROUGH THE ONE MAN, JESUS CHRIST;

WHAT THIS PHRASE MEANS:?

> ## "..HE SHALL BE BOUND IN HEAVEN.......DO "IT WILL BE LOOSED IN HEAVEN?"

This tells us that anything that the believer **tie** and **untie** is based on what it has already been tied **"in heaven"** the same **Lord Jesus Christ**.

Then what is **what the Lord has already tied and that has given us power to tie again?** **Jesus Christ** teaches us as well:

MATTHEW 12, 29
OR AGAIN, HOW CAN ANYONE ENTER A STRONG MAN'S HOUSE AND CARRY OFF HIS POSSESSIONS UNLESS HE FIRST TIES UP THE STRONG MAN? THEN HE CAN ROB HIS HOUSE.

Jesus explains that you can control the demons and do to obey him because he already tied the strong man, Satan.

The fact that the demons obey you proves you that Satan has been tied.

Satan was already **"bound in heaven"** by the power of the heavens. The power of Satan is broken and the key has been given to us. We also have power over him. Amen!

The Greek word for tying is **deo** which means:

> - **TIE TIGHTLY.**
> - **AS WITH CHAINS.**
> - **LIKE WHEN AN ANIMAL IS TIED TO PREVENT IT MOVES.**

When Satan is tied up you do anything further. It loses its ability to act against us.

God shows us that these strong men were already defeated and tied by the power of the heavens.

In the book of Toby, there is a passage that reveals also that the angel Raphael (Brother Azarias) tied the devil.

Toby 8, 3 (one of the Deutero-canonical or Apocryphal books)

THE DEVIL, IN THE DELL'OLIO THAT SMOKE; FLED TO UPPER EGYPT, WHERE THE ANGEL TIED HIM.

1 JOHN 3, 8b
THE REASON FROM THE BEGINNING, THE REASON THE SON OF GOD APPEARED WAS TO DESTROY THE DEVIL'S WORK.

We have been given the **"keys of the Kingdom"**. There is power to rule over the forces of darkness. The battle was already won in heaven **and we are to attach what has already been bound in heaven on Earth.**

TESTIMONY:

One of the experiences that taught me the importance of tying, was as follows; a nurse asked me to pray for her 15-year-old daughter because of her daughter inappropriate behavior and her lack of respect toward her.

A Saturday she came in with her daughter and we started to talk, as soon as we ask for the presence of the Holy Spirit, an evil spirit started to manifest, I immediately started to say a prayer of liberation and in the name of Jesus I cast out the spirit, in my ignorance in those days, I had not sealed with the blood of Jesus Christ the people in my house, my properties and my animals at the time of the expulsion; our pet dog, named Pancho, all of the sudden started to run around in circles as if crazy, he must to leap some 25 to 30 laps and immediately fell dead; Unfortunately this spirit entered the dog until he died.

After this experience, I learned the importance of sealing the house and protect us with the blood of Jesus to all my loved ones, animals, including objects and things in the home and to TIE.

The curious thing is that I remembered then the herd of pigs which Jesus had allowed the demons that were in the Gadareno to enter them. Jesus in His infinite goodness allowed to enter the dog and not my children and the people who were in the house.

BIND THE STRONG MAN.

Tie the evil spirit saying, **LORD:**

- ➢ **YOUR WOUNDS.**
- ➢ **YOUR POWER.**
- ➢ **YOUR LOVE.**
- ➢ **YOUR BLOOD.**
- ➢ **YOUR CROSS.**

In the name of Jesus, I tie at this moment all evil spirit, come from where you may come:

- ➢ **THE AIR.**
- ➢ **THE WATER.**
- ➢ **THE FIRE.**
- ➢ **THELAND.**
- ➢ **THE ABYSS.**
- ➢ THE SKY.
- ➢ DISEASE.
- ➢ OF SORCERY.
- ➢ MUTE.
- ➢ DEAF.
- ➢ EVIL SPIRIT.

- BAD SPIRIT.
- MALIGNANT SPIRIT.
- SPIRIT OF FEAR.
- ETC. ETC.

Coming from where it comes, call it as you call, you are ordered in **THE NAME OF JESUS OF NAZARETH, THE CHRIST, THE SON OF GOD MADE FLESH:**

I BIND AND I COMMAND YOU:

- **DO NOT MOVE.**
- **NOT MAKE ANY DEMONSTRATION.**
- **OR DO ANY ACT THAT MILLSTONE.**
- **ANY SUCH ACT OF FUSS.**

IN THE NAME OF JESUS, I ORDER YOU TO BE TIED:

- **BY THE BLOOD OF CHRIST.**
- **BY THE HOLY NAME OF JESUS.**
- **BY HIS PRECIOUS SORES.**
- **BY HIS CROWN OF THORNS.**

WHICH I ORDERED TO BE TIED, TO STAY TIED.

TO BIND THE STRONG MAN YOU HAVE THE CONTROL OF THE RELEASE, AND IN THE NAME OF JESUS, BIND THE STRONG MAN.

BY TYING SEVERAL DEMONIC SPIRITS.

So that said:
I BIND what remains there.
I BIND out all the other spirits that may be there.

The spirit may be causing a stir or making **THE PERSON act** or do something like:

> - **A YAWN.**
> - **SHOUTING.**
> - **SHOCK.**
> - **DROP ON THE FLOOR.**
> - **ANY REPRESENTATION.**

I don't know how many spirits there are, but refuse or I realize that there is more than one and say:

I CAST OUT ALL OF THESE AND ORDER THEM TO STAY BOUND and then working with one single.

They are to be **ISOLATED**, I am sure that one realizes which is especially true of the three, four or five, that are **BOUNCING, ACTING, AND PERFORMING AN INTERACTION** (a spirit communication with another), what one is seeing is a **DEMONIC ACTOR.**

Then the **INDIVIDUAL BACKFIRES** and one sees another **DEMONIC ACTOR,** it may be another **SPIRIT,** one works with **ONE,** then **ANOTHER** and **THEN** with **THIS ONE.**

While one works with **ONE SPIRIT, ISOLATE** the others and **TIE** them, then always place **THE CROWN OF THORNS IN A CIRCLE,** and **ALL THE BLOOD FROM THE THORNS** around **THE SPIRIT** with which we will begin to work so that it's **SURROUNDED BY THE BLOOD OF JESUS AND CAN NOT MOVE AROUND.**

THE SPIRIT is TIED up and CAST OUT from the rest, so one is working ONLY ONE BY ONE, while the others are waiting their turn.

Once you take that decision:

> ➢ ONE MAINTAINS CONTROL OF THAT.
> ➢ NOT BEGIN TO EXAGGERATE HIS ROLE.
> ➢ NOT BEGINS TO DESTROY THE PERSON.
> ➢ AND ALWAYS HAVE CONTROL OF THE SITUATION.

Remember this; TIE IS THE KEY.

THE RELEASE of several spirits may take several hours TYING, without doing anything other than TO TIE, TIE AND TIE.

Then we ordered with power in the **Name of JESUS** and the **Spirit** will be cast out, **THIS RELEASE** could take **only 20 minutes** what otherwise would have taken a day, maybe more.

TESTIMONY:

During the liberation of a 15-year-old girl who came accompanied by a friend who belonged to the prayer group, when the liberation was taking place, the spirit had power and brought in another demon who entered in the friend that had accompanied her, immediately I placed a Crown of thorns around the person and tied the spirit and ordered it not to move.

This young girl with the spirit, had remained as a statue not moving only it swung a little, I went on with the release of the 15-year-old until the Lord in His immense mercy released it and immediately the spirit of the other girl was also released , then we did the inner healing and they forgave their parents. All honor and Glory to Our God.

THE ASPECTS OR FORMS OF THE SPIRITS

Once is **ISOLATED** to achieve **ASPECTS,** when a spirit begins to **ACT** on one, one knows that **THE ASPECTS** are **EXAGGERATING** the role.

Let us take as an example **THE SPIRIT OF ANGER:**

I have it and keep it there, the person said, **"I'M AFRAID" FEAR** is an **ASPECT** of the **ANGER.**

Then **THE SPIRIT** says:
YOU CAN NOT REMOVE ME! This is a spirit of **MOCKERY as ASPECT,**

He says:
I will not be cast out! You have **"CHALLENGE"** as **ASPECT,** everything **THE SPIRIT** says, reveals it's **ASPECTS = FORMS.**

One begins to **TIE,** but one does not begin to pursue another thing, one is now **ISOLATING** and **WORKING** with one thing until it is **GONE.**

Is **ISOLATED,** the **ASPECTS** are caught and if **THE SPIRIT** is exaggerating the role played, it's just a look that is manifested, the **ASPECT** is **TIED UP.**

When one has **BOUND** it by **LOVE OF GOD** becomes the **INNER HEALING, THE HEALING OF THE PERSON.**

ONE DOES NOT RELEASE SPIRIT, ONLY PEOPLE, HUMAN BEINGS THAT HAVE:

- ➤ **SHOCKS.**
- ➤ **FEARS.**
- ➤ **NEEDS.**
- ➤ **WOUNDS.**

They have been there for a long time, **THE PERSON** is **WOUNDED,** and we are going to touch these **WOUNDS,** let's heal that person through **THE DIVINE LOVE OF JESUS.**

Contrary to many **BOOKS** and **WRITERS** that I have read about **THE SPIRITUAL BATTLE,** we are not going to be caught **IN A BATTLE,** we are therefore making a **WORK OF HEALING** and as **THE HEALING** is done, **THE SPIRIT IS CAST OUT IN THE NAME OF JESUS.**

STEP 4
LEGAL RIGHT

NAME OF THE SPIRITS

I ORDER YOU IN THE NAME OF JESUS:

- ➤ **WHAT IS YOUR NAME?**
- ➤ **WHAT IS YOUR REAL NAME?**
- ➤ **WHAT IS YOUR FUNDAMENTAL NAME?**
- ➤ **WITH WHAT RIGHT OR AUTHORITY ARE YOU IN THAT BODY?**

The team must be attentive to **THE ASPECTS OF THE DEMON OR DEMONS.**

THERE ARE THREE KINDS OF SPIRITS NAMES.

It is **THE BASIC** name as **FEAR;** the same spirit may have **THREE LEVELS OF NAME OR THREE CLASSES OF NAME** one spirit.

It is possible to have three names, but not necessarily, some may have only one or two.

THE SPIRIT OF FEAR.

You may also have other names such as:

> ➢ **I CAN NOT.**
> ➢ **I WILL NOT.**

One asks **THE SPIRIT, "IN THE NAME OF JESUS, TELL ME YOUR NAME"** and responds:

> ➢ **"I CAN NOT."**

And then you say **"NO"** in **"THE NAME OF JESUS, tell me YOUR NAME",** his name is **"NOSENSE,"** the spirit will always give one name, if we ask in the **NAME OF JESUS.**

When one asks for the name to a **MOCKING SPIRIT,** it will always give its name and the name is:

> ➢ **"THAT."**

If one continue in prayer and continue asking it in the **NAME OF JESUS** his name you will recognize:

> ➢ **IS DIFFICULT TO TELL YOU.**
> ➢ **OR IT WILL TELL YOU, I CAN NOT SAY THAT.**

You just pay attention to what they are saying and **JOIN THE CAMMON WORDS** and that is **THE NAME** of the spirit.

THEY KNOW THE HAVE TO GIVE YOU THEIR NAMES THEY HAVE TO GIVE THEM; the spirits know more than one, they have to comply with a mandate in **THE NAME OF JESUS.**

MATTHEW 28, 18
THEN JESUS CAME TO THEM AND SAID,"ALL AUTHORITY IN HEAVEN AND EARTH HAS BEEN GIVEN TO ME."

JOHN 16, 33
I HAVE TOLD YOU THESE THINGS, SO THAT IN ME YOU MAY HAVE PEACE. IN THIS WORLD YOU WILL HAVE TROUBLE. BUT TAKE HEART! I HAVE OVERCOME THE WORLD.

LUKE 10, 19
HAVE GIVEN YOU AUTHORITY TO TRAMPLE ON SNAKES AND SCORPIONS AND TO OVERCOME ALL THE POWER OF THE ENEMY; NOTHING WILL HARM YOU.

They know that they have to obey and therefore have a **MIDDLE NAME.**

THE GREAT MISTAKE is that **5 THINGS** could happen at the same time, in other words one can have **6 or 7 SPIRITS** and all operate at the same time, bouncing off each other.

THE FIRST.

The first thing one wants to do into **THE RELEASE** is to find out with whom one is working.

LUKE 8, 30
JESUS ASKED HIM, "WHAT IS YOUR NAME?" "LEGION" HE REPLIED, BECAUSE MANY DEMONS HAD GONE INTO HIM.

THEIR NAME, we have **TO KNOW THE NAME OF THE SPIRITS** and against whom **WE ARE** working with.

IF THE SPIRIT IS TELLING THE TRUTH, **IT IS DONE.**

> - IF THE DEVIL HAS SAID WHAT RIGHT HE IS IN THAT BODY WITH, OR IF IT GIVES US THEIR NAME, THIS GIVE US CLUES TO MAKE THE INNER HEALING OF THE PERSON.

If malignant spirits are manifesting to the person we are liberating and we have tied them, and we already know why they are in that body or if we have received in words of knowledge, telling us the root of the problem, we order the spirit of the person to return to it's body and take possession of it, soul and spirit and proceed to do **THE INNER HEALING.**

TESTIMONY:

While visiting a Christian Church in Miami I heard the Pastor say "**I DON'T WASTE MY TIME IN ASKING THE SPIRIT WHAT IS HIS NAME" I JUST CAST THEM OUT!** I am sure that with authority and in the name of **JESUS,** the demons are out.

I respect that pastor very much I have read many books and several wonderful courses written by him and has a resurgent Church in Miami, United States.

The point is that we know that the demons are cast out, but if we don' find out the names of the spirits, we don't have any clue to make the inner healing and if there is no inner healing we know that the demon returns and returns with 7 more of the worst kind and will find their house swept and clean.

The issue is not simply the demons, is to heal the person from his wounds so that they do not return and have a fulfilling life in abundance as **CHRIST** promised us.

Be very careful about wanting to have conversations with **THE DEVIL** to find curiosities and things that we are not allowed, **DO NOT BE**

CURIOUS, do not let him take control, **we have the CONTROL**.

When you find **A NAME** you decide to work with one and not with six at a time, one will be working with **a single SPIRIT and begins to isolate it.**

It works with the principle of the INSULATION, ISULATE YOUR-SELF FROM THE POWERS:

> ➤ **THE AIR.**
> ➤ **THE WATER.**
> ➤ **THE FIRE.**
> ➤ **THE LAND.**

> ➤ FROM UNDER THE EARTH.
> ➤ NATURE.
> ➤ FROM THE DEPTHS.

And all those things are **ISOLATED** from the other spirits that can be conducting an **INTERACTION** in the room or place **THE RELEASE** being performed.

I have 5 or 6 things and say:

I TIE YOU ALL IN THE NAME OF JESUS, AND TO SPIRIT OF ANGER.. that somehow are looking at me , if it is exaggerating **HIS PERFORMANCE** (their manifestations) I tell: **I TIED YOU (TIE YOUR ACTION) ("WHATEVER IS DOING)** and ordered **"STAY THERE"**.

The person who is **MINISTERING** must remember that one is **IN CONTROL OF THE SITUATION**, must never allow **THE DEMON** to take **THE CONTROL** of the situation.

One has **THE CONTROL OF THE RELEASE IN THE NAME OF JESUS, AND TIE THE STRONG MAN.**

MATTHEW 12, 29
OR AGAIN, HOW CAN ANYONE ENTER A STRONG MAN'S HOUSE AND CARRY OFF HIS POSSESSIONS UNLESS HE FIRST TIES UP THE STRONG MAN? THEN HE CAN ROB HIS HOUSE.

NAME OF THE MAIN SPIRITS:

➢ SPIRIT UNCLEAN OR IMPURE, IT IS THE MOST FREQUENT:

  o MATTHEW 12, 43
  o MARKS 1, 23. 26. 27; 3,11; 5, 2. 8. 13; 7, 25
  o LUKE 4, 33.36; 6, 18; 8, 29; 9, 42; 11,24

➢ MUTE SPIRIT: MARK 9, 17
➢ DEAF AND DUMB SPIRIT: MARK 9, 25b
➢ BAD SPIRITS: LUCAS 7, 21; ACTS: 19, 12
➢ EVIL SPIRITS: LUKE 8, 2
➢ SPIRITS SEER; ACTS 16, 16
➢ SPIRITS OF EVIL: EPHESIANS 6, 12
➢ SEDYCUBG SPIRITS: 1 TIMOTY 4, 1

COMMON GROUPS OF DEMONS

1. **SORROW**
   LOAD
   MELANCHOLY
   OPPRESSION
   DISGUST
   SADNESS

2. **CHARGE**
   CRITICAL
   FINDING FAULTS
   TRIAL

3. **ADDICTION AND COMPULSION**
   ALCOHOL
   CAFFEINE
   DRUGS
   GLUTTONY
   DRUGS
   NICOTINE

4. **INVOLVEMENT**
   COMEDIAN
   FORGERY
   HYPOCRISY
   CLAIM
   DRAMA

5. **BITTERNESS**
   LACK OF FORGIVENESS
   HOMICIDE
   IRE
   GRIEF
   HATE
   RETALIATION

RESENTMENT
VIOLENCE

6. **SELF-ACCUSATION**
SELF-CONDEMNATION

7. **SELF-DECEPTION**
SELF SEDUCTION
MISTAKE
PRIDE

8. **JEALOUSY**
DISTRUST
SELFISHNESS
ENVY
SUSPECT

9. **GREED**
MATERIAL GREED
GREED
KLEPTOMANIA
DISCONTENT
NONCONFORMITY
THEFT
STINGINESS

10. **COMPETITION**
ARGUMENTATIVE
COMPULSIVE
EGO
PRIDE

11. **CONFUSION**
FRUSTRATION
INCOHERENCE
OBLIVION

12. CONTEST
ALTERCATION
CONTAINMENT
DISPLEASURE
FIGHT

13. CONTROL
DOMAIN
SORCERY
POSSESSION

14. GUILT
CONDEMNATION
BEWILDERMENT
INDIGNITY
USELESSNESS
SHAME

15. DEPRESSION
ANXIETY
DEFEATISM
DISCOURAGEMENT
MORALE
DESPAIR
DESPAIR
DESPOTICAL
INSOMNIA
MORBIDITY
DEATH
SUICIDE

16. DOUBT
SKEPTICISM
LACK OF FAITH
UNBELIEF

17. DISEASE
ANY ILLNESS OR DISEASE

18. MENTAL DISEASE
HALLUCINATIONS
DEMENTIA
DISPOSITION
SCHIZOPHRENIA
MADNESS
MANIA
PARANOIA
MENTAL RETARDATION
SENILITY

19. DECEPTION
DISTORTION
MISREPRESENTATION
HYPOCRISY
LIE
PRIDE
DEFAULT

20. ESCAPE
ALCOHOL
DRUGS
STOICISM
INDIFFERENCE
PASSIVITY
DROWSINESS

21. SPIRITUALISM
SPIRIT GUIDE
NECROMACIA
SESSION

22. SCHIZOPHRENIA
SCHIZOPHRENIA
MADNESS
DEMENTIA

23. FALSE CHARGE
FALSE COMPASSION
FALSE LIABILITY

24. FATIGUE
TIRED
DISCOURAGEMENT
DEFEAT
WEAR
SLOTH
SOPOR

25. GLUTTONY
SELF-PITY
SELF-ESTEEM
COMPULSION (TO EAT)
ESCAPE
FRUSTRATION
NERVOUSNESS
IDLENESS
RESENTMENT

26. INHERITANCE
EMOTIONAL
PHYSICAL
CURSE
MENTAL

27. HYPERACTIVITY
COMPULSION
ICONCERN
OPPRESSION

28. MENTAL IDOLATRY
EGO
INTELLECTUALIZATION
PRIDE
RATIONALIZATION
PRIDE
VANITY

29. IMPATIENCE
AGITATION
CRITICAL
FRUSTRATION
BIGOTRY
RESENTMENT

30. SEXUAL IMPURITY
ADULTERY
BESTIALITY
CONCUPISENCIA
DEPRAVASION
EXHIBITIONISM
LUSTFUL FANTASIES
FETISH
FORNICATION
FRIGIDITY
HOMOSEXUALITY
INCEST
LESBIAN
LUST
MASTURBATION
NYMPHOMANIA
PROSTITUTION
VIOLATION
VOYERISM

31. INDECISION
CONFUSION

DELAY
ESCAPE
INDIFFERENCE
OBLIVION
RETARDATION
DELAY
FEAR

32. INSECURITY
SELF-PITY
SCARY
INEPTITUDE
INFERIORITY
FAILURE
SOLEDAD
SHYNESS

33. CURSE
BLASPHEMY
JOKE
MOCKERY
SLANDER
GOSSIP
CRITICAL
CONTEMPT
MURMURING
REBATE

34. TIED MIND
CONFUSION
SPIRITS OF SPIRITUALISM
SPIRITS OF OCCULT
FEAR OF FAILURE
FEAR OF MAN

35. DEATH
HANDS AND LEGS PARALYZED
TURNING EYE

36. NERVOUSNESS
ANXIETY
HEADACHE
DECEPTION
WANDERING
EXCITATION
NERVOUS HABITS
CONCERN
INSOMNIA
TENSION

37. OCCULT
DIVINATION (ANY)
CHARMS
WRITING ANALYSIS
ASTROLOGY
WITCHCRAFT
LETTERS
SPELLS
CHARMS
SPELL
AUTOMATIC WRITING
FETISH
SPELLS
HYPNOSIS
HOROSCOPE
LEVITATION
WHITE OR BLACK MAGIC
EVIL EYE
PALM OF YOUR HAND
PENDULUM
PERCEPTION EXTRASENSORY
IRRIGATION

SPELLS
BOARD
TAROT
SNAIL AND THE LIKE

38. PRIDE
HAUGHTINESS
ARROGANCE
EGO
IMPORTANCE
RIGHTEOUSNESS
PRIDE
VANITY

39. PARANOIA
JEALOUSY
CONFRONTATION
DISTRUST
ENVY
PERSECUTION
SOSPECT
FEARS

40. PASSIVITY
DISTRACTED
NEGLECT
INDIFERENCE
LETHARGY
RETREAT

41. PENALTY
DISTRESS
SORROW
CRUELTY
CRYING
GRIEF
DADNESS

42. PERFECTION
CRITICAL
EGO
FRUSTRATION
INTOLERANCE
IRE
IRRITABILITY
PRIDE
VANITY

43. PERSECUTION
INJUSTICE
FEAR OF CHARGE
FEAR OF DOOM
FEAR OF JUDGEMENT
FEAR OF REPROBATION
SENSITIVITY

44. CONCERN
ANXIETY
APREHENTION
AFRAID
FEAR

45. DEFAULT
DISOBEDIENCE
FAILURE TO SUBMIT
OBSTINACY
STUBBORNNESS

46. REJECTION
SELF-REJECTION
LONELINESS
FEAR OF REJECTION

47. FALSE RELIGIONS
BUDDHISM
CONFUCIANISM
HINDUISM
ISLAM
SHINTO
TAOISM
OTHER

48. RELIGIOUS
ERRORS OF DOCTRINE
FORMALISM
LEGALISM
OBSESSION DOCTRINAL
RELIGIOSITY
RITUALISM
SEDUCTION AND DECEIT
FEAR OF GOD
FEAR OF LOSING THE SALVATION
FEAR OF HELL
FEAR LOSING LOVED ONES

49. RETALIATION
CRUELTY
DESTRUCTION
HURTFUL
HATE
GRUDGE
SADISM

50. WITHDRAWAL
GRUMBLE
REVERIE
FANTASY
UNREALITY
CLAIM

51. SECTS
BAHAISM
CHRISTIAN SCIENCE
GNOSTICISM
LODGES AND SOCIETIES
MORMONISM
ROSICRUCIANISM
SUBUD
THEOSOPHY
JEHOVAH'S WITNESS
UNITARIANISM
OTHER

52. SENSITIVITY
SELF- AWARENESS
COWARDICE
FEAR OF DISAPPROVAL
FEAR OF MAN

53. SUICIDE
SELF-PITY
DESPAIR
ESCAPISM
GRIEF
REJECTION
LONELINESS

54. FEAR OF AUTHORITY
DECEPTION
LIE

55. FEARS
PHOBIA (ALL KINDS)
HYSTERIA

STEP 5
INNER HEALING

The inner healing can be:

- ➢ **BEFORE THE LIBERATION.**
- ➢ **DURING THE LIBERATION.**
- ➢ **AFTER THE LIBERATION.**

We must remember that the release comes within the context of the integral healing of the person, body, soul and spirit.

Failure to do that gives place to what Jesus himself tells us in His word:

LUKE 11, 24 – 26
24
WHEN AN EVIL SPIRIT COMES OUT OF A MAN, IT GOES THROUGH ARID PLACES SEEKING REST AND DOES NOT FIN IT. THEN IT SAYS, I WILL RETURN TO THE HOUSE I LEFT.

25
WHEN IT ARIVES, IT FINDS THE HOUSE SWEPT CLEAN AND PUT IN ORDER.

26

*THEN IT GOES AND TAKES SEVEN OTHER SPIRITS MORE
WICKED THAN INSELF, AND THEY GO IN AND LIVE THERE
AND THE FINAL CONDITION OF THAT MAN IS WORSE THAN
THE FIRST.*

Proceed to heal the wounds of the person.

Dear reader you can acquire books on inner healing which illustrate on
how to proceed; if God permits it soon we will be publishing a book
about "Inner healing".

STEP 6
UNTIE,
UNTIE AND UNTIE

WHAT IS REFERRED TO UNLEASH?

Unleash is leave the captives free. Through the Ministry of healing, the liberation which is part of the Ministry of healing, the captives are freed from the chains of slavery that Satan has placed around them.

LUKE 4, 18
THE SPIRIT OF THE LORD IS ON ME, BECAUSE HE HAS ANOINTED ME TO PREACH GOOD NEWS TO THE POOR. HE HAS SENT ME TO PROCLAIM FREEDOM FOR THE PRISONERS ANS RECOVERY OF SIGHT FOR THE BLIND, TO RELEASE THE OPPRESSED,

This read it the book of Isaiah Jesus on the day of rest in the synagogue and said after winding the book:

> ➤ **TODAY THIS SCRIPTURE BEFORE YOU HAS BEEN MET.**

In Mark we find a passage from the word of Jesus to all who believe in him.

MARK 16, 15 – 18

15

HE SAID TO THEM, GO INTO ALL THE WORLD AND PREACH THE GOOD NEWS TO ALL CREATION.

16

WHOEVER BELIEVES AND IS BAPTIZED WILL BE SAVED, BUT WHOEVER DOES NOT BELIEVE WILL BE CONDEMNED.

17

AND THE SIGNS WILL ACCOMPANY THOSE WHO BELIEVE: IN MY NAME THEY WILL DRIVE OUT DEMONS; THEY WILL SPEAK IN NEW TONGUES;

18

THEY WILL PICK UP SNAKES WITH THEIR HANDS; AND WHEN THEY DRINK DEADLY POISON, IT WILL NOT HURT THEM AT ALL; THEY WILL PLACE THEIR HANDS ON SICK PEOPLE, AND THEY WILL GET WELL.

The mission that Jesus came to accomplish is the same as the last commandment which He gives us before He is received in heaven and sitting at the right hand of God.

When Jesus released the crippled woman in the day of rest, Saturday the following happened:

LUKE 13, 11 – 12

11

AND A WOMAN WAS THERE WHO HAD BEEN CRIPPLED BY A SPIRIT FOR EIGHTEEN YEARS. SHE WAS BENT OVER AND COULD NOT STRAIGHTEN UP AT ALL.

12

WHEN JESUS SAW HER, HE CALLED HER FORWARD AND SAID TO HER, "WOMAN, YOU ARE SET FREE FROM YOUR INFIRMITY."
When the main Rabbi of the synagogue was angry because this release had been made on the Sabbath day Jesus answered them:

LUKE 13, 15 – 16
15
THE LORD ANSWERED HIM, YOU HYPOCRITES! DOESN'T EACH OF YOU ON THE SBBATH UNTIE HIS OX OR DONKEY FROM THE STALL AND LEAD IT OUT TO GIVE IT WATER?

16
THEN SHOULD NOT THIS WOMAN, A DAUGHTER OF ABRA-HAM, WHOM SATAN HAS KEPT BOUND FOR EIGHTEEN LONG YEARS, BE SET FREE ON THE SABBATH DAY FROM WHAT BOUND HER?

The Word Greek to unleash in this text is **luo. Luo** is defined in the lexicon of Thayers as:

> ➤ **LEAVE LOOSE SOMETHING TIED OR TIGHT.**
> ➤ **LOOSEN OR UNLEASH SOMEONE CAPTIVE.**
> ➤ **RELEASED.**
> ➤ **GET OUT OF THE PRISON.**
> ➤ **PUT IN FREEDOM FROM SLAVERY OR DISEASE.**

The victory over the demonic spirits was already won by Jesus.

1 JOHN 4, 4
YOU, DEAR CHILDREN, ARE FROM GOD AND HAVE OVERCO-ME THEM, BECAUSE THE ONE WHO IS IN YOU IS GREATER THAN THE ONE WHO IS IN THE WORLD.

WHAT IS LIBERATION?

The Random House Dictionary has the following definition:

> TO RELEASE OR FREE: THEY WERE FREED FROM SLAVERY:

- o   EMANCIPATING.
- o   RELEASE.

Emancipate and releases are two synonymous with this definition.

Jesus instructs us and sends us to put it into practice. Therefore every Christian must have the capacity and the knowledge to cast out demons

UNTIE, UNTIE AND UNTIE.

All prayer must be in the name and power of Jesus Christ.

In your name we pray to The Father and resist the snares of the enemy

With His power we are freed from all **Oppression** and **Obsession.**

THE RELEASE OF OPPRESSION AND OBSESSION HAS TWO ASPECTS:

> PRAY TO THE FATHER IN THE NAME OF JESUS SC THAT YOU RELEASE THE PERSON FROM EVERY THING IT IS ENSLAVING.
>
> EXERCISE THE POWER OF CHRIST SAID: MARK 16 17 *"IN MY NAME THEY WILL DRIVE OUT DEMONS;"*

HERE WE MUST NOTE NOT IS A REQUEST BUT **AN ORDER** TO LET IN PEACE AND RELEASE THE PERSON.

THIS AUTHORITY IS EXERCISED IN THE NAME OF JESUS CHRIST.

Simple and effective prayer is found in St. Paul:

ACTS 16, 18
"IN THE NAME OF JESUS CRIST I COMMAND YOU TO COME OUT OF HER!"

To say the prayer of liberation it is necessary to first ask for the protection of the Lord.

> **BY LIVED EXPERIENCE WE MUST ALSO PROTECT:**

- **OUR FAMILIES.**
- **THINGS.**
- **ANIMALS.**
- **LINTELS AND DOOR AND PLACE WHERE IT MAKES LALIBERACION.**

PRAYER OF RELEASE.

"Lord Jesus",
You gave your life on the cross for my sins and rose from the dead.

I have been redeemed by your precious blood, and for your immense love you made me a servant, you know that I belong to you and don't live I but that you live in me.

Clean me Lord of all my faults and all my sins, consciously or unconsciously, I regret wholeheartedly for having offended you and ask mercy and your forgiveness and cleanse me of all my sins.

I waive any practice of occultism which has been made in the past and all the evil work and untie any tie in the name of Jesus.

I forgive everyone who have offended and hurt me, and I'm sorry if I've caused offense and hurt to my neighbor conscious or unconscious.

Clean me with your precious blood and if my sins are as scarlet cleans and whitens my Body, Soul and Spirit to be able to serve you as a useless servant I am and that I can meet with your commands.

Give me your holy spirit with power and authority, and in the name of "Jesus", to be able to release (name)...................... all evil spirit and the demon siege.

AMEN.

YOU SPIRIT:

- ➢ **DIABLICAL.**
- ➢ **EVIL.**
- ➢ **VAGRANT.**
- ➢ **JESTER.**
- ➢ **DEAR.**
- ➢ **MUTE.**
- ➢ **DEAF AND DUMB.**
- ➢ **SEX.**
- ➢ **SORCERY.**
- ➢ **ETC., ETC. (REMEMBER THAT THERE ARE SPIRITS FOR EACH THING).**

NAMED WHATEVER IS NAMED,
I ORDERED IN THE NAME OF JESUS:

- ➢ **FOR HIS BLOOD.**
- ➢ **BY HIS POWER.**
- ➢ **FOR HIS LOVE.**
- ➢ **BY HIS WOUNDS.**
- ➢ **BY HIS CROWN OF THORNS.**

> THAT COME OUT OF THIS BODY, CALL AS YOU
> CALL.

THIS CHILD (IF YOU HAVE THE NAME OF THE PERSON
SAYING IT) IS "SON OF GOD."

AND YOU DO NOT HAVE A PART IN IT; NOBODY EXCEPT
JESUS HAS RIGHT TO BE IN IT, BECAUSE IT IS JESUS
WHOM HE BELONGS.

IN THE NAME OF JESUS, I COMMAND AND ORDERED OUT
OF THIS BODY AT THIS TIME.

Depending on how the person reacts and if the evil spirit has gone, can
speak in tongues.

SPEAK AND PRAY IN TONGUES.

Many times we do not know to ask what should be and then the Holy
Spirit comes to our aid, and with their urge to speak in languages.

> SPEAKING IN TONGUES HOLDING THE HANDS OF
> THE PERSON THAT WE ARE MINISTERING TO.

ROMANS 8, 26 - 27
26
*IN THE SAME WAY, THE SPIRIT HELPS US IN OUR WEAK-
NESS. WE DO NOT KNOW WHAT WE OUGHT TO PRAY FOR,
BUT THE SPIRIT HIMSELF INTERCEDES FOR US WITH
GROANS THAT WORDS CANNOT EXPRESS.*

27
*AND HE WHO SEARCHES OUR HEARTS KNOWS THE MIND OF
THE SPIRIT, BECAUSE THE SPIRIT INTERCEDES FOR THE
SANINTS IN ACCORDANCE WITH GOD'S WILL.*

1 CORINTHIANS 14, 2
FOR ANYONE WHO SPEAKS IN A TONGUE DOES NOT SPEAK TO MEN BUT TO GOD. INDEED, NO ONE UNDERSTAND HIM; HE UNTERS MYSTRIES WITH HIS SPIRIT.

Note: Verse 27 says "who speaks in tongues"

Small Leroosse illustrated says among other things:

> ➤ TALK, PRAY, INTERCEDE.

TESTIMONY:

A testimony that caught my attention is that of Catholic priest Emilianc Tardif, in his book "JESUS LIVES TODAY".

He was celebrating a mass in a church he was invited to with his niece and a friend in Los Angeles. It reads as follows:

After reading the Gospel in French, I wanted to comment on it, bu something curious happened: I felt my cheek went numb and I started tc speak in a language I didn't understand. It was not neither French, no English, nor Spanish.

When I finished talking, I exclaimed shocked:

> ➤ DON'T TELL ME THAT I HAD JUST RECEIVED THE GIFT OF TONGUES....
> ➤ THAT IS WHAT YOU HAVE ALREADY RECEIVEI RESPONDED MY NIECE. YOU WERE SPEAKING II TONGUES.

So much that I had made fun about the gift of tongues and the Lord gave it to me at the time that I was to preach. So I discovered this beautiful gift of the Lord.

TESTIMONY:

Something very similar happened to me in a charismatic ladies prayer group to which I was invited; they were going to pray for my daughter who was very ill with a tumor in her brain.

They were praying and suddenly almost all the people started to pray in tongues and I said to myself: "Look at this group of women suffering from lack of men, who have nothing to do". After few years I asked God's forgiveness for such a thought.

We are ignorant and we have little experience about this wonderful gift that God gives us to communicate with Him and to ask what is convenient to us.

TESTIMONY:

At a meeting at my home in Ocala Florida, United States we invited a group of people to pray, I then asked if any of them could speak in tongues to do so, we were praying for some sick people. I noted that only a group spoke in tongues, while the great majority of the others didn't. I asked them if they have not received the gift of speaking in tongues and they answered they didn't, I asked if they would like to have it, and they said yes, we prayed to the Lord to endow these people with that gift and after a short while most of them started to speak in tongues. After thanking the Lord for such wonderful gift, they all left. A week later we were invited to their group and to our unpleasant surprise they told us that their spiritual director has forbidden them from praying in tongues.

During the meeting, the group expressed that it was not necessary to pray in tongues because they didn't understand what it was said, unless they would have someone who interpreted it that was said.

This seemed very well known because it comes from the pastors or people who are not charismatic or that do not have the gift of tongues and are based on the following:

1 CORINTHIANS 14, 13 – 19

13

FOR THIS REASON ANYONE WHO SPEAKS IN A TONGUE SHOULD PRAY THAT HE MAY INTERPRET WHAT HE SAYS.

14

FOR IF PRAY IN A TONGUE, MY SPIRIT PRAYS, BUT MY MIND IS UNFRUITFUL.

15

SO WHAT SHALL I DO? I WILL PRAY WITH MY SPIRIT, BUT I WILL ALSO PRAY WITH MY MIND; I WILL SING WITH MY SPIRIT, BUT I WILL ALSO SING WITH MY MIND.

16

IF YOU ARE PRAISING GOD WITH YOUR SPIRIT, HOW CAN ONE WHO FINDS HIMSELF AMONG THOSE WHO DO NOT UNDERSTAND SAY "AMEN" TO YOUR THANKGIVING, SINCE HE DOES NOT KNOW WHAT YOU ARE SAYING?

17

YOU MAY BE GIVING THANKS WELL ENOUGH, BUT THE OTHER MAN IS NOT EDIFIED.

18

I THANK GOD THAT I SPEAK IN TONGUES MORE THAN ALL OF YOU.

19

BUT IN THE CHURCH I WOULD RATHER SPEAK FIVE INTE-LLIGIBLE WORDS TO INSTRUCT OTHERS THAN TEN THOU-SAND WORDS IN A TONGUE.

Note: Verse 16 says "if I pray and my spirit prays."

Small Lerousse illustrated says among other things:

➢ **PRAYER**: PRAYER, PRAY MENTALLY.

We will make a small recount of this:

FIRST.
As we read in Romans 8, 26-27 and 1 Corinthians 14, 2, who spoke in languages, speaks to God and it is the Holy Spirit that comes to our aid to ask what should be.

SECOND.
St. Paul speaks that he preferred in the Church not to pray in tongues, but we are talking here about a charismatic prayer group where they were supposed to be Charismatic.

THIRD.
There is confusion in the following:

IN SPEAKING IN TONGUES AND PRAY IN TONGUES:

To pray in tongues you need one who interpreted.

Speaking in tongues is the Holy Spirit who comes to you to ask what is good.

TESTIMONIALS.

FIRST TESTIMONY:

I have had the experience of being present and read testimonials speak and pray in tongues.

In one of those testimonials that I read, tells about Father Tardif who, while in another country, preaching the Gospel, utter a few words, which he didn't understand absolutely nothing, despite the fact that he spoke English, French and Spanish, a person approached him and I asked him "Do you know what you just said?" and humbly he replied with a NO...The person then said: "You gave a message in Russian."

SECOND TESTIMONY:

I have seen and heard several people who pray, receiving messages and sing in languages completely unknown. But I can give testimony that when these happen even when some people do not understand, they are filled with the Holy Spirit.

THIRD TESTIMONY:

An unforgettable experience happened while in a charismatic retreat in Santo Domingo school, we received more than 2,500 people at the same time driven by the Holy Spirit talking in tongues, it was wonderful. That place trembled and we were all filled with the Holy Spirit.

Other experiences of speaking in tongues have been testimonies of physical healings, inner healing and above all, releases.

When we speak in tongues while we are ministering to a person and impose hands and we hear moans ineffable, if the person or persons are receptive and open to the Holy Spirit, almost all have a rest in the spirit, God only knows what happens in that moment with these people, I have seen physical healings and inner healings, releases especially change of life that operates in every one of those people.

Speaking in tongues, comes from the Greek words **"Glossa"** meaning language or dialect and the **"Laleo"** word that means talk or emit sound.

These combined words **"Glossolalia"** is what is described in the Greek text as **"Speaking in tongues"**.

In the book Rev. of Robert DeGrandis with the title The Gift of languages" makes clear the issue:

There is the following:

> ➤ **THE GIFT OF TONGUES OF PRAYER.**
> ➤ **THE GIFT OF TONGUES MINISTERIAL.**

THE GIFT OF TONGUES OF PRAYER.

It is a permanent gift in which we are built. The spirit prays in us according to Romans 8, 26.

The main purpose of prayer in tongues is praising God, can also be in a song of praise.

The Gift of languages, while praise God has as goal to allow the interpretation or proclaim God's message;

Praying in tongues is a permanent gift.

331

Example:
Today I prayed in tongues in the Church.

Example:
When I arrived at the Conference, the spirit touched me and I spoke in tongues. Then someone gave the interpretation.

THE GIFT OF TONGUES MINISTERIAL

It really is **"SPEAKING"** in tongues.
When it will Minister to the community through a anointed expression, this is speaking in tongues.
Speaking in tongues in a transitional gift that is used only when anointing.

CONCLUSION.

We have seen different forms of this gift:

> ➤ SPEAKING IN OTHER LANGUAGES.
> ➤ RECEIVE A MESSAGE IN TONGUES AND INTER-
>   PRETATION.
> ➤ SONGS IN TONGUES.
> ➤ SOUNDS IN TONGUES.
> ➤ PRAYER AND SUPPLICATION IN TONGUES.

We want to conclude this point with several quotes from the word of God, **"THE BIBLE."**

1 CORINTHIANS 4, 20
FOR THE KINGDOM OF GOD IS NOT A MATTER OF TALK BUT OF POWER.

1 CORINTHIANS 2, 14
THE MAN WITHOUT THE SPIRIT DOES NOT ACCEPT THE THINGS THAT COME FROM THE SPIRIT OF GOD, FOR THE ARE FOOLISHNESS TO HIM, AND HE CANNOT UNDERSTAND THEM, BECAUSE THEY ARE SPIRITUALLY DISCERNED.

1 CORINTHIANS 2, 5
SO THAT YOUR FAITH MIGHT NOT REST ON MEN'S WISDOM, BUT ON GOD'S POWER.

1 THESSALONIANS 5, 19
DO NOT PUT OUT THE SPIRIT'S FIRE;

1 THESSALONIANS 4, 8
THEREFORE, HE WHO REJECTS THIS INSTRUCTION DOES NOT REJECT MAN BUT GOD, WHO GIVES YOU HIS HOLY SPIRIT.
SORT THE DEMONS DO NOT RETURN.

Many times we cast out in the name of Jesus the evil spirit, because in the name of Jesus, they have to leave, but we will not ban their return forgetting that word of the Gospel:

MATTHEW 12, 43 – 45
43
WHEN AN EVIL SPIRIT COMES OUT OF A MAN, IT GOES THROUGH ARID PLACES SEEKING REST AND DOES NOT FIND IT.

44
THEN IT SAYS, I WILL RETURN TO THE HOUSE I LEFT. WHEN IT ARRIVES, IT FINDS THE HOUSE UNOCCUPIED, SWEEPT CLEAN AND PUT IN ORDER.

45
THEN IT GOES AND TAKES WITH IT SEVEN OTHER SPIRITS MORE WICKED THAN ITSELF, AND THEY GO IN AND LIVE THERE. AND THE FINAL CONDITION OF THAT MAN IS WORSE THAN THE FIRST. THAT IS HOW IT WILL BE WITH THIS WICKED GENERATION.

PROCEED TO:

➤ SEAL THE PERSON SO THAT THOSE SPIRITS WILL NOT RETURN.

➤ SEND THE EVIL SPIRITS AT THE FEET OF JESUS FOR HIM TO DISPOSE OF THEM.

It is necessary to give the order to:

MARK 9, 25
"AND NEVER ENTER HIM AGAIN". OTHER TRANSLATIONS SAY: OUT OF, AND DO NOT ENTER MORE IN HIM.

We must learn from past mistakes and experiences:

➤ NOT ENOUGH GET THE SPIRIT BUT IT IS NECESSARY TO PROHIBIT THE RETURN (Mk 9, 25) AND SEND IT TO THE FOOT OF THE CROSS AND CHRIST TO DISPOSE OF THEM.

➤ THIS PRAYER IS CONVENIENT FOR SMALL COMMUNITARY GATHERINGS BUT NOT IN LARGE GROUPS; SOMEWHERE WHERE IS PRIVATE, AND THERE MUST NOT BE CHILDREN PRESENT.

➤ BY THE BLOOD OF CHRIST AND HIS PRECIOUS WOUNDS WE TAKE AUTHORITY OVER ALL TIE AND WE UNTIED THEM IN THE NAME OF JESUS.

It is of utmost importance to make the person's inner healing so the demons will not return, if the person is keeping the doors open the demons will returned:

This is why we must:

➤ HEAL THE WOUNDS THAT WERE THE ROOT OF THE PROBLEM.

- ➢ IT IS NECESSARY TO TURN ON THE LIGHT OF CHRIST THRU (BAPTISM IN THE HOLY SPIRIT).
- ➢ PROVIDE MONITORING AND GROWTH IN JESUS CHRIST ANNOUNCING HIS KINGDOM AND EVANGELIZING TO THE PERSON.
- ➢ IF IT IS POSSIBLE TO INTEGRATE IT TO A GROUP IN THE CHURCH.

LUKE 11, 22
BUT WHEN SOMEONE STRONGER ATTACKS AND OVERPOWERS HIM, HE TAKES AWAY THE ARMOR IN WHICH THE MAN TRUSTED AND DIVIDES UP THE SPOILS.

JOHN 1, 5
THE LIGHT SHINES IN THE DARKNESS, BUT THE DARKNESS HAS NOT UNDERSTOOD IT.

Remove spirits by removing them makes no sense; I would say that it is worse because we expose the person to the evil that will come back 7 times worse.

Jesus sent his Apostles first not to expel demons but **ANNOUNCE HIS KINGDOM.** The expulsion of demons is a consequence of evangelization.

MATTHEW 10, 7 – 8
7
AS YOU GO, PREACH THIS MESSAGE: THE KINGDOM OF HEAVEN IS NEAR.

8
HEAL THE SICK, RAISE THE DEAD, CLEANSE THOSE WHO HAVE LEPROSY, DRIVE OUT DEMONS. FREELY YO HAVE RECEIVED, FREELY GIVE.

STEP 7
TEST IF
THE SPIRIT LEFT

> ➤ MAKE THE PERSON ACKNOWLEDGE AND CONFESS THAT JESUS CAME IN THE FLESH, AND WAS BORN FROM THE HOLY SPIRIT AND MARY.

1 JOHN 4, 1 - 3

1
DEAR FRIENDS, DO NOT BELIEVE EVERY SPIRIT, BUT TEST THE SPIRITS TO KNOW WHETHER THEY ARE FROM GOD, BE CAUSE MANY FALSE PROPHETS HAVE GONE OUT INTO THE WORLD.

2
THIS IS HOW YOU CAN RECOGNIZE THE SPIRIT OF GOD EVERY SPIRIT THAT ACKNOWLEDGES THAT JESUS CHRIST HAS COME IN THE FLESH IS FROM GOD,

3
*BUT EVERY SPIRIT THAT DOES NOT ACKNOWLEDGE JESUS
IS NOT FROM GOD. THIS IS THE SPIRIT OF THE ANTICHRIST,
WHICH YOU HAVE HEARD IS COMING AND EVEN NOW IS
ALREADY IN THE WORLD.*

When we ask the person we are liberating to say that Jesus came in the
flesh; The evil spirit can't pronounce or recognize that Jesus came in
flesh, this gives us a safe sample that the person has been released or
not, if the person can say that Jesus is the son of Mary and came in flesh,
this person is released, but if not, the evil spirit will re-appeared again.

If you know the person has been freed, then thank God; His beloved son,
and the Holy Spirit.

STEP 8
BAPTISM IN
THE HOLY SPIRIT

AFTER ORDERING THE SPIRIT OUT OF THAT BODY, AND
YOU ARE SURE THAT THE SPIRIT IS OUT, IMPOSE THE
HANDS THAT ARE THE HANDS OF JESUS, GOD AND THE
SPIRIT ON THE PERSON.

> ➤ FEEL HOW THE HOLY SPIRIT FLOWS INTO US AND
> PASSES TO THE PERSON WE HAVE RELEASED IN
> THE NAME OF JESUS.

PUT YOUR HANDS IN THEIR HANDS OR ON THEIR HEAD:

NOTE:
YOU MUST HAVE DONE THE INNER HEALING.
We must be careful not to impose hands ahead of time, we must rely on
the impulse of the Holy Spirit, it may be before, in the middle or after
the release, we are sealed with the blood of Christ and the coat of arm
and the armor of God.

But it is advisable to do so at the end, unless the Holy Spirit tell us otherwise.

1 TIMOTHY 5, 22
DO NOT BE HASTY IN THE LAYING ON OF HANDS, AND DO NOT SHARE IN THE SINS OF OTHERS. KEEP YOURSELF PURE.

Where is the light of Christ, there will not be darkness, many who minister impose hands during the liberation, I repeat it is important that we feel when is the right time indicated by the Holy Spirit for discernment of spirit.

WHAT HAPPENS IF THE EVIL SPIRIT IS STILL IN THE PERSON?

> ➢ **IF THE SPIRIT DOES NOT WANT TO LEAVE, ASK IT WHO SENT YOU? IN THE NAME OF JESUS HAS TO RESPOND.**

> ➢ **WHAT'S YOUR NAME? TELL ME YOUR REAL NAME IN THE NAME OF JESUS. (PERHAPS THE NAME IT WAS GIVEN IN THE BEGINNING IS NOT THEIR REAL NAME).**

IF THE SPIRIT IS TELLING THE TRUTH, IT IS DEFEATED.

USUALLY IT WILL GIVE A NAME THAT IS NOT REAL OR A DECEIVING NAME.

REMEMBER THAT SATAN IS THE FATHER OF LIES, IT WILL ALWAYS LIE. BUT IN THE NAME OF JESUS HAVE TO SAY HIS NAME.

YOU WILL SAY:

YOU'RE THE DEVIL COME OUT OF THAT PERSON IN THE NAME OF JESUS; YOU KNOW YOU HAVE TO LEAVE.

THE DEVIL CAN NOT SAY THE TRUTH BECAUSE IS THE FATHER OF LIES.

TOGETHER WE PRAISE AND THANK GOD.

> GIVE PRAISE AND THANKS TO GOD.

LUKE 17, 15 – 18
15
ONE OF THEM, WHEN HE SAW HE WAS HEALED, CAME BACK, PRAISING GOD IN A LOUD VOICE,

16
HE THREW HIMSELF AT JESUS FEET AND THANKED HIM – AND HE WAS A SAMARITAN.

17
JESUS ASKED, WERE NOT ALL TEN CLEANSED? WHERE ARE THE OTHER NINE?

Jesus loves you praise and we give thanks for favors received, many times we forget to say thank you Lord by so much love.

EVEN IF YOU FEEL THAT THE SPIRIT HAS NOT LEFT:

> BAPTIZE THE PERSON IN THE HOLY SPIRIT.

> ALTHOUGH THE DEVIL IS MANIFESTING HIMSELF OR IS POSSESSED, STILL BAPTIZE THE PERSON:

WHEN THE LIGHT SHINES, THE DARKNESS LEAVES.

PRAYER TO THE HOLY SPIRIT:

COME HOLY SPIRIT,
COME SPIRIT OF GOD,
MAKE YOUR LIGHT SCARE AWAY ALL DARKNESS,
GIVE TO (Name)... PEACE, JOY AND
TRANQUILITY.

COME HOLY SPIRIT,
BAPTIZE THIS PERSON AND FILL HIM IN YOUR LOVE.

STEP 9
THE BLOCK

IF THE SPIRIT is not manifesting, **WHY IS THAT?**:

- ➤ **I KNOW IS THERE.**
- ➤ **IS NOT MANIFESTING.**
- ➤ **WHY?**

PRAY and ask the **LORD** to help you through his **HOLY SPIRIT.**

The Lord will GUIDE YOU. There are 5 points that will help:

1. **WE HAVE THE WRONG NAME.**

As we know they lie, lie to you until you **TIE THEIR LIES OF THEIR TRICKS.**

If you have not **BOUND** yet their tricks, they can lie; once one **TI THEIR TRICKS AND LIES, THEY ARE DEFEATED.**

THERE ARE THREE THINGS:

- ➤ **TRICKS.**
- ➤ **THE LIES.**
- ➤ **THE INHERITANCE.**

Those above could be aspects. You can say to them:

- ➤ **I TIE YOUR LIES.**
- ➤ **I TIE YOUR DISAPPOINTMENT.**
- ➤ **I TIE YOUR TRICKS.**

2. TAKING POWER.

By gaining power from a power source.

WHAT IS AN ENERGY SOURCE?:

- ➤ **ANY OBJECT OF OCCULT.**
- ➤ **THERE IS A BEWITCHED OBJECT IN THE ROOM.**
- ➤ **A BOOK ABOUT WITCHCRAFT.**
- ➤ **ANY KIND OF OBJECT FROM WHICH POWER FLOWS.**

Many of us have discovered these objects and know that we need to get rid of them:

- ➤ **BURN THE BOOKS OF WITCHCRAFT.**
- ➤ **GET RID OF HORNS/CHARMS THAT PEOPLE WEAR AROUND THEIR NECK OR ANY OTHER OBJECT.**
- ➤ **HOROSCOPES.**
- ➤ **HEAVY METAL MUSIC, ROCK, ETC.**

These objects are like a source of energy that gives power or they can be used as a communication tool.

343

TIE COMMUNICATION again, perhaps there is another ASPECT, or in another room, another person or team **spirit**.

THIS ISTAKING POWER FROM another **spirit** one has **TO TIE IT AGAIN.**

3. IS STUCK OR GLUED.

That means he is SUSPENDED from something.

BUT WHAT?

INNER HEALING IS NEEDED, it is possible that one has not made **ADEQUATE INNER HEALING** and it has to be more **PROFOUND**.

Yet the spirit is still **IN THE FEAR** of a person, the person has not healed from the **FEAR**.

Perhaps the person does not want to get rid **OF THE FEAR**, or **DO NOT WANT TO FORGIVE**, we think that, many times the person does not want to get rid of **THE FEAR**.

REMEMBER.
No one can be released unless the person so desires.

4. SPIRIT OF LUST.

How does the person being liberated reacts to a spirit of lust?

WHAT HAPPENS IF IS RID OF THAT?

Sometimes they say, where am I if that spirit leaves? **"Yes"** I wanted it to be gone from me, but the reality is that it was very funny.

The truth is that the person has not yet decided and **the spirit knows what is THE OPTION OF THE PERSON** and sometimes one has to do more work in the decision.

Many times the **DESIRE**; or perhaps it is a **SIN THAT HAS NOT BEEN CONFESSED.**

THE AREA OF DARKNESS:

> ➤ **IF THERE ARE DARKNESS IT BELONGS TO THE DARKNESS.**
> ➤ **THAT IS THEIR TERRITORY.**
> ➤ **THAT IS WHERE IT SHOULD BE.**
> ➤ **WHERE SHOULD BELONG AND HAS RIGHT TO BE IN THE DARKNESS.**

So if there is darkness in **THE PERSON** as long as **A SIN HAS NOT BEEN CONFESSED,** if the spirit is in that same **AREA, there** is where it has to be.

One needs to verify:

> ➤ **IF TAKING POWER.**
> ➤ **SO WE ARE GIVING POWER.**
> ➤ **IF IS ATTACHED TO SOMETHING.**

Perhaps we need to TIE IT MORE.

Many times they are doing:

> ➤ **PLAYING WITH US.**
> ➤ **CHALLENGING US.**
> ➤ **DISOBEYING US.**

Other times this kind comes combined:

- ➤ CHALLENGE.
- ➤ DISOBEDIENCE.
- ➤ REBELLION.
- ➤ NEGATIVISM.

5. THE SPIRITS MAY BE DEAF AND MUTE.

THEY COULD BE **DEAF**.
YOU HAVE TO TIE IT'S DEAFNESS OR HIS MUTENESS

MARK 9, 25
WHEN JESUS SAW THAT A CROWD WAS RUNNING TO THE SCENE, HE REBUKED THE EVIL SPIRIT. "YOU DEAF AND MUTE SPIRIT," HE SAID, "I COMMAND YOU, COME OUT OF HIM AND NEVER ENTER HIM AGAIN."

MATTHEW 9, 32
WHILE THEY WERE GOING OUT, A MAN WHO WAS DEMON-POSSESSED AND COULD NOT TALK WAS BROUGHT TO JESUS.

SPIRIT WITH MENTAL RETARDATION.

 ASPECT of **MENTAL RETARDATION**, the person began to **ACT** as a **MENTALLY RETARDED** and the spirit said:

"I DO NOT UNDERSTAND WHAT YOU ARE SAYING; and remained saying the same; you have to tie his mental retardation, and says: YOU HAVE TO **UNDERSTAND WHAT I SAY, AND LEAVE**.

THE LABEL.

It may be that one is working with **A LABEL** present, perhaps there was **A DEDICATION** that you don't know; many people are not aware that they have been dedicated and if the **DEDICATION** was made before they were born.

TESTIMONY:

The servant of God with whom I worked on release told me that on one occasion they brought to him a priest with spiritual problems, and he told me that during a mass, evil spirits manifested thru him, after an investigation it was discovered that their parents had dedicated him to Satan before birth.

Over the years Satan which was legally entitled for the dedication came to find its prey.

Thanks to God and his beloved Son, such dedication was broken and the priest was free of those spirits.

TESTIMONY:

I read the following in a book:

In Florida, a group worked in something very serious and bad that it happened to a person.

THE PERSON HAD A CHANGE OF PERSONALITY VERY REMARKABLE, TORMENTS OF FEAR AND ANXIETY this person was on the verge of a nervous breakdown.

Summarizing all in one thing:
THE FACT THAT SHE HAD ATTENDED A SPIRITUALIST SESSION;

She was attending a healing service for the sick and there were two rows of people to be prayed for. All of the sudden an evil spirit started to manifest on her, we approached her and one of the persons on the team received a word of knowledge :

"SHE WAS DEDICATED."

We asked her parents if she had been dedicated and they denied it, meanwhile the young woman was moving violently on the ground.

Well, where was **THE DEDICATION?**

When she attended **THE SPIRITUALIST SESSION**, the woman who led **THE MEETING**, was wearing a ring in the form of a serpent and in the mouth had a ruby and before the session started the woman said to her:" I feel that you should take the ring and wear it" that ring was **THE MARK OF SATAN** and thru the taking and wearing of that ring, the young woman was being dedicated to **SATAN,** and the woman who ran the spiritualist session, **WAS A TRUE WITCH.** The evil spirits then entered the young woman and she was marked as **THE PERSON WHO WOULD BE DESTROYED.**

THE FIRST THING I DO IS: BREAK THE DEDICATION

It was something that was done against her will or if she knew, she was disobedient by going to a **SPIRITUAL SESSION**, she was out of God's protection and was riding in **THE TRAIN OF SATAN**, from the beginning she did wrong, but worse, she was **MARKED**.

SHE WAS DEDICATED, therefore they **INVOKED THE SPIRITS** or whatever is done in the spirits sessions, I know that they **INVOKED THE SPIRITS, AND THEY ENTERED IN THE YOUNG WO-MAN.**

YOU WILL SEE, THE SORCERERS AND WITCHES have to **DESTROY X** a number of people a year and give account to **SATAN** about this before the end of the year.

THEY NEED MORE PRAYER AND FASTING

It could be that this kind of spirit needs more prayer and fasting to be able to be expelled.

> ➢ **IT SHOULD BE A CHAIN OF PRAYER.**
> ➢ **FASTS AND PREPARE WELL FOR THE RELEASE.**

MARK 9, 29
HE REPLIED, "THIS KIND CAN COME OUT ONLY BY PRAYER AND FASTING."

STEP 10
RECOMMENDATION AND MONITORING

IMPORTANT POINTS:

➢ THE PERSON HAS TO WANT TO BE RELEASED OTHERWISE NO ONE WILL BE ABLE TO RELEASE IT.

➢ IF THERE IS NOT AN INNER HEALING THE SPIRITS CAN RETURN WITH 7 OF THE WORST KIND SO MUST SEAL THE PERSON SO SPIRITS CAN NOT RETURN.

➢ THERE HAS TO BE A TRUE REPENTANCE AND CONVERSION.

➢ WE MUST FOLLOW THIS PERSON UP TO BE KEPT IN FAITH AND AWAY FROM SIN.

➢ IT IS ADVISABLE TO ANOINT WITH OIL.
   o OIL.
   o HOLY WATER

➢ IF IT IS POSSIBLE TO RECEIVE THE HOLY COMMUNION , READ THE WORD OF GOD (THE BIBLE)

➢ ATTEND CHURCH AND A PRAYER GROUP.

HOME RELEASE

Many times when we acquired items for our home we don't realize, whether deliberately or by lack of knowledge that what we have acquired can have influences that gives the devil the legal right to affect our home, polluting the atmosphere, our lives and our children's.

When we visit the home of an acquaintance or a friend, many times we have this estrange feeling and may say **"This house feels heave"**, referring to the atmosphere of that home that breathes and feels heavy, sometimes we say **"It feels so good to be here",** and we don't want to leave.

We ourselves realize the difference between a home and another.

In the home:

> ➤ CONSTANT FIGHTING.
> ➤ DO NOT READ THE BIBLE.
> ➤ DO NOT PRAY.
> ➤ NOT PRAISE GOD.
> ➤ DO NOT PLAY SONGS WITH RELIGIOUS THEMES.
> ➤ NO HARMONY.

It is logical that they will have a heavy or loaded atmosphere.

Some of us have the custom or habit, either by inheritance or by our sinful nature to keep objects in our homes for "good luck" or as shelter and protection for home or for ourselves, these objects are:

> **PROTECTION.**

- CERTAIN HERBS.
- ALOE VERA INTO TRIANGLES ON IN EACH COR-NER OF THE HOME.
- A GARLIC BRAIDS.
- CLEAN THE HOUSE WITH LEMON WATER CUT DIAGONALLY.
- AN OPEN BIBLE.
- IN THE CAR A ROSARY HANGING FROM THE MIRROR OR OTHER FETISHES OR AMULETS.
- A BROOM ABOVE THE DOOR, ETC.

> **GOOD LUCK.**

- A HORSESHOE ABOVE THE MAIN DOOR.
- ALOE VERA ON THE MAIN DOOR.
- AN ELEPHANT WITH THE BACK FACING THE DOOR.
- A GLASS OF WATER WITH CAMPHOR, A FEW CENTS.
- A CUP WITH A SUNFLOWER.
- A BALLOT OF TWO DOLLARS OR A COIN OF STONE.
- SESAME SEEDS OR COINS ON THE FLOOR OF THE HOUSE, ETC.

> SUPERSTITION.

- USE A CHARM OR AMULET.
- DO NOT GO UNDER A LADDER.
- DO NOT GO OUT ON FRIDAY THE 13TH.
- RETURN TO YOUR HOUSE IF YOU SEE A BLACK CAT.
- USE A CHARM, ETC.

When we acquire possessions, these may be contaminated and can come to take various forms:

> **STATUES OF FOREIGN GODS.**
> **CHARMS "MAGIC".**
> **SOUVENIRS OF PAST SINS.**
> **ROCK OR HEAVY METAL MUSIC.**
> **MAGAZINES CONTAINING HOROSCOPES.**
> **BOOK OF MAGIC OR OCCULT, ETC.**
> **PAINTINGS OF PAINTERS INSPIRED BY THE DEVIL OR PAINTING WHILE DRUGGED.**

God tells us in his Holy Word that He does not want us to own impure objects, because they invite demons to do disaster in our homes, in our lives and in our hearts.

Christ wants us to live as in St. Paul says:

1 CORINTHIANS 10, 20
"I DO NOT WANT YOU TO BE PARTICIPANTS WITH DEMONS."

We must know that the cross and the resurrection of Jesus Christ have established our authority over demons.

As Jesus has given us his authority, we must live on the offensive.

MATTHEW 10, 1
HE CALLED HIS TWELVE DISCIPLES TO HIM AND GAVE THEM AUTHORITY TO DRIVE OUT EVIL SPIRITS AND TO HEAL EVERY DISEASE AND SICKNESS.

LUKE 19, 10
FOR THE SON OF MAN CAME TO SEEK AND TO SAVE WHAT WAS LOST.

EPHESIANS 6, 10
FINALLY, BE STRONG IN THE LORD AND IN HIS MIGHTY POWER.

For these reasons we should never fear the devil and his demons.

Jesus gave the example when taught us to pray:

MATTHEW 6, 13
AND LEAD US NOT INTO TEMPTATION, BUT DELIVER US FROM THE EVIL ONE.

The release of the Lord is always there for those who choose to walk in the path of righteousness.

We need to clean the atmosphere of our homes and our hearts.

This cleaning often involves the removal of certain physical possessions. What are they?

This book gives us guidelines to teach us to walk with prudence and to exercise spiritual discernment.

1 CORINTHIANS 2, 15
THE SPIRITUAL MAN MAKES JUDGMENTS ABOUT ALL THINGS, BUT HE HIMSELF IS NOT SUBJECT TO ANY MAN'S JUDGMENT:

EPHESIANS 5, 15
BE VERY CAREFUL, THEN, HOW YOU LIVE NOT AS UNWISE BUT AS WISE,

> ➤ **PAGAN RELIGIOUS BOOKS.**
> ➤ **BOOKS IN THE OCCULT.**
> ➤ **HOROSCOPES CONTAINING MAGAZINES.**
> ➤ **NEWSPAPER HOROSCOPES CONTAINING.**
> ➤ **GAMES OCCULT.**
> ➤ **MAGIC GAME, ETC.**

Satan is also known as Beelzebu the Lord of the flies.

MARK 3, 22
AND THE TEACHERS OF THE LAW WHO CAME DOWN FROM JERUSALEM SAID, "HE IS POSSESSED BY BEELZEBUB! BY THE PRINCE OF DEMONS HE IS DRIVING OUT DEMONS.

The flies are attracted by the manure; the demons are attracted by the darkness.

The books of magic and everything that has to do with this and Occult are an open invitation to the demonic spirits which give them the legal right to pollute our homes, prosecute you and your family.

Many adornments and artifacts may seem harmless, but may have a meaning for the satanic spirits, these ornaments and artifacts are used so that the demons are in your homes and the spirits of evil can acquire power thru these objects so that they may not be expelled from your home.

The phrase "Delivered to the idols", from the Greek Kateidolos is where Luke describes in Athens:

ACTS 17, 16
WHILE PAUL WAS WAITING FOR THEM IN ATHENS, HE WAS GREATLY DISTRESSED TO SEE THAT THE CITY WAS FULL OF IDOLS.

Athens was the capital of the idols in the ancient world, possibly very

similar to Kyoto, Japan in our days.

THE IDOLS

They are made of wood, stone, or metal, some people not even worry about their presence.

However they are not pieces of wood, stone, or metal, they have been carefully created by humans, intending to set to form in the visible world in which the forces of the invisible world of darkness have permission to control the lives of people, families and their homes and an entire city and locked its inhabitants in spiritual darkness.

That is why Paul said that "his spirit is mad seeing the city delivered to idolatry."

TESTIMONY:

One Monday attending a prayer group, we met at the home of the leader of the group, at once the Lord Jesus through the Holy Spirit showed me in Word of knowledge a fan of burnished metal, the kind that are placed on the walls for decoration. I advised at that meeting that those decoration objects were not from God and the person who owned it must get it out of the home at once, nobody there admitted owning it and I asked that if they saw one in any house to let the person know that it was important to get rid of it.

The following week, again I had the same vision thru Word of knowledge and I say it again, no one admits to have one; during the weekend the leader of the group sent me a message with a great friend of mine named Ruben, whom, by the way thanks to God first and then to him and his wife Eugenia I'm walking with the Lord, tells me to be very careful how I talk, because my message about the metal fan has not been confirmed and that they did not want me to speak about any "vision" thru word of knowledge. I told Ruben that I could not attend that prayer group anymore because I could not disobey the mandate of Jesus and what Jesus thru his Holy Spirit revealed to me for the benefit of its people.

The word of God says: **put not a muzzle to the ox that thresh.**

In the next two weeks I did not return to the group, but the following Saturday Luis Gómez calls me and asked me if I could go with him to help him pray for a family that have been visiting witches and fortune tellers and these witches had given each of them charms, spells, fetishes and the like.

Being at the home of Luis Gómez we made a prayer to renounce to all of the above and to accept Jesus as their Savior and proceeded to make a prayer of liberation by the family, the mother and her two daughters.

One of her daughters had problems with her husband and they were about to divorce, as we were told, she asked us to pray for liberation in the home because they felt the atmosphere very estrange and heavy and that they could not sleep at night.

Luis asked me to come to their home to pray for liberation, that same day we went, she lived in the top floor of a building and we started by

357

asking her the witch had given her amulets or charms, if there were any books or magazines containing horoscopes or books relating to witchcraft, we filled a box with these garbage, and prayed in every room of this person's home.

The biggest surprise of my life was when we entered her bedroom, and there it was! The metal fan that God had revealed to me before was there hanging as an ornament in the back wall of their bed, exactly as I had seen it; This fan of burnished metal had a few Chinese goddesses carved in it.

When I saw it, the expression of my face was so transformed that the lady asked what was wrong. I explained to her the revelation I had and what had happened in the prayer group.

I told her I knew that these ornaments cost lots of money, but that I strongly advise her to take it down and throw it away into the sea and break any alliance with it; She asked me to take it and I did.

As a flawed human being, I said to myself, this is my opportunity to show them in the prayer that I was always right when I told them about the fan.

That night started to rain and about 11: 00 o'clock, my phone at home rang; It was the lady, crying and telling me that they had had to tie the maid because she wanted to jump from the balcony, she was acting very strange and wanted to commit suicide.

I told her to leave the apartment immediately and that the following day we will go with a group to pray and we would be fasting.

Knowing the influence that these objects which were given to the lady by the witch have and that they give power to the demons thru those Chinese goddesses carved in the fan, I immediately get up from my bed and drove to the nearest boardwalk; in my country there is a beautiful boardwalk which borders the coast of the city giving view to the Caribbean Sea, though the night was stormy and rainy I took all the objects that had been removed from that home and throw them into the sea in the name of Jesus and by His name broke any influence of the demon on that home and the people who lived in it.

The following day I go back to the woman's apartment with my friend and brother in Christ Ruben, and his wife Eugenia, and explained to them what had happened and that the infamous metal fan had been in the couple's bedroom, and therefore it was a confirmation from God of what I had said at the prayer group, everything is for the glory of God.

We pray and everything was liberated thanks to the Precious Blood of our Lord Jesus Christ.

All of these was a learning experience for me, not only for the confirmation of the fan but for the wonderful work done by Jesus in that family, but also taught me how to be humble and that His Glory is for Him alone.

TESTIMONY:

One evening at my home arrived a friend who was accompanied by a lady friend, my friend asked me when it would be possible for me to pray for this woman; I asked her what her problem was and my friend tells me that the lady was about to be divorced from her husband and her 15-year-old son was very rebellious, and several members of her family had felt strange noises in the house.

I asked her if she had visited some magician, sorcerer or healer and she denied it, then I gave her an appointment to come the next day at two o'clock in the afternoon.

I usually fast before praying and have a chain of people praying for that person.

The following day the lady came promptly at two o'clock in the afternoon, we sat in a small courtyard and commend us to God, His beloved son Jesus, and the Holy Spirit that enlightened us and to guide us during this inner healing prayer.

A part of the inner healing prayer that caught my attention was the forgiveness.

Us men don't realize the evil that we do when we are unfaithful to our spouse, not only the woman suffers but the children as well suffer the consequence of possible divorce, children are not dumb, and they realize immediately the lack of love between their parents and home.

"When we started to talk about that issue, I asked the lady if she was willing to forgive the infidelity of her husband, she said yes. We must remember that we condition God to forgive us as we forgive, it cannot be a pardon halfway, it has to be a total and honest forgiveness, the devil will always want to remind us of the moments of suffering and is at this time that we should say in our hearts and our minds" **"I have already forgiven him in the name of Jesus"**, and thus to strengthen us spiritually.

By following our prayer the Holy Spirit put in my heart the following question **"Have you ever been unfaithful to your husband?"**, she responded quickly and emphatically, **"No, never"**, we continued our prayer and after a while the Lord puts again in my mind the same question, **"Have you not been unfaithful to your husband...ever?"** again she answered with a **"NO"**.

Almost at the end of the afternoon, it was 6 pm, we were almost finishing our prayer and the Lord again puts in my heart the same question I said to her: You have to forgive me but the Holy Spirit tell me that you can fool me but not God and sends me to ask again **"Were**

you unfaithful to your husband?", the Lord who knows everything, in His infinite goodness and wanting to always heal us inwardly as he did with Peter, gave this lady three times the opportunity to repent of her sin and recognize it and forgive herself, she said between tears and sobs: **"Yes, I was unfaithful"** then we agreed to meet at her home the next day at 9: 30 am to say a prayer of liberation much needed in her home.

The following day I went to her home, I could felt the heavy atmosphere, as it is in every place that there are only fights and discord.

Upon entering her 15 year old son's bedroom we found several posters of famous singers of Rock and Heavy Metal, including multiple cds, I made the woman aware about the danger of this kind of music not only for the youth but also for her home, then we proceeded to remove a few books and magazines about horoscopes, witchcraft, and other related materials; After filling a box with different objects like elephants for good luck, Buddha's, etc., we sat in the living room to pray to the Lord Jesus for release of the home of these demonic influences.

While seated, something caught my attention at the coffee table in the center of the room, was a small crystal bell, calmly I lifted it and I saw how the pendulum of the same began to move slowly at first and gradually was gaining speed as a centrifugal.

The woman had not noticed what was happening and I just couldn't believe what I was watching, slowly I raised the bell again and slowly began to move until it reached an incredible speed, the lady looking at me said: **Are you making the bell spin?,** I answered **"No"**, and again very slowly lift it and began to spin and spin very rapidly.

The woman rose from her chair, white as a sheet of paper and told me: "Take all of these out of here", referring to the box with all the objects and the glass bell. We prayed and threw all these contaminated material into the sea in the name of Jesus.

OBJECTS HAVE A SPIRITUAL MEANING.

DEUTERONOMY 32, 16 – 18

16
THEY MADE HIM JEALOUS WITH THEIR FOREIGN GODS AND ANGERED HIM WITH THEIR DETESTABLE IDOLS.

17
THEY SACRIFICED TO DEMONS, WHICH ARE NOT GOD – GODS THEY HAD NOT KNOWN GODS THAT RECNTLY APPEA-RED, GODS YOUR FATHERS DID NOT FEAR.

18
YOU DESERTED THE ROCK, WHO FATHERED YOU; YOU FOR-GOT THE GOD WHO GAVE YOU BIRTH.

When one disobeys God it brings the curse. Disobedience is inherent to the worship of strange gods (idolatry) which in fact is the worship of demons.

In the Bible we have evidence of physical things that can have a spiritual meaning:

> - THE BLOOD OF THE LAMB (SEE EXODUS 12, 7-13).
> - THE TABERNACLE, its ORNAMENTS AND UTENSILS (SEE EXODUS 26 AND 27).
> - BAPTISM BY WATER (SEE LUKE 3, 21-22).

- ➢ THE LAST SUPPER (SEE MATTHEW 26, 28) (SEE CORINTHIANS 11, 23-25).
- ➢ THE HANDKERCHIEFS AND APRONS MIRACLE (SEE ACTS 19, 11-12).
- ➢ HEAL WITH OIL (SEE JAMES 5, 14).

NUMBERS 21, 5 – 9

5

THEY SPOKE AGAINST GOD AND AGAINST MOSES, AND SAID, "WHY HAVE YOU BROUGHT US UP OUT OF EGYPT TO DIE IN THE DESERT? THERE IS NO BREAD! THERE IS NO WATER! AND WE DETEST THIS MISERABLE FOOD".

6

THEN THE LORD SENT VENOMOUS SNAKES AMONG THEM; THEY BIT THE PEOPLE AND MANY ISRAELITES DIED.

7

THE PEOPLE CAME TO MOSES AND SAID, "WE SINNED WHEN WE SPOKE AGAINST THE LORD AND AGAINST YOU. PRAY THAT THE LORD WILL TAKE THE SNAKES AWAY FROM US." SO MOSES PRAYED FOR THE PEOPLE.

8

THE LORD SAID TO MOSES, "MAKE A SNAKE AND PUT IN UP ON A POLE; ANYONE WHO IS BITTEN CAN LOOK AT IT AND LIVE".

9

SO MOSES MADE A BRONZE SNAKE AND PUT IT UP ON A POLE. THEN WHEN ANYONE WAS BITTEN BY A SNAKE AND LOOKED AT THE BRONZE SNAKE, HE LIVED.

This bronze serpent, offered the sons of Israel a solution to their sins. That metal snake had the power to heal those who had been bitten by poisonous snakes. Today we understand the significance of such metal snake: **symbolizes Christ** becoming SIN for us, when he was put on the cross as a living sacrifice for all of us.

900 years later, when King Hezekiah cleaned the temple **(2 Kings 18, 4)**

He took high places and broke the images, and cut the symbols of **Aseras, and shattered to pieces the bronze serpent made by Moses, because until then burned you incense Israel children**; and he called it **"Nehustàn"**.

An object designed by God for the health of Israel had become a God who loved Israel!

THE SUPERSTITION:

Superstition is to put faith in a person, thing, or place other than the Almighty God and his word infallible.

Nowdays is not the time to be weak or superstitious, but that we must learn to walk with wisdom and spiritual discernment.

THERE ARE THINGS THAT ARE PROHIBITED TO POSSESS.

God made us and saved us, making us **"a new creation"**.

Paul tells us:

2 CORINTHIANS 5, 17
THEREFORE, IF ANYONE IS IN CHRIST, HE IS A NEW CREA TION; THE OLD HAS GONE, THE NEW HAS COME!

Because of our new life in Christ, God expects that we live in a new way, remove the old and get what's new.

EPHESIANS 5, 8 – 11 SAY:
8
FOR YOU WERE ONCE DARKNESS, BUT NOW YOU ARE LIGHT IN THE LORD. LIVE AS CHILDREN OF LIGHT.

9
(FOR THE FRUIT OF THE LIGHT CONSISTS IN ALL GOOD-NESS, RIGHTEOUSNESS AND TRUTH)

10
AND FIND OUT WHAT PLEASES THE LORD.

11
HAVE NOTHING TO DO WITH THE FRUITLESS DEEDS OF DARKNESS, BUT RATHER EXPOSE THEM.

In **Exodus 20, 3** God banned children of Israel from having other gods.

God is a jealous God, jealous of our confidence **(see Deuteronomy 4, 24 and 5, 9).**

EXODUS 20, 3
YOU SHALL HAVE NO OTHER GODS BEFORE ME.

God forbade them to participate in witchcraft and astrology. He explained to them that these activities and practices are an abomination before Him.

DEUTERONOMY 18, 9 – 13
9
WHEN YOU ENTER THE LAND THE LORD YOUR GOD IS GI-VING YOU, DO NOT LEARN TO IMITATE THE DETESTABLE WAYS OF THE NATIONS THERE.

10

LET NO ONE BE FOUND AMONG YOU WHO SACRIFICES HIS SON OR DAUGHTER IN THE FIRE, WHO PRACTICES DIVINA- TION OR SORCERY, INTERPRETS OMENS, ENGAGES IN WITCHCRAFT,

11

OR CASTS SPELLS, OR WHO IS A MEDIUM OR SPIRITIST OR WHO CONSULTS THE DEAD.

12

ANY ONE WHO DOES THESE THINGS IS DETESTABLE TO THE LORD, AND BECAUSE OF THESE DETESTABLE PRAC- TICES THE LORD YOUR GOD WILL DRIVE OUT THOSE NA- TIONS BEFORE YOU.

13

YOU MUST BE BLAMELESS BEFORE THE LORD YOUR GOD.

In the Bible we see a list of things that dishonor God and which must no be placed in his people in the Old Testament. These things suggest tha there are other gods, which violates the first four commandments.

DEUTERONOMY 4, 15 – 19; 23 – 24
15
YOU SAW NO FORM OF ANY KIND THE DAY THE LORD SPO KE TO YOU HOREB OUT OF THE FIRE. THEREFORE WATCH YOURSELVES VERY CAREFULLY,

16

SO THAT YOU DO NOT BECOME CORRUPT AND MAKE FOR YOURSELVES AN IDOL, AN IMAGE OF ANY SHAPE, WHE THER FORMED LIKE A MAN OR A WOMAN,

17

OR LIKE ANY ANIMAL ON EARTH OR ANY BIRD THAT FLIE IN THE AIR,

18

OR LIKE ANY CREATURE THAT MOVES ALONG THE GROUND OR ANY FISH IN THE WATERS BELOW.

19

AND WHEN YOU LOOK UP TO THE SKY AND SEE THE SUN, THE MOON AND THE STARS – ALL THE HEAVENLY ARRAY – DO NOT BE ENTICED INTO BOWING DOWN TO THEM AND WORSHIPING THINGS THE LORD YOUR GOD HAS APPOR-TIONED TO ALL THE NATIONS UNDER HEAVEN.

23

BE CAREFUL NOT TO FORGET THE COVENANT OF THE LORD YOUR GOD THAT HE MADE WITH YOU; DO NOT MAKE FOR YOURSELVES AN IDOL IN THE FORM OF ANYTHING THE LORD YOUR GOD HAS FORBIDDEN.

24

FOR THE LORD YOUR GOD IS A CONSUMING FIRE, A JEA-LOUS GOD.

All this is still valid today. Our Father feels sadness if we have or possess statues of other gods, or objects that seek to gain power from any source spiritual, being the only true God. These objects are prohibited because they open door to the demons and supernatural de-ception and take us away from God; prevent our physical and spiritual health.

Many times as I explained above, by ignorance we buy objects and ornaments that for us represent no harm, but that those who manu-facture these objects give a meaning of different gods as normally happens with Chinese and Japanese objects which figures are usually gods or goddesses and are dedicated for them objects which greatly influence in us and in our homes.

The use of these objects can set a spiritual significance; many objects are not neither good nor bad in themselves. However, the use that is given to them can set its spiritual meaning.

It is customary in many countries when a baby is born to put a charm in his or her clothing as a guard against "evil eye" etc. In our ignorance we do not realize that what we are doing is telling God, we do not need your protection and a charm has more power than God and you are no longer needed. That is what we do without realizing that we are exchanging the protection of our God for a charm or amulet.

Today we see many vehicles with a rosary placed in the rear view mirror and I wonder does vehicles pray the Rosary?, honestly it would be a surprise for me to know that vehicles pray the Rosary. What really happens is that people use it to protect them against an accident, and are turning rosary beads into an amulet and supplanting the protection of God and our Lord Jesus Christ by a rosary that is nothing other than a string with plastic balls or any other material.

On several occasions I've read in books of Evangelical people say that the Rosary is diabolical, I sincerely believe that they are in error, but the use that is being given to be used as an amulet of protection can't deny that they are absolutely right.

We must not let go God's protection for anything in this life, God is who protects us and has given us according to the Bible, two angels to protect us and by ignorance we exchange the protection of God, of Jesus and their angels, by a charm or anything else.

Let us put our protection only in God our Creator.

When we are in God's ways, He always shows us things that are impure and that dishonor Him.

God has given us His spirit, and the spirit will always tell us when an object or things are impure and dishonor to the Father.

Jesus promise:

JOHN 16, 13
BUT WHEN HE, THE SPIRIT OF TRUTH, COMES, HE WILL GUIDE YOU INTO ALL TRUTH. HE WILL NOT SPEAK ON HIS OWN; HE WILL SPEAK ONLY WHAT HE HEARS, AND HE WILL TELL YOU WHAT IS YET TO COME.

When looking for purity before our Father and ask Him to show us if any of our belongings are dishonorable. He will let us know. The truth is what God reveals, to be able to heal!

It is important for our welfare and our health to keep our homes free from objects and polluted things and now let us be guided by the Holy Spirit before purchasing any objects or things.

What do we do with objects and polluted things?

In the New Testament we read about the revival in the city of Ephesus:

ACTS 19, 18 – 20
18
MANY OF THOSE WHO BELIEVE NOW CAME AND OPENLY CONFESSED THEIR EVIL DEEDS.

19
A NUMBER WHO HAD PRACTICED SORCERY BROUGHT THEIR SCROLLS TOGETHER AND BURNED THEM PUBLICLY. WHEN THEY CALCULATED THE VALUE OF THE SCROLLS, THE TOTAL CAME TO FIFTY THOUSAND DRACHMAS.

20

IN THIS WAY THE WORD OF THE LORD SPREAD WIDELY AND GREW IN POWER.

Then everything that offend God and is impure before Him, must be burnt, all books, magazines, records, tapes, cd, dvd and anything that defies our God, must be destroyed, if can't be burnt, throw it into the sea, river or lake, and everything we do is in the name of Jesus.

Bless your home in the name of the Father of the Son Jesus and of the Holy Spirit.

Change your home's environment, play songs of praise to God, to His Beloved Son and to the Holy Spirit.

May God continue to bless you.

BIBLIOGRAPHY

He Came to Set the Captives Free
Rebecca Brown, MD

Jesus Live Today
Emiliano Tardif, MSC
José H. Prado Flores

The Demon, Symbol or Reality?
René Laurentin

The Children's Bread Release
Guillermo Maldonado

Satan, You Can't Have My Children
Iris Delgado

Pigs in the Parlor
Frank & Ida Mae Hammond

Spiritual Housecleaning Workbook
Eddie & Alice Smith

Fight Against Principalities Demonic
Lic. Rita Cabezas

Sects and Satanic Cults
Giuseppe Ferrari
Eugenio Fezzotti
Mons. Mario Moronta R
Lucia Musti
Andrea Pocarelli
Mons. Ángelo Scola

Exorcism in the 21st Century
Jesús Yánez Rivera

The Battle to Man's Soul
Graham Powell

Manual for the Deliverance Worker
Frank Marzullo
Tom Snyder

Inner Healing and Deliverance
Guillermo Maldonado

How to Cast out Demons
Doris M. Wagner

Listen to Me Satan!
Carlos Annacondía

Angels and Demons
Raúl Berzosa Martinez

Give It Back!
Kimberly Daniels

Texts Bible
Several biblical texts had been used, mainly from Reina Valera 1960